David Marrani approaches the study of contemporary institutions of justice carrying a rich multidisciplinary toolbox. He uses the tools of philosophy, particularly work associated with structuralism and post structuralism, psychoanalysis, Freud and Lacan, anthropology, art criticism, architecture, film theory, and jurisprudence to name a few to reflect on a number of pressing issues intimately associated with the delivery of justice. Chapters include a study of judicial authority and courtroom ritual. Two others explore the space of justice. One examines the modern architectural jurisprudential preoccupation with transparency revealing the new opacity that it generates. The second focuses on the impact of the dematerialisation of justice, as cameras turn the institutions of justice into just another TV show. This is a rich, thoughtful and provocative study that is a must-read for anyone interested in the nature and place of justice in contemporary society.

Leslie J. Moran, Professor of Law, Birkbeck, University of London

Space, Time, Justice

This book merges philosophical, psychoanalytical and legal perspectives to explore how spaces of justice are changing and the effect this has on the development of the administration of justice. There are as central themes: the idea of transgression as the starting point of the question of justice and its archaic anchor; the relation between spaces of justice and ritual(s); the question of use and abuse of transparency in contemporary courts; and the abolition of the judicial walls with the use of cameras in courts. It offers a comparative approach, looking at spaces of justice in both the civil and common law traditions. Presenting a theoretical and interdisciplinary study of spaces of justice, it will appeal to academics in the fields of law, criminology, sociology and architecture.

Dr David Marrani studied law, philosophy and psychoanalysis in France and in the UK. He is Professor and Director at the Institute of Law, Jersey. He teaches undergraduate and postgraduate students on Common Law Reasoning, Comparative Law, Comparative Public Law, Jurisprudence and Critical Studies. He is a visiting professor at several European and international universities. His research relates to comparative public law and the intersections between law, philosophy and psychoanalysis. He is Series General Editor for Routledge Research in Constitutional Law and the SLS Convenor for comparative law.

Space, Time, Justice
From Archaic Rituals to Contemporary Perspectives

David Marrani

Routledge
Taylor & Francis Group
LONDON AND NEW YORK

First published 2018
by Routledge

2 Park Square, Milton Park, Abingdon, Oxfordshire OX14 4RN
52 Vanderbilt Avenue, New York, NY 10017

Routledge is an imprint of the Taylor & Francis Group, an informa business

First issued in paperback 2020

British Library Cataloguing-in-Publication Data
A catalogue record for this book is available
from the British Library

Library of Congress Cataloging-in-Publication Data
Names: Marrani, David, author.
Title: Space, time, justice: from archaic rituals to contemporary perspectives / David Marrani.
Description: Abingdon, Oxon; New York, NY : Routledge, 2017. | Includes bibliographical references and index.
Identifiers: LCCN 2017020039 ISBN 9781138703254 (hardback) | ISBN 9781351787444 (adobe reader) | ISBN 9781351787437 (epub) | ISBN 9781351787420 (mobipocket)
Subjects: LCSH: Judicial process—Philosophy.
Classification: LCC K2100. M377 2017 | DDC 340/.114—dc23
LC record available at https://lccn.loc.gov/2017020039

ISBN: 978-1-138-70325-4 (hbk)
ISBN: 978-0-367-59400-8 (pbk)

Typeset in Galliard
by RefineCatch Limited, Bungay, Suffolk

Contents

Illustrations

Tables

Figures

Acknowledgements

Even though this book is a collection of essays I have been writing for almost a decade, it is also the result of a collective and interdisciplinary reflection, visits to *palais de justice* and courthouses in France, Spain, Italy, the UK, the USA, Australia and New Zealand. It is also the result of discussions and debates with friends and colleagues.

I was lucky enough, years ago, to come across Professor Pascal Richard who awakened me and brought me to the other side of the law. I wish to thank him for that and for his constant support and friendship.

I also would like to thank Professor Peter Dews, who helped me rediscover psychoanalysis; Professors Guillaume Tusseau and Pierre Brunet for their critical reading of part of the book; Me. Jean-Michel Urbani, for looking at it from within the law. Also, Richard Cornes, Linda Mulcahy, David Tait, JC Remotti, Andreas Philippopoulos-Mihalopoulos, Jacques Commaille, Laurence Dumoulin, Antoine Garapon, Geoffrey Samuel, James Lambert, Cliona O'Dunlaing and Lucy Jewel. Thanks go to Cairis who kindly proofread all the chapters.

In particular, thank you Giulia and Sadb, for allowing me to spend time on this, rather than with you.

As a series of essays, this book comprises several studies I have undertaken with presentations at several high-profile institutions or international conferences. I wish, particularly, to thank the Law and Society Association and all the colleagues I have met there over the years.

Foreword

Professor David Marrani situates his book on the intersections between law and philosophy, architecture and psychoanalysis. The result is a complex and sophisticated book. It sheds light on many cultural expressions, which are fundamental to our understanding of the law in society. Following the Freudian revolution, as Marrani notes, legal science must take in consideration how the architecture, the symbols, and the rituals surrounding the law are themselves capital for a proper grasp of some legal behaviours and customs. That is, a theory to study the cultural symbolism attached to the legal world is in many ways important for legal philosophy. It gives depth to the world where attorneys plea, where magistrates write judgements, and where criminals get their due. The representational settings attached to the architecture of courthouses, for instance, permit us to better understand such events, which is an important contribution of Marrani's study.

Two books, *Totem and Taboo* as well as *Moses and Monotheism* by Sigmund Freud, offer to Marrani the key to a genealogy about the origins of the law, and its contemporary functioning. Though Freud has not written anything specific about the law, this should not prevent us from using his valuable insights in legal philosophy. Freud was profoundly attached to the Hobbesian image of humans as selfish beings, moved by motives of personal gratification. Humans are too often wicked, immoral, and non-civilised. The law, conversely, is engaged in an effort of civilisation. Humanity struggles with humankind. In a way, the law is a sacrifice, both collectively and individually. It rules out certain behaviours, such that we may have civilisation and a peaceful social life, secured by a stable social and political order. The cultural setting of the law, however, influences how it is then used in a courthouse, as Marrani explains in this book.

David Marrani shows us how the law inserts itself in the legal symbolic of our modern societies. Because there have been numerous cultural shifts, for example in the architecture of courthouses, the law has also been accompanied by many different rituals. The law, in a way, is constantly changing, adapting to our modern culture, and perhaps, now, to a postmodern culture. Hence, applying the law, Marrani notes, is exercising a power, which is intimately tied to a given cultural context and a given symbolic order.

It is common in psycho-legal theories today to understand Freud through the impressive work of the French thinker Jacques Lacan, and indeed it leads us to a sophisticated philosophical interpretation of the Freudian revolution. In this Lacano-Freudian tradition, the unconscious is "structured as a language", which we may access in the form of linguistic signifiers and cultural symbols. Such a viewpoint offers us an original way to approach the law, one with which most practitioners will not be familiar. It is nonetheless fundamental to what we may call the execution of the law. Legal rituals are often taken for granted, and yet a proper understanding of such rituals will make us better understand, for instance, the power of judgedom, that is, the realm of judges. It will also lead us to a critical examination of the rituals of justice, which may be more important than most of us would expect in the administration of justice.

Marrani explains how the creation of new narratives too often overcomes critical scrutiny and reflection. I must admit that I love the pages where he analyses the "narratives" used today by architects to explain why they design courthouses as "shopping-malls" in the name of "transparency". This is indeed an abuse of the concept of transparency, a new opacity as Marrani brilliantly notes, which ought to be studied further. What do we mean when we invoke the idea of transparency? And what can it mean for the law or for the administration of justice? One will find in this book an analysis of many interesting questions like these, which will give a new meaning to what Supreme Court Justice Felix Frankfurter once said – "Justice must satisfy the appearance of justice."

Professor Marrani convincingly demonstrates that the Lacano-Freudian theory of law has yet something to teach us. He offers a comprehensive view of the representational world where the law operates. Furthermore, he gives us a solid account of the Lacano-Freudian theory. The contribution of this theory to understand the symbolic world where law take place is such that it cannot be ignored.

Bjarne Melkevik
Bjarne is professor of legal philosophy at Université Laval, Quebec.

Introduction

In my research, I have been trying to consider something quite complex; the intersection between law and philosophy, architecture, art theory and psychoanalysis. My ideas are sometimes quite radical, I suppose, especially for lawyers who are not accustomed to the abstract world. Sometimes my ideas seem quite naïve, because I may not be an expert on everything, but simply an apprentice that tries and tries again to perfect and polish his work.

That said, I have tried to make accessible, as much as possible, the radical (and naïve) knowledge I have introduced here, in order to propose an abstract and theoretical work that can be comprehended, I hope, simply, by those of you who will give me the pleasure of reading me.

As I mentioned, this book is based on my ongoing research on courts, judges and justice. If what is important for justice is to be seen to be done, the place where justice is or is supposed to be rendered has a pivotal part to play in its administration. The place of justice for neo-Classical architects was a Palace of Justice, 'speaking through allegorical and metaphorical forms', contrasting the 'temple illuminated by justice' and the 'dark places devoted to crime'. There is therefore, in spaces of justice, a very present and perhaps permanent idea of separation, of dichotomy, almost like a black and white vision. The place where justice has to be rendered has to show contrasts between light and darkness, highlighting the light of the truth, the legal truth. Spaces of justice are not just any other places, they are sacred places transcended through ideas of power and authority. This complex system of values is, via rituals, connected to the 'speaking architecture': the building, which imposes the solemnity of the state, illuminating this authority. We therefore need to think about and rethink spaces of justice. This is the objective of this research monograph. We particularly need to think about it in what is said to be a postmodern period. If we are after (post)modernity, we should consider the potential changes that have occurred between preceding periods and that time of modernity, and not simply in one geographical area or jurisdiction, but in a comparative way. For instance, does the idea of power and authority transfer to 'post modernity' or do we have something else, something different? One could argue that, in fact, a judge may not represent justice anymore because the changes introduce a lack of distance, where the power and authority vanish completely.

This is a circular problem, a revolution. Moving from a ceremonial, very formal judge, in a temple-like court building, to a business-like judge in an office-like court building affects the position of the judge. This book questions whether a judge in a contemporary building, or a judge viewed through cameras, represents *something someone somewhere*, in the same way as it did before.

In the first chapter I introduce the ideas and concepts that are, in my opinion, central to a work based on intersection between philosophy, psychoanalysis and law. The transgression of the fundamental law 'you shall not kill' acts at the foundation of a micro society and establishes the law, repressed, through psychological mechanisms. Notions such as totem, taboos, Oedipus, the killing of the father by the brothers and the repression of the law are introduced here. The brothers must kill the father to exist as a group, a social organisation. But should they kill again, then the group would cease to exist. Hence 'you shall not kill' becomes the foundation of a (civilised) society. That essential moment of time is re-enacted during the legal event of trial, where the 'brothers' will be judged in front of an audience, for transgressing the law. That is when the 'where' is needed, when the consideration for spaces of justice arises. I argue that law courts operate like a microcosm of the social organisation, where rituals of birth and re-birth take place, alongside the re-creation of the original transgression that marked the first step towards society.

In Chapter 2, I analyse, in depth, the relationship between time and space in the legal event. It applies the psychoanalytical notions introduced in the previous chapter specifically to the administration of justice. It also offers a comparative approach, looking at the judge in the spaces of justice, both in the civil and common law traditions. I define how the judge relates to the idea of 'totem' and to the Oedipus complex, and how it can be compared in the two legal traditions on this basis. Specifically, it develops the idea of quality and quantities of 'totemic position/s' according to the specific legal traditions. I then consider elements that I believe to be conditioning the symbolic position of the judge, and compare these in both traditions. Finally, I offer a connection between time and space through ritual(s).

In Chapter 3, I focus on analyses of the link between the architecture of courts of justice and the respect for the law. I consider how court architecture may influence the efficiency of the law, in terms of individual case resolution, which has an impact on the cohesion of society. I analyse the impact of courthouse designs and their importance because of the long-term investments they constitute and because of the specific message of authority they convey. Courthouses are looked at as specific spaces where the law is 'spoken' and where 'divine justice' results. I examine how, in the past, the original myth of authority was represented by neo-classical (in civil law countries such as France) or gothic revival architecture (in common law countries such as the UK) in 'palaces of justice'. I then consider that in more recent years, we have witnessed a radical shift in courthouse design. The representation of authority through judicial architecture has now been replaced by a contemporary 'post-modern' approach that seems to modify the original myth. This chapter is more about examining the use of transparency, or what is termed here 'the new opacity', as an integral aspect of contemporary courthouse design.

In Chapter 4, I look at how the psycho-social perspective on the legal event of trial is challenged by technology. This chapter concerns, once more, the concept of 'authority' in the process of justice. If justice has to be seen to be done, the appearance of justice becomes what is spoken of: its image becomes its new foundation. The technology deployed in courts modifies the archaic, sacred, spatio-temporal space of the court. It leaves an empty box in which there is literally no-one. Will it become a void that is related not to 'real' justice but to a digital representation of justice? Let us remind ourselves that we, subjects, seek to articulate ourselves in a signifying field that is necessarily fragile (a representation rather than a reality) and that we may be creating a lack of justice. This void-consequence is the subject of the signifier – that is, a retroactive effect of the failure of its own representation. That is why the failure of representation is the only way to represent it. The focus is mainly on the Crime and Courts Act 2013 that relaxes the rules on filming court proceedings in the UK. I then consider how filming, recording and broadcasting might be a new legal Janus, with one positive side and one negative side. It appears on the one hand as a continuation of the (real) audience, the public present at a trial, through a 'techno-legal' transparency; while on the other hand it may appear as though drifting towards voyeurism. I finish by using Baudrillard's and Barthe's work on media to complete the illustration on this chapter about cameras in courts.

Chapter 5 offers some conclusions.

1 Transgression as the 'big bang' of society*

Le collectif n'est rien que le sujet de l'individuel.
Lacan, J., *Écrits 1*, Paris: Seuil, 1999, p. 211 note 6.

Transgression seems to invite us to act. We want to advance; cross borders, pass onto the other side of something, or somewhere, or go beyond limits, while it whispers words such as *good* and *bad*, what is permitted and what is forbidden, in our ears.

Transgression is therefore an invitation to go further but also a process of limitation between what is allowed and what is forbidden. It is a situation that delineates a space which is more or less real: it allows us to exist. Transgression shows what is possible, through the delimitation of what is and cannot be. To transgress is, in law, to breach a rule, or to violate a law. The act of transgressing sets down the issue of the rule and its breach. We understand how this passes beyond the idea of sanction. Transgression defines, therefore, what is good and what is bad, not only psychologically but also legally. However, it is also the path from the law to the outlawed, from the permitted to the forbidden, a forbidden that is identified by the transgression itself. Transgression also, then, means the guarantee of the creation of a social space.

Without transgression, there cannot be a rule that can be qualified 'a rule'. It highlights the point that only the respected rules, with sanctions as corollary, are 'true' laws. Only with the possibility of transgression are sanctions necessary. We may consider here the thoughts of Bentham or Austin who told us about the nature of an obligation to respect the law: 'to be obliged to do . . . is to be liable . . . to a sanction'.[1] This is not without reminding us of themes developed by Kelsen either: 'Rules of law, if valid, are norms. They are, to be more precise,

* A version of this chapter was presented as 'La transgression ou l'acte de naissance de la société humaine', during the Colloque sur la transgression, 25 November 2011, USTV, Toulon, France. A French version was subsequentely published as 'La transgression ou l'acte de naissance de la société humaine', in Jean-Jacques Sueur and P. Richard (eds), *La Transgression* (Bruxelles: Bruylant, 2013).

1 Austin, J. and Campbell, R., *Lectures on Jurisprudence, Or, The Philosophy of Positive Law, Volume 1,* Clarck: The Lawbook Exchange Ltd, 2005, p. 444.

norms stipulating sanctions'.[2] Norms can only be laws positing sanctions. In addition, sanctions appear to be anticipated: what is 'illicit' is not a negation of the law but an action that the law prohibits and subjects to a sanction that is forecasted, anticipated.[3] Sanctions are required because we must keep in mind that *la chair est faible,* the flesh is weak, and that our world is not an utopia; rules are not always permanent, and may be a result of the sanction that would eventually follow an offence. Transgression may at the same time be imagined as progression or regression according to whether or not the rule is respected. What is forbidden, and the sanctions for not respecting what is forbidden, are linked, and we will then see taboos, crimes and incest appearing as the norm. Indeed, to be civilised we need to have laws making it impossible to transgress.

It is quite simple to consider that a society cannot really develop without laws, and sanctions of these laws. A society cannot develop without a corpus of rules with sanctions, conceived as the only way for the rules to be respected. Sanctions are the corollary of rules and then of the structuring of a society. That is a theory that reminds us of the myth of creation of a primitive society, as explained by psychoanalysis. According to Lacan,

> la première situation dont encore nous sommes redevables à l'initiative freudienne d'avoir amené la notion en psychologie pour qu'elle y trouve à mesure des temps la plus prodigieuse fortune – première situation, disons-nous, non comme confrontation abstraite dessinant une relation, mais comme crise dramatique se résolvant en structure –, c'est justement celle du crime dans ses deux formes les plus abhorrées, l'Inceste et le Patricide, dont l'ombre engendre tout la pathogénie de l'Œdipe. Il est d'autant plus significatif de la reconnaître dans la succession des crises, sevrage, intrusion, Œdipe, puberté, adolescence qui refont chacune une nouvelle synthèse des appareils du moi dans une forme toujours plus aliénante pour les pulsions qui y sont frustrées, toujours moins idéale pour celles qui y trouvent leur normalisation.[4]

As a consequence, we discover that the primordial crime is at the foundation of universal law, and that it is with law and crime that mankind, that the civilised

2 Kelsen, H., *General Theory of Law and State*, Clarck: The Lawbook Exchange Ltd, 2009, p. 30.

3 'Ce qui est "illicite" n'est pas une négation du droit mais une action que la loi prohibe et dont la sanction est prévue d'avance, anticipée'. Balibar, E., 'The Invention of the Super-Ego, Freud and Kelsen 1922', p. 15 Balibar, E., 'The Invention of the Super-Ego, Freud and Kelsen 1922', p. 15. www.google.co.uk/url?sa=t&rct=j&q=&esrc=s&source=web&cd=1&ved=0CCgQFjAA&url=http%3A%2F%2Fwww.soundandsignifier.com%2Ffiles%2FBalibar_The_Invention_of_the_Superego_NEW.doc&ei=yot9T-y6J8HC0QXW_9jQDQ&usg=AFQjCNEsz0XbjYJ9P2y0bEZ_A9JizcMPSQ&sig2=As2ov-fL8SOwZdJx1UoKJw www.google.co.uk/url?sa=t&rct=j&q=&esrc=s&source=web&cd=1&ved=0CCgQFjAA&url=http%3A%2F%2Fwww.soundandsignifier.com%2Ffiles%2FBalibar_The_Invention_of_the_Superego_N.EW.doc&ei=yot9T (accessed 17 February 2017)

4 Lacan,J., *Écrits 1*, Paris: Point Seuil, 1999, pp. 128–129.

man, starts; through the game of transgression and refusing to transgress that law. Without crime punishment would not be, and the coercive characteristic of the law would remain a fiction. It is possible to conceive a crime as affirming that law is a compulsory norm, a necessity for crime to exist.[5] But further, it is also the foundation of the social ensemble. As highlighted by Balibar, Laplanche, in his deciphering of Freud, shows the existence of a transition from a first level of complexity, that corresponds to a simultaneous and ambivalent presence of love and hate, admiration and fear, to a second level that corresponds to the simultaneous prescription of obedience to the law and transgression, bringing, paradoxically, the creation of the guilty via sanctions.[6]

The original crime, the original laws, are elements of a game that develops only because of the 'limits' forced by crime and its rejection. This constitutes the basis of a primitive micro-social organisation, something similar to the transformation of the state of nature into the state of civilisation. As explained by Lévi-Strauss, the structures of the society are symbolic,[7] and in addition, 'the social [is] constituted by relations of communication and symbolic exchange.'[8] Furthermore, 'In order that social order shall be maintained . . . it is necessary to assure the permanence and solidarity of the clans which compose the society'.[9] It is then quite interesting to analyse Freud's writings in their social dimension and not simply on the individual level. When undertaking research on incarnations of power (such as the Head of State or the judge),[10] we ought to put forward what is too often hidden; the father figure. Looking at the description that Legendre made on Lortie, we understand that the Oedipus complex and the figures of the judge and the Head of State are in positions similar to that of a triangle.[11]

To sum up, it is the interference between the individual and the group in Freud's thoughts that we contemplate here, an interference not always simple to see and even less to describe but an interference that is truly present. This interference begins with the mixing of Oedipus and the myth of the primitive horde, between a schema supposed to apply to individuals and one supposed to apply only to the group. Both are a narration of the same thing. Both talk to us about transgression. In this chapter, I analyse the notion of individual and collective via transgression, then how 'you shall not kill' interacts with transgression and the group, before considering the variation in the account of transgression.

5 Balibar, 'The Invention of the Super-Ego', p. 15.

6 Ibid., p. 31

7 Lacan, *Écrits 1*, p. 131. Les structures de la société sont symboliques.

8 Dews, P., *Logics of Disintegration, Post-Structuralist Thought and the Claims of Critical Theory*, London: Verso, 2007, p. 128.

9 Lévi-Strauss, C., *Totemism*, London: Merlin, 1964, p. 60.

10 Thank you to Pierre Brunet for suggesting this and making this link for me.

11 Legendre, P., *Le Crime du Caporal Lortie, Traité sur le Père*, Paris: Champs Flammarion, 1989, p. 74. We note specifically that Lortie declared that the government of Quebec had the face of his father: 'Le gouvernement du Québec avait le visage de mon père'.

One for transgression, transgression for all

Freud's work does not simply focus on isolated individuals. It concerns associated individuals, which are the individuals in a group and as constituents of that group. Freud in *Totem and Taboo* recognises that 'the totemic system is, as we know, the basis of all the other social obligations and moral restrictions of the tribe'.[12] The totemic system is composed of totems and taboos. It presents various characteristics: a) it is an organisation; b) it is an organisation that concerns a group; c) it is an organisation that 'organises' that group, bringing order to it, as basis of the rules which manage the group. We note that the term 'horde' is used by Freud as a small ensemble of people; that the group, he made reference to, appears to us as a renewal of the primitive horde.[13]

The primitive form of social human formation is the horde, led by a powerful male in a despotic fashion.[14] The father persecutes the brothers equally. They fear him equally.[15] He will be violently eliminated by the horde's members, his sons, which will transform the paternal horde into a community of brothers.[16] This horde, resulting from a transgression, becomes a community. The father of the horde becomes a god: the totemic clan appears.[17] The totemic system is therefore a micro-social organisation that is at the origin of the taboos and originates from taboos. Freud acknowledges this to define the notion of taboo: 'the meaning of 'taboo', as we see it, diverges in two contrary directions. To us it means, on the one hand, 'sacred', 'consecrated', and on the other 'uncanny', 'dangerous', 'forbidden', 'unclean'.[18] He acknowledges, as do anthropologists and sociologists, that the word 'taboo' has two meanings, which he sums up under the term *religious interdiction*.[19] That *religious interdiction* is manifested 'essentially expressed in prohibitions and restrictions'.[20] In fact, for Freud, the taboo is something that cannot be tackled because it is sacred and provokes fear, terrifying fear, expressed mainly under the form of forbidden elements and restrictions. We may note the Oedipal identification that concerns the father as original totem, and the original crime, essential to society, where guilt, aggression, the killing of the father and rivalry between brothers seem to structure the subject.[21]

We have a working hypothesis laid down by Freud; the idea that taboos are forbidden things, frontiers that culture or various cultures place around a large catalogue of phenomena such as specific objects, places, people, including the

12 Freud, S., *Totem and Taboo*, London: Ark, 1950, p. 9.
13 Freud, S., 'The Group and the Primal Horde', in 'Group Psychology and the Analysis of the Ego', *SE* 18, London: Vintage Hogarth Press, 2001, pp. 67–134, esp. pp. 122–123.
14 Ibid., p. 122.
15 Ibid., p. 125.
16 Ibid., p. 122.
17 Ibid., p. 124.
18 Freud, *Totem and Taboo*, p. 18.
19 Ibid., p. 19.
20 Ibid,. p. 18.
21 Lacan, *Écrits 1*, pp. 100–123, esp. p. 116.

father of the horde, and also actions. Taboos, Freud tells us, are principally expressed through what is forbidden. The wild man, a sort of guinea pig, sees his life structured by those taboos which permit the birth of a micro-societal life. In a permanent yo-yo between individual and group, we find that we are close to what happens with a child who, through socialisation, is presented with what is forbidden. The parents explain what is forbidden when they order the child not to do something. To say 'no' and create limits,[22] through the idea of '*ne fait pas ci, ne fait pas ça*'[23] is in fact a proto normative structure with rules that allow a social life to be organised; its first version being family life. Those rules allow us to become 'civilised'.[24] But what is forbidden produces desire. What is forbidden, which is behind the barrier, behind the frontier, which is potentially dirty, or impure or taboo, produces desire: the desire to cross, to go beyond the limit, a desire that needs to be repressed and condemned, creating the comprehension of *transgression*. We are confronted here with the same dilemma as Narcissus, or the famous cartoon character Mandrake, and their reflection in the mirror, their image.[25] Narcissus looks at himself in the water and sees his reflection, as he would see it in a mirror. He comes closer to the image, to the frontier that constitutes the surface of the liquid. Narcissus goes further and crosses that frontier, that limit; he transgresses. Going too far, means that the water 'mirror' becomes the water 'window', making him cross to the other side. If the story of Narcissus offers a fatal ending, Mandrake and his double, the one behind the mirror, his inverted *image inversé* Ekardnam, warn us of what could happen. His double is evil. Mandrake/Ekardnam symbolises the historical and heroic battle between good and evil. Narcissus drowns transgressing, Mandrake reveals the secret of our consciousness, of the good and the evil inside us, at individual and group levels.

Freud offers an initiation into the tight links between anthropology and the development of the individual. The explanation of taboos highlights the nature and origin of consciousness at both the level of individual and society. Indeed:

> If I am not mistaken, the explanation of taboo also throws light on the nature and origin of conscience. It is possible, without any stretching of the sense of the terms, to speak of a taboo conscience or, after a taboo has been violated, of a taboo sense of guilt.[26]

22 Halmos, C., *L'autorité Expliquée aux Parents*, Paris: Nil, 2008, p. 11.
23 As popularised by the singer J. Dutronc.
24 Halmos, *L'autorité Expliquée aux Parents*, p. 49. C. Hamos illustrates parental authority explaining its necessity in the process of child civilisation. She analyses it in four principles. Principle 1: in a civilised society, we may think about anything, say anything but we cannot do everything. Principle 2: We cannot have everything. Principle 3: sexuality is subjected to rules (horror of incest, consenting partner, private dimension of the act). Principle 4: necessity imposed by the reality of price to pay (effort and reward).
25 Ekardnam ('Mandrake' in reverse) is the diabolical twin of Mandrake that exists on the other side of the mirror.
26 Freud, *Totem and Taboo*, p. 67.

It is possible to use the idea of conscious taboo, and if a taboo is violated a sense of guilt is attached to the taboo, in the same way as crossing the mirror for Mandrake. The conscious taboo as moral conscious, internal perception of the repudiation of certain desires we feel,[27] brings an internal condemnation of accomplished actions.[28] The conscious taboo is probably the most primitive form of consciousness that includes the establishment of what we know as *good and evil*. For Freud,

> this same characteristic [conscience] is to be seen in the savage's attitude towards taboo. It is a command issued by conscience; any violation of it produces a fearful sense of guilt which follows as a matter of course and of which the origin is unknown.[29]

If it seems evident that Freudian theory is more concerned with the individual self, we cannot eliminate the social dimension from Freud's writings. For him, taboo is a social formation.[30] His analysis of the socio-cultural phenomenon lets us imagine also that the transgression has to be thought in this specific context. We need to bear in mind that the connection between individual and group seems to go through neurosis, which, even if Freud clearly explains that it is different from taboo, has elements so similar that he uses some analogies:

> The asocial nature of neuroses has its genetic origin in their most fundamental purpose, which is to take flight from an unsatisfying reality into a more pleasurable world of phantasy. The real world, which is avoided in this way by neurotics, is under the sway of human society and of the institutions collectively created by it.[31]

The fear in primitive tribes that the violation of taboos would be followed by punishment, serious illness or death, is characteristic. Indeed, 'It is feared . . . that the violation of a taboo will be followed by a punishment, as a rule by some serious illness or death'.[32] But it is not necessary for the punishment to really exist. The threat of possible punishment following a transgression is enough. This echoes what Bentham proposes: it is less the punishment than the idea of punishment, apparent, or what comes from a real punishment (the idea of the punishment) that matters.[33] However, if the transgression is not followed by 'real' punishment, the group must be punished:

27 Ibid.
28 Ibid.
29 Ibid., p. 68.
30 Ibid., p. 105.
31 Ibid., p. 74.
32 Ibid., p. 71.
33 Tusseau, G., *Jeremy Bentham, la guerre des mots*, Paris: Dalloz, Les sens du droit, 2011, p. 155.

> Only if the violation of a taboo is not automatically avenged upon wrong-doer does a collective feeling arise among savages that they are all threatened by the outrage; and they thereupon hasten to carry out the omitted punishment themselves.[34]

There is a necessity felt by the group, a social necessity, towards applying a real punishment, which is understood as an essential element of the cohesion of the group. We can easily see hidden here the beginning of a sort of solidarity that really seems to push the solitary individual into a forced association. In fact,

> If one person succeeds in gratifying the repressed desire, the same desire is bound to be kindled in all other members of the community.[35]

We then understand that criminal law, Freud's human criminal law, is based on the hypothesis that impulses are the same for the guilty and the one avenging the victim; 'one of the foundations of the human penal system'[36] keeping in mind that 'the punishment will not infrequently give those who carry it out an opportunity of committing the same outrage under colour of an act of expiation.'[37] There is a sort of mechanism here too, which demonstrates a certain dose of solidarity,[38] a *bricolage* that reinforces social norms.

Transgression, 'you shall not kill', and 'masks' of the group

In *Civilisation and Its Discontent*, Freud considers again the borders between the individual and the collective and seems to focus on the irreconcilable antagonism between instinctual demands and restrictions imposed by civilisation. This point has to be linked to the idea of human criminal law and the relation between 'that the prohibited impulses are present alike in the criminal and in the avenging community'.[39] What Freud establishes here is a spatial dimension of the world as society: the civilisation. We may ask ourselves here if it is not possible to consider that 'civilisation' was defined by Freud as a synonym of the State in Kelsen. Indeed, for him the State is an association of people based on psychological interaction.[40] This one is maintained by an organic repression, the ego emerging from that constraint. The social link begins then in repression.

34 Freud, *Totem and Taboo*, p. 71.
35 Ibid., p. 72.
36 Ibid.
37 Ibid.
38 Ibid.
39 Ibid.
40 Kelsen, H. (1924), 'The Conception of the State and Social Psychology – With Special Reference to Freud's Group Theory', *International Journal of Psycho-Analysis* 5, pp. 1–38, esp. p. 3.

Transgression continues to develop by transforming into morality. It is perhaps here that the individuals' assimilation into a group can then take shape and grow beyond civilisation. Transgression or the possibility of transgression becomes a point of view that affects the lifestyle and builds social stratification (through transgression; deviance), interacting between individual and group. This is the beginning of the creation of the superego and that is not far from the State concept, Kelsen considering that for Freud, the State has a 'group mind'.[41] Kelsen himself will attempt to apply the Freudian theory of totemism to legal theory; totemism imagined as the collective consumption of the same animal killed by the tribe, by all members of the tribe, as an act of identification.[42] If one refers to the exchange between Freud and Kelsen on the consideration of the superego and the State, one realises that it is designed as enlargement of the Father in parent-authority. The Father itself is imposed as the 'third instance' which initiates social functioning,[43] and is already reminiscent not only of the problem of authority in the group, whose superego is one element, but also of what will be discussed later, the issue of legal event, the trial that according to Ost is 'the ritualised staging, institutionalised by words which have layers'.[44] The superego is the other face of the Name of the Father, his mask.[45] One needs to recall this phrase of Lacan; 'It is in the name of the father that we must recognise the support of the symbolic function, which . . . identifies himself with the figure of the law'.[46] In addition, the pure logic of Oedipus means that to the capricious desire of the mother, origin of the superego, we must oppose the law that applies to all, the pacifying effect of the Name of the Father.[47] But this State of which Kelsen speaks resonates here as the best group for the individual:

> 'Like all other social groups, the state, the most significant of them all, is the specific unity of a multitude of individuals, or at any rate, of individual activities, and the inquiry into the nature of the state is fundamentally an inquiry into the nature of this unity'.[48]

41 Ibid., p. 19.

42 Jabloner, C., 'Kelsen and his Circle: The Viennese Years', *European Journal of International Law*, 9 (1998), pp. 368–385, esp. p. 383.

43 Halmos, *L'autorité Expliquée aux Parents*, p. 149.

44 Ost, F., 'L'invention du tiers, Eschyle et Kafka', *Esprit*, Autumn–September 2007, p.149. Furthermore, we note that the absence of the figure of the third party in a society brings automatically a trial similar to Kafka's one (p. 155), absence that reflects the absence of the Father as carrying the law (p. 156): 'la mise en scène ritualisée, institutionnalisée de la parole qui fait tiers'.

45 Miller, J. A., *Theorie de Turin*, www.causefreudienne.net/index.php/ecole/textes-fondateurs/theorie-de-turin (accessed 5 April 2012). Miller, too, brings Kafka here: 'Un monde sans juge, où la loi n'aurait pas d'interprète, où l'inhumanité universalisante de la loi s'appliquerait sans médiation au particulier, ne serait pas un monde de Kant, mais un monde de Kafka'.

46 Lacan, *Écrits 1*, p. 276: 'C'est dans le nom du père qu'il nous faut reconnaître le support de la fonction symbolique qui . . . identifie sa personne à la figure de la loi.'

47 Miller, *Theorie de Turin.*

48 Kelsen, 'The Conception of the State and Social Psychology', p. 1.

It is also the best example of community:

> The state, too, as a social bond, is manifested in the idea of a definite community, of common organisation, of common territory, etc. Here, again, an extra-psychological conception of the state must be assumed whose psychic reflex-its precise kind is irrelevant-may create this feeling of fellowship in the minds of the people forming the state.[49]

The heart of the superego manifestations oscillates between two extremes: critical monitoring or surveillance, in fact self-critique, and severity and harshness towards oneself, the anticipation of punishment for things that have not been committed 'in the real'.[50] The state constraint seems to be associated with the law in analysing the ambivalent effects produced in the individual unconscious.[51] Without this connection, no social standard is effective, and compliance to standards does not cause excessive guilt and need for punishment, which Freud describes as characterising the severity or even the cruelty of the superego that finally establishes equivalence between respect for the law and its transgression.[52]

It is through a psychic court that the creation of 'his' world is defended: the excessive guilt and cruelty of the superego not only establishes an equivalence between respect for the law and its transgression, but also between court and '*for interieur*'.[53] Humans become civilised, if we look again at the myth of the primal horde as narrated in *Totem and Taboo*, only at the time of renunciation, when the border between the psychic court and the future judicial court is no longer clear. We know that in the horde, the sons, the brothers, are forced to kill the father in order to take his place. But this is not the only consequence. In fact, the father must be killed in order to implement this prohibition of killing. The only original pact is the implementation of 'thou shalt not kill'. But it is a pact that can only arrive after the patricide. It should first be a transgression of the pact, even though it does not yet exist, so that it can be imposed. According to Freud, 'we feel not the slightest temptation to violate any of these prohibitions – the commandments to "do no murder", for instance – and that we feel nothing but horror at the notion of violating them.'[54] This first, and most important, effect of the commandment is to block the *passage à l'acte*. We must repress the desire to kill the father, renounce transgressing, to create a social bond. The assemblage, or 'weaving',[55] is a psychic one, a symbolic weaving with a social impact, which creates social ties; a court judging permanently, by creating this superego, which prevents the patricide from happening again. It is well understood that this operates both at the individual level and at group level. It includes moving

49 Ibid., p. 6.
50 Balibar, 'The Invention of the Super-Ego', p. 8.
51 Ibid.
52 Ibid.
53 Ibid., p. 11.
54 Freud, *Totem and Taboo*, p. 69.
55 Halmos, *L'autorité Expliquée aux Parents*, pp. 148–149

from the pleasure principle to the reality principle. As Marcuse says '[t]he radical hypothesis of *Beyond the Pleasure Principle* would stand: the instincts of self-preservation, self-assertion'.[56] For Freud, human history began in repression, the beginning of civilisation occurs when humans 'give up'.[57] One can venture this hypothesis: that civilisation began in crime and its renunciation, when man gave up the idea of transgressing.

In the group we do find this. The pleasure principle, party time, *le temps de la fête*, the state of nature, is a state of complete satisfaction of everything and anything. It precedes the application of the principle of reality when we should repress a number of things, starting with renouncing killing our neighbour according to 'thou shalt not kill'. From the psychic court to the place of justice, there is actually only one small step, but one giant leap for mankind. Places of justice are there to narrate something much broader than the settlement of a dispute between parties. They are there to help us with special devices to present a play, allowing us to put on the clothes of an actor, framed by law, through specific rituals.[58]

We refer to these fictions so decried by Bentham, these 'intellectual or ideological constructs of large scale such as the social contract'.[59] It is well known that according to the state of nature, the social contract theories of Hobbes and Locke, that Rousseau considers that time without the direct experience of continuity is an almost magical space-time: hypothesis 1, which is used as a marker to another almost magical space-time; and hypothesis 2, where one lives the experience of discontinuity.[60] Humans will be civilised when we renounce the satisfaction of 'all' desires. We do it for ourselves, but also, consciously or not, willingly or not, for the group. By becoming civilised, we can, or can hope to, live with others. Under the mask of civilised man remains the (original) crime, their renunciation, transgression. Civilised humans renounce transgression and aggression toward their peers. Civilised humans must therefore make huge efforts to not transgress anymore because it is this renunciation that creates social ties. It is therefore not surprising that in their desire for civilisation, humans retain their desire for aggression. In the state of nature, where the pleasure principle (or the lack of it) was the rule, humans could do whatever they wanted. Crime, transgression of the future pact, was permanent. The state of civilisation is a space-time where the reality principle that becomes the rule is applied, (or is present), making the transgression of the pact a crime. We should not forget that the crime is committed only because there is something else in front of us as an obstacle for our enjoyment. Primitive man, son in the horde, knows this well and knows the obstacle: the father. For Freud the first crime, the crime *par excellence*, is patricide. We must kill the father, obstacle to pleasure; our pleasure. He must be killed because he, the father, is the foundation of the law. He both forces and

56 Marcuse, H., *Eros & Civilisation*, London: Abacus, 1972, p. 73.
57 Ibid., p. 29.
58 See following chapters on that point.
59 Tusseau, *Bentham*, p. 38.
60 Derrida, J., *De la Grammatologie*, Paris: Les Éditions de Minuits, 1967, p. 372.

prevents pleasure. He forces it because without something forbidden, he does not exist. He prevents it because it 'brings' reality. We must transgress once at least, to be sure of the sustainability of 'thou shalt not kill'.

From one story of transgression to another

Almighty God created the Garden of Eden, a paradise, whose image is reminiscent of the state of nature. Yet it is a somewhat peculiar state of nature because Adam can do everything except one thing. Adam can do whatever he wants in the garden, except eat the forbidden fruit of the tree of knowledge. The 'Father' prohibits his 'son' from doing this but we feel that if he does not transgress there cannot be anything else. So we may well have here a state of nature time-1 of the state of civilisation. It touches tangentially the state of civilisation through this prohibition that must be transgressed, especially as we know what comes after . . . We anticipate transgression, as it is anticipated in the relationship rule; punishment/sanction. By imposing this rule, a development through what is forbidden is allowed, by transgression. One could think of Adam not touching the forbidden fruit. So he does not come out of this state of nature of a particular kind. This is a particular state of nature because it is created by the divine with a limit that must necessarily be exceeded: Adam must absolutely not touch the forbidden fruit but must also do it (this is expected) to found human society. When Adam contravenes this prohibition, there may then be the development of humanity. It is a transgression that is also a foundation. The divine prohibition in the time-1 offers a space of reality not unrelated to the Freudian reality principle. The divine prohibition and its transgression create man/humanity.

Humans are facing rules, taboos, that they cannot (or can no longer) break. Yet these are the rules that they gave themselves. These taboos; sacred, consecrated, disturbing, dangerous, forbidden, impure are related to totems. They work around the will of the father, either in agreement with it, or against it. The totem is marked by taboos attached to it, which constitute its heart: the members of the horde cannot kill the totem (horror of patricide) while the rule of absolute abstinence to all women, as totem (horror of incest) also exists. The myth of the primal horde, the totem and taboo, creates the story of the desire to transgress and of the law, of not to transgress.[61] To become civilised, patricide must be contained by the original law, the basic/fundamental law, the simplest of the state of civilisation that is the rule of 'thou shalt not kill', an essential rule and commandment included in the Decalogue, and therefore a foundation. From the moment this law is 'there', present, human society can be said to be civilised. The myth works as a pact, an alliance between the brothers; members of the horde. They will not kill (or not anymore) the father, because they become civilised. Until this transgression is repressed, the horde knows nothing other than freedom. For Marcuse, the absence of repression is the

61 Derrida, *Grammatologie*, p. 372. For Freud, laws are prohibition of patricide and of incest. It is at the time of *la fête* that incest becomes a crime too. Before that time, there is no incest, no crime, because there is no prohibition of incest as there is no society.

archetype of freedom; civilisation is the struggle against it.[62] The substitution of the reality principle to the pleasure principle is the largest traumatic event in human development, personal and social. It happens when the young child learns to submit to his parents, but it was there in the primitive horde, when the father controlled power and pleasure and forced his children, brothers, to give up their freedom.[63] Basically, the myth of the primitive horde, and the assassination of the Father, demonstrates that the history of individuals is also that of the group, of civilisation, and vice versa. The development, the move from the pleasure principle (which was used as the equivalent to the state of nature) to the reality principle (the same for the state of civilisation), in Freudian theory, involves a chronological social time, a time when everything is done for and by the acquisition and integration of social rules, code of conduct, morality. Time, as Levinas says, is not the act of an isolated subject, alone, but is the relation itself of the subject in otherness, illustrating again a social dimension.[64]

But the transition to the reality principle, to the state of civilisation, does not mean the end of the crime. Thus the pleasure principle remains in the unconscious, archaic memory of the patricide, and may resurface.[65] A mechanism is needed to resolve disputes, a specific legal event that permits them to reconsider the renunciation and to bring back the social bond. This event will, as a result, be conceived as a staging or a play repeating the original pact, the transgression, and its repression. Rousseau considered the original pact to be the birth of human society: 'It is sacred to him only one institution, one fundamental agreement: it is the Social Contract, the order social itself, the right of law, the Convention that is the basis for all agreements.'[66] In a brief effort of memory the brothers will be reunited to be judged and sentenced. We will recall the original act of patricide; this original crime that was in fact not one in our state of total freedom, and that has become one since we qualified it as a transgression. As said by Marcuse, Freud's individual psychology is essentially social.[67] The social bond is 're-woven' through this reconstruction, in the legal event, then trial,[68] each participant identifying the criminal and reliving the crime scene. The specificity of this event, as shown by Garapon, is a meeting, mediated by specific forms, of several persons whose imputation of their actions is recognised, as well as their ability to justify themselves by narrating stories'.[69] This event appears as a ritual link between the

62 Marcuse, *Eros & Civilisation*, p. 31.
63 Ibid.
64 Levinas, E., *Le Temps et l'Autre*, Paris: PUF, 1983, p. 17.
65 Marcuse, *Eros and Civilisation*, p. 31.
66 Derrida, *Grammatologie*, p. 373: 'Il n'est sacré à ses yeux qu'*une seule* institution, *une seule* convention fondamentale: c'est, nous dit le *Contrat social*, l'ordre social lui-même, le droit du droit, la convention qui sert de fondement à toutes les conventions.
67 Marcuse, *Eros and Civilisation*, p. 31.
68 For an analysis of the differences between trial and *procès*, see Marrani, D., 'Confronting the symbolic position of the judge in western European legal traditions: A comparative essay', *European Journal of Legal Studies* 3 (1) (2010), pp. 1–31.
69 Garapon, A., 'Le Droit mis à l'Epreuve', *Esprit,* August–September 2007, p. 208.

space of justice and what 'accounts' for the individual and for the group, the society. In places of justice, the ritual concern allows a metamorphosis of everyday life, where one comes to the transformation of what is mundane.[70] There is therefore an urgent necessity for the process of justice, for the device or the judicial apparatus, to allow the smooth functioning of society, which is also that of group harmony. The places of justice are charged with orchestrating that harmony by using rituals to contribute to the restoration of some order. For Eliade, myth and ritual are connected:[71] the ritual abolishes the profane, chronological, time, and recovers the sacred time of myth.[72] The sacred time meets the sacred place in the places of justice through rituals of justice. But it connects, it communicates, with the myth, in particular that of the primal horde.

The judicial ritual functions as memory, reminding us of the fundamental ambivalence of legal events. It allows us to link the psychic court and the 'social' court. In fact, behind the judicial ritual hides the sacred, the religious, magically linking time and space.[73] Humans who are not free as they were 'before' have now overthrown their 'masters' and hidden their commands in their mental apparatus.[74] We know that the particular characteristic of an event, its movement, is well known; a frantic march bringing us from the outside to the inside. The boundary between the outside and the inside is a wall of separation between two spaces, in and out. We move from outside to inside the sacred space of justice, the walls of which are an enclosure separating the sacred from the profane; the place where the social bond is 're-woven', where the return to the primal scene is taking place. When we consider what happens abstractly within a place of justice, we have inside or outside a feeling that is the same for everybody, that here and now there is something about the law and its application.[75] This event is framed by specific rituals that merge time and space, a theatrical ritual, where the development of mankind, passing through transgression, will replay through some *mise en scène*.

Spaces of justice, playing with the natural movement of the Earth and the Sun, day and night, life and death, light and darkness, between the 'temple illuminated by justice to the dark places devoted to crime',[76] offer not only a representation of the psychic court but also of the myth of the horde and the patricide. They impose the separation between good and bad, right and wrong, real and/or

70 Bowie, F., *The Anthropology of Religion*, London: Blackwell Publishing 2000, excerpts from Chapter 7 'Ritual Theory, Rites of Passage, and Ritual Violence', pp. 151–168, citing Alexander, B., p.139.

71 Eliade, M., *Aspect du Mythe*, Paris: Gallimard idées 1963, p. 10

72 Ibid, p. 172.

73 On that specific point related to ritual, see Reik in Reik, T., *Ritual, Four Psychoanalytic Studies*, New York: Evergreen, 1962 (1946).

74 Marcuse, *Eros and Civilisation*, p. 32

75 Goodrich, P., 'Europe in America: Grammatology, Legal Studies and the Politics of Transmission', *Columbia Law Review*, 101 (8) (2001), pp. 2033–2084, esp. p. 2077.

76 Markus, T., *Buildings and Power, Freedom and control in the origin of modern building types*, London: Routledge, 1993, pp. 34–35.

symbolic.[77] The court contributes to this connection between justice and human development.[78] It is a sacred place, illuminated by the light of truth, which contrasts with the darkness of the crime scene,[79] a place where people are physically face to face, where 'justice is . . . inseparable from the experience of human plurality, appearance (in court) becoming a metaphor for human coexistence'.[80]

In places of justice, there is the presence of a specific ritual, a complex system of values which forces solemnity. There is theatre creating a space where time is organised to produce a symbolic moral system. It allows the movement from the darkness, a chaotic moment, disorganised and terrible, which follows the dispute, coming after the outlawed time, that continues on from the transgression of the law, to the light of the system of morality. This revives the pact, and repeats a journey of initiation, from the beginning, from the pre-transgressive state, to the post-transgressive state, enabling a fresh start, and then finally a re-birth. In a courthouse, a microcosm of a primitive world, the development of humanity is replayed, from the time of birth to the time of the dispute. Within the legal event, this drama's primal scene is played and replayed, reminding us of where we came from and how we arrived at where we are: remembering the transgression. Ritual, myth . . . we see the renewal, a transformation affirmed and confirmed by an existing link between the myth of birth and rebirth.[81] Also, the work of the judge, as explained by Professor Assier-Andrieu, is to reformulate what was: what originates in the past.[82] The *stare decisis*, so important to the trial, is illustrated by the idea of tradition, an endless chain of rules, which is handed down in time 'by the institution of the jury, the voice of the people itself.'[83] Understandably, the trial (by jury) is an important legal event for the common law. It is a flagship event that carries both powerful magic and value judgment. It is, in fact, the legal event *par excellence*. In the courtrooms and in the classrooms of our law schools, one can legitimately call the trial an 'event' and see through the judicial process what should or should not be – in the present time for the parties, and in the future for society. The trial is also an expression of a certain kind of magical thinking. It is therefore an open and specific expression of the *raison d'etre* of common law lawyers, which is brought about through dramatisation. The common law through

77 The term trial owes its origin to the French word *triable*, sortable, and thus is closely tied to that which can be sorted or separated. This dynamic process, understood as an event for the parties and for society, must achieve a result: the separation of the good from the bad. See also Klein, M., 'L'amour, la culpabilité et le besoin de réparation' in Klein, M., *L'Amour et la Haine*, Paris: Payot 2001 (1937), pp. 87–88.

78 This works as a reminder of one of the reasons we may have used temple as signifier of justice over centuries, in development of societies we may qualify of post primitives.

79 We may with Lacan consider that 'Truth begins to be established only once language exists'. Lacan, J., *My Teaching*, London: Verso, 2008, p. 29.

80 Garapon, 'Le Droit mis à l'Epreuve', p. 215.

81 Reik, *Ritual*, pp. 91–166, esp. p. 156.

82 Assier-Andrieu, L., *L'Autorité du Passé, Essai anthropologique sur la common law*, Paris: Dalloz, Les sens du droit Essai, 2011, p. 111.

83 Ibid., p. 63.

precedent reminds us of the past, and brings to our present an unconscious fear of power and authority. The voice of the people, the cry of the horde . . . the judicial rituals go beyond the solely individual frame as they allow the brothers to rebuild social bonds, and to remember the transgression as a founding act. As highlighted by Balibar, the judicial time of subjectivity, conceived as the moment when the superego is considered as structure; a system individualising social relationships mediated by guilt, by integrally moving the logic of negative identification at the scene of the unconscious, permits the proposition that there is only transgression, and that only this statement makes our membership of or belonging to the legal order possible.[84]

In this chapter I analysed the original transgression and how this moment may be considered as the foundation of the social construct. I considered how the individual and the group are actually linked and how the magical mechanism totem and taboo are related to judicial ritual and the specific space and time of justice: the object of the next chapter.

84 Balibar, 'The Invention of the Super-Ego', p. 15.

2 Judicial spaces and ritual(s) of justice

The relation between time and space in the trial*

Introduction

According to Paul Ricœur's words,

> the delivery of justice is not merely a matter of arguments, but one of making decision. Here lies the heavy responsibility of the judge, the last link in the proceedings' chain, in any stages. When the last word of the judge is one of sentencing, the judge reminds us that he is the holder of the balance as well as the sword.[1]

With this beautiful definition given by the philosopher, we will keep in mind the idea of the argument and of the decision, the balance and the sword, of the proceedings and of the judge as an agent in the delivery of justice, of all these characteristics of judicial practice '[which] allow to define . . . justice formalism'.[2] By focusing on the idea of formalism, we quickly realise that behind what Ricœur calls 'judicial practice characteristics' is hidden the appearance, or even the aesthetic aspect, of justice, which is equally, if not more, important than its reality. However, the idea of proceeding and of practice requires us not to consider justice as motionless but as dynamic. Such formalism is bound to ritual and is

* This is a revised, amended and updated version of a 2011 book chapter published in French as 'Rituel(s) de justice? – Essai anthropologique sur la relation du temps et de l'espace dans le process'. Parts of the book were presented as papers: 'Réflexions autour des rituels de justice', 18 May 2012, Université Laval, Quebec ; 'Ritual, Law, Justice: The Question of Time and Space', Staff Seminar, 24 May 2010, New Zealand Centre for Public Law, Victoria University of Wellington, New Zealand; 'Essay on Rituals of Justice', Third Justice Environments Conference (Justice Research group, University of Western Sydney), 20–22 May 2010, Sydney, Australia.

1 Ricœur, P., *Amour et Justice*, Paris: Seuil, Point Essais, 2008, p. 27: 'l'exercice de la justice n'est pas simplement un cas d'arguments, mais de prise de décision. C'est ici la lourde responsabilité du juge, dernier anneau de la chaîne de procédures, à quelque degré que ce soit. Quand ce dernier mot du juge est un mot de condamnation, le juge se rappelle à nous comme porteur non seulement de la balance mais du glaive'.

2 Ibid. 'toutes ces caractéristiques de la pratique judiciaire [qui] permettent de définir . . . le *formalisme* de la justice'.

more or less already noticeable in primitive societies, and perfectly visible in archaic and pre-modern societies.[3] Here, formalism is articulated with religion, magic and law, within the context of the value and of the normative system of each social organisation.[4] As Garapon underlines 'before rules, law, judges, courthouses, there was ritual'.[5]

If we consider law in primitive societies, a number of examples of ritual(s) linked to justice can be found. Tribal courts, such as Tribal Councils of American Indians, or of the Ashanti, are, for instance, striking illustrations. One may, from these examples, note the absence of temporal permanency – which is not unrelated to Garapon's ideas. There is no continuity in time, as courts sit temporarily. Furthermore, there are no permanent structures which could remind us of our 'courthouses'. Finally, there are, occasionally, the use of (compulsory) procedures or a judicial apparatus which includes 'several things/elements: a body of written laws/rules, tribunals or courts of justice, committed in the function of stating the law, judges.'[6] However, two elements are generally found: accountability and authority. Indeed, the liability of the author of the 'wrongdoing' and authority of the group (or of one individual in the group acting or reacting on behalf of the group) are almost always present.

Likewise, the presence of a certain method or process can be found: a comparatively developed and complex procedure. If we can hardly imagine the absence of continuity, however, we understand the latter elements very well in our modern societies.[7] Only the preconceived ideas of modern or postmodern man are likely to stop us considering these ancient practices as institutions which, like our current ones, are essential to the delivery of justice but also of making law effective or even 'alive'. Thus, in primitive societies, justice expresses itself as social practice, as defined by Ricœur. It is obviously less formal than the one we know: it means applying rules which are not always written, expressing opinions in places which are not always built 'physically', and operating thanks to judges who are not truly judges but 'individuals like us [here like them], deemed [more or less] independent and responsible for pronouncing the just sentence in a particular circumstance', that is to say 'a higher instance' responsible for 'deciding between claims of parties with competing rights or interests'.[8] In addition, primitive societies will always be concerned with focusing on a social dimension of the wrongdoing and the restoration of the right (social) order. Furthermore,

3 Hoebel, E. A., *The Law of the Primitive Man*, New York: Atheneum 1976, p. 257.

4 Ibid., p. 267.

5 Garapon, A., *Bien Juger*, Paris: Odile Jacob, 2001 (1997), p. 23: 'Avant qu'il y est des lois, du droit, des juges, des palais de justice, il y avait un rituel'.

6 Ricœur, *Amour et Justice*, p. 27: 'plusieurs choses: un corps de lois écrites, des tribunaux ou des cours de justice, investis de la fonction de dire le droit, des juges.'

7 Hoebel, *The Law of the Primitive Man*, p. 24.

8 Ricœur, *Amour et Justice*, pp. 26–27: 'des individus comme nous [comme eux ici], réputés [plus ou moins] indépendants et chargés de prononcer la sentence juste dans une circonstance particulière', that is to say 'une instance supérieure' is responsible for 'trancher entre des revendications [claims] de parties porteuses d'intérêts ou de droits opposés'.

this is confirmed in non-European modern societies where the overriding objective is not the truth, but rather harmony and peace.[9]

Primitive societies, in this sense, must be seen as important examples because they influence what is and what happened 'after', which shaped our vision, with the help of ritual(s). Thus, a very primitive level of justice does not necessarily require the presence of a third party, such as our judge. From this absence, it is worth noting, for example, that their court will occur in a space and a time very different from the one we know with the justice of today, but will, however, respect a precise and certain legal chronology. This 'procedure', accepted by the tribesmen, will be sanctioned in last resort by public opinion, emanating from the whole tribe.[10] Justice is done as soon as public opinion of the tribe accepts and acknowledges that the procedure followed by the plaintiff is correct, the sentence is adequate, and the guilty person agrees to accept it.

Thus, the court will be constituted by the plaintiff, and with public opinion which supports him, the procedure will be supposed 'legal'.[11] The court and the sanction become landmarks for the law. Indeed, law cannot exist without a sentence pronounced to enforce it, with the court as the special space where the authority is manifested. Professor Sacco claims, 'Law is rooted in man's willingness to obey'.[12] Thus, any legal apparatus would only be there to revive in man this willingness. Even in the most primitive societies, law should pass the test of the court, which is the only tool to allow an order, a command, to become a legal rule.[13] What about, then, the difficulties that we sometime face concerning the recognition of courts? In primitive societies, it is clear that a flexible model is favoured, one which corresponds to cosmogony, of a cosmogonic vision of the world, of the myth of its creation and so of the ritual as recreation of the original myth.[14] Eliade underlines, 'the original myth of medicines is always integrated in the cosmogonic myth'.[15] There is thus a parallel relationship between the cure and justice – this relationship is also present in the presence of the shaman, the magician, or the sorcerer, as an affirmation of the supernatural origin of authority.[16] The magical side of justice is present in most primitive societies. In some Eskimo tribes, the legal instrument of dispute resolution, and restoration of the relations between the members of the community, is the sung duel, alone or with the support of the family of the accused. One of the litigants will receive a 'judgment' in its favour. This judgment will be followed by a psychological 'reward' but no

9 Nader L. and Sursock, A., 'Anthropology and Justice', in Cohen, R. (ed.), *Justice: Views from the Social Sciences*, New York: Springer, 2006, pp. 205–230, esp. p. 209.

10 Ricœur, *Amour et Justice*, p. 24.

11 Ibid., p. 25.

12 Sacco, R., *Anthropologie Juridique, Apport à une micro histoire du droit*, Paris: Dalloz, 2008, p. 170.

13 See Hart, H.L.A., 'Positivism and The Separation of Law and Morals', in Dworkin, R.M., (ed.), *The Philosophy of Law*, Oxford: OUP, 1977, pp. 15–37.

14 Eliade, M., *Aspects du Mythe*, Paris: Gallimard, Idées, 1963, p. 33.

15 Ibid., p. 42.

16 Sacco, *Anthropologie Juridique*, pp. 122–123.

real 'reward' or compensation.[17] The sung duel operates like the duel which takes place between the lawyers and the parties. Another illustration can be found in the case of the Ifugao. The Ifugao have a very precise procedure to respect. This requires the use of an intermediate; the Monkalun, who is neither a judge, nor an arbitrator, but a mediator, whose only objective is to restore the balance, the good order in the community. Chosen by the plaintiff, he is the facilitator of both parties, contributing to an embryo of a legal institution.[18] One will notice here the parallel between balance and good order and the use in the justice symbol of the balance for the equilibrium and of the sword for the good order.

But we will focus a little longer on the case of the Ashanti. Their procedure is really codified. The parties (first defendant and second defendant) are presented to the Speaker or the Okyeame who starts the hearing, describes the facts, and proposes a date for the trial. The day of the trial, both parties are presented to the chief and to the elders. The Okyeame asks the first defendant to present his facts orally and concludes by saying, 'if the presentation I made is not the truth, and if I made up anything, then I am ready to undergo the punishment, because I uttered the forbidden words'. Therefore, he relies on the court. The second defendant presents himself, and explains his own version of the case by repeating the same sentence as the first one. The presentations are diametrically opposite. The Okyeame must then corroborate both versions by repeating them. He asks the first one 'Is it the words of your mouth or am I lying'. If the words are not identical, he may request they be corrected, but this is rare. The statement is therefore confirmed. Idem for the second statement. Two truths oppose one another, 'by confronting reasons for or against, supposedly plausible, communicable, worthy to be discussed by the other party'.[19] Like barristers, the elders will cross-examine the two parties, while the chief remains discreet. The public may then ask questions, and one can call a witness, who will be called by the Okyeame. Only one witness will be called. Indeed, the Ashanti system relies on a very firm religious belief. It is not possible to believe that one witness will be more or less in favour of one of the parties. Moreover, the power of the oath and of the death penalty, along with the lie, a sort of sin, in short, makes the presence of two witnesses impossible. The elders will ask the chief to present the witness via messenger. The latter should take the oath, in particular to not tell anyone of the hearing, otherwise he will die. Now, everything relies on the testimony. The Okyeame informs the chief 'Great sire, we will introduce the main support' and he warns the parties that the witness will be decisive in the decision making. Then, the witness arrives with the messenger and should take the oath before the gods to tell the truth. The Okyeame appeals to the gods to kill the witness if he lies, and orders the witness to swear three times that he will not lie. The elders must then decide, of the two parties, whose story is best supported by that of the

17 Hoebel, *The Law of the Primitive Man*, pp. 96–99.

18 Ibid., pp. 114–115.

19 Ricœur, *Amour et Justice*, pp. 26–27: 'en confrontant des raisons pour ou contre, supposées plausibles, communicables, dignes d'être discutées par l'autre partie'.

witness. The Okyeame then tells the losing party: 'you heard what the witness stated', explaining that what he did was similar to the fact of coming to the court and hitting the Okyeame with sticks, and therefore he was guilty. Everyone present then shouts: 'E, e, e, e, e!'[20] Then the sentence will be pronounced by the King. The various examples presented above show a certain vision of justice.

Understandably, the work of the anthropologist, or of the lawyer, is not the same as the work of the preceptor or of the fabulist. Yet, we dare to express the idea that justice presented in these illustrations closely corresponds to fables narrated by La Fontaine. From the umpire who 'Never held to their discretion [the parties' discretion] an equal balance',[21] and the tree or monkey judge[22] before which the trial takes place, and the pleas are done 'Not by a lawyer, but by each party, as Themis did not work' ('No lawyers called to twist the laws; Each client pleaded his own cause),[23] to Rabelais' caricature of the judge, Perrin Dandin/Sir Nincom, mentioned in La Fontaine's fable, who 'made him' judge and 'draw the cash, and leave the parties only purse and cards'.[24] One likes to think that this judge, so powerful, so close to the sovereign, can only be corrupted, and that we can notice the difference of treatment between the judge of the seventeenth century and that of primitive societies. Yet it is obvious that what La Fontaine portrayed corresponds to a time of transition between a society which seems primitive and a more rational justice. This judge is corrupted: 'The parties leaving for their shares, The shells (and shells there might be moister), From which the court has sucked the oyster.'[25] The tree or monkey judge would not be considered as caricatures in primitive societies. We nevertheless understand that something is already changing. The judge's dress, coated with fur, appears like one of his strong and important characteristics: 'A saintly mouser, sleek and fat, An arbiter of keenest wit. John Rabbit in the judge concurred.'[26] But the clothes do not make him more convincing:

> And off went both [the weasel and the young rabbit] their case to broach
> Before his majesty, the furred.
> Said Clapperclaw, 'My kids approach,
> And put your noses to my ears:
> I'm deaf, almost, by weight of years.'

20 Hoebel, *The Law of the Primitive Man*, pp. 246–251.

21 La Fontaine, J., 'Le Juge arbitre, l'Hospitalier et le Solitaire', Livre XII fable 25, in *Fables*, Paris: Hachette, 1929, p. 511: 'Jamais ne tenait à leur gré [au gré des parties] la balance égale'.

22 Ibid., 'L' Homme et la Couleuvre', Livre X, fable 1, p. 383.

23 Ibid., 'Le Loup plaidant contre le Renard par devant le Singe', Livre II, fable 3, p. 55: 'Non point par avocat, mais par chaque partie, Thémis [n'ayant] pas travaillé'.

24 Ibid., 'L' Huître et les Plaideurs', Livre IX, fable 9, p. 355. 'constitue' en cour et 'tire l'argent à lui, Et ne laisse aux plaideurs que le sac et les quilles'.

25 Ibid., 'Les Frelons et les Mouches à miel', Livre I, fable 21, p. 47. 'On fait tant, à la fin, que l'huître est pour le juge, Les écailles pour les plaideurs.'

26 Ibid., 'Le Chat, la Belette et le petit lapin', Livre VII, fable 16, p. 265.

And so they did, not fearing anything.
The good apostle, Clapperclaw,
Then laid on each a well-armed paw,
And both to an agreement brought,
By virtue of his tusked jaw.[27]

Furthermore, as Garapon highlights when he quotes the fable of the *Donkey carrying relics*: 'It's thus a brainless magistrate, is honoured for his robe of state'.[28] Basically, behind the judge hides the man, a human corrupted or not. His function keeps dignity, thanks to this fur, to the judge's uniform. The fur helps to keep the dignity of the function.

The link with the archaic memory of these rituals is often highlighted by psychoanalysis. Unconscious ideas particularly influence criminal law, where, for example, we see the affirmation of the *lex talionis*, the law of retaliation, or even revenge, as mentioned in the Old Testament: an eye for an eye and a tooth for a tooth.[29] It can also be found in many codes such as the Hammurabi code.[30] Freud refers to this law in *Totem and Taboo*: 'the law of retaliation, which is so profoundly rooted in human feelings, considers that a murder can only be atoned for by the sacrifice of another life'.[31] We will see that it is in this crime; the first crime and all the mechanisms established to prevent it, that the drama of life is played and played again. It seems that looking for justice is a permanent cause for most, if not all, societies. According to Nadr and Sursock, the belief in justice, the behaviours which are associated with it, but also the reasons for justice, are universal phenomena. However, the signification of this phenomenon varies with the socio-cultural context, thus creating different forms of justice.[32] To this end, La Fontaine also enlightens us.

Understandably, if justice is both considered as a set of universal phenomena and also as an asymmetrical concept which depends on socio-cultural context, a specific space and time consists in a universal ritual or particular rituals. These always depend upon the vision that the individual and the group will have in their archaic memory of the third-party judge, which revolve around a totem or totems; these archaic social micro-organisations then define more or less 'design rituals'.

Because this book is written in a European context, it will first take European examples, mostly from French law and English law (sometimes British law). It will focus on the analysis of the judge, relying of course, on law, but also on philosophy and psychoanalysis. It will show how a parallel may be drawn between

27 Ibid.

28 Garapon, *Bien Juger*, p. 12: 'd'un magistrat ignorant, C'est la robe qu'on salue.'

29 For in depth analysis see Fish, M., 'An Eye for an Eye: Proportionality as a moral principle of punishment', *Oxford Journal of Legal Studies* 28 (1), pp. 57–72, (2008); Waldron, J., 'Lex Talionis', *Ariz. L. Rev.* 34 (25) (1992), pp. 25–51.

30 Schoenfeld, C.G., *Psychoanalysis and the Law*, Springfield, Charles Thomas, 1973, pp. 18–21.

31 Freud, S., *Totem and Taboo*, London: Ark, 1983, p. 154.

32 Nader and Sursock, 'Anthropology and Justice', p. 205.

the judge and the totem and how the judge might play a role in a specific narrative of the Oedipus story. In this chapter, I will present the characteristics attached to (the) legal totem(s), and its, or their, quantitative and qualitative differences. Then, the idea of ritual(s) and its (their) links with law and justice will be considered.

Judge, totem and Oedipus

Before considering the relationship between the three objects here, we will make a preliminary comment on the judge and the legal event in Western legal traditions.

The judge and the legal event in Western legal traditions

According to Legrand, the two legal traditions present in Western Europe, known by the terms of civil law, and common law, interact within a general legal framework: The Treaty of Rome.[33] Basically, these two legal traditions remain discursive formations of sufficient homogeneity, which generate 'autonomous discursivities'. They allow us to define two ways of understanding the reality (which reflects the two basic mythologies).[34] On this basis, and knowing that, on one hand, comparative law is, as Richard explains, an anamorphosis of legal theory,[35] and on the other hand, for Legrand, a commitment to the interdisciplinary,[36] it seems crucial to look closely at the place of the judge in these two legal traditions. The objective here is to operate this analysis through the prism of what Wittgenstein believes to be a mere mythology, a powerful mythology; the psychoanalytic theory,[37] because if we are confronted with 'autonomous discursivities' it seems that an important space should be given to the language.[38]

The judge, in the two major legal traditions, operates in a legal institution which seems to be similar, but uses a different terminology: trial and *procès*. The legal institution described by the trial and the *procès* may be understood through

33 Legrand, P., 'How to Compare Now', *Legal Studies* 16 (1996), pp. 232–242, esp. p. 232.
34 Ibid., p. 240.
35 Richard, P., 'Les Apports de Wittgenstein à la Réflexion Comparatiste', *RIDC* 4 (2005), pp. 899–920, esp. p. 900.
36 Legrand, 'How to Compare Now', p. 238.
37 Bouvresse, J., *Wittgenstein reads Freud: the myth of the unconscious*, Princeton: New French Thought, 1995, p. 52.
38 We know that Lacan reckons that the unconscious is designed like the language. According to Freud, language substitutes something for another thing. Lacan considers this second thing as the most important element. We should indicate that my comments will be restricted to Western Europe and solely to common law and civil law cultures. The concept of major legal systems will not be used because we will interpret the research of Legrand and Samuel as showing that the common law cannot be considered as a system. Legrand, P. and Samuel, P., *Introduction to Common Law*, Paris: La Découverte, 2008, esp. p. 8. We will also use English law as prototype of the common law and French law as civil law prototype. Finally, we may use the terms of Romano-Germanic and tradition of civil law equivalently.

the concept of legal event. It is a flagship event, powerful – or even magical – which carries value as a specific judgement. It is, in fact, the legal event *par excellence.* It is something, in the courtrooms and in the classrooms of law schools, one can legitimately call an 'event' and that enlightens the judicial process, in particularly by giving an idea of order, of what should or should not be. It is also the expression of a certain kind of magical thinking. It is therefore an open and specific place for the expression of a *raison d'être*, through dramatisation. It is, indeed, what Garapon proposes, when he notices that 'the legal event is part of justice as well as law: it is the foundation'.[39]

Nevertheless, the use of different words, trial and *procès,* may be a good way to distinguish the particularism of legal events, while highlighting the power of the words (in two different traditions).[40] It is necessary to keep in mind what Heidegger explained regarding the translation from Greek to Latin, which we will here apply by analogy: it is a closing and alienating process.[41] In seeking to theorise both institutions, we may diminish their meaning. The scope of certain facts may be so important, and so exceptional, that these facts influence both the individual and society. Beforehand, the meaning of these realities may be enlightened by using comparative linguistics. The term 'event' implies, through its Latin etymology *évenire* (*e* which means on, *venire* which means coming) that facts *come* and give a result (come out). The term 'trial' in the Anglo-Saxon world, which owes its origin to the French word *triage*, thus is closely tied to what can be sorted or separated. This dynamic process, understood as an event for the parties and for society, must achieve a result: the separation of the good from the bad.

According to the Oxford dictionary, the trial etymologically comes from the word *triage*, from ancient French, which is an act of separation of the good from the bad. This slightly Manichean dichotomy, expressed in this definition of the legal trial institution, is quite different from that of its 'Romano-Germanic' version, although the French equivalent, the *procès*, does not share this idea of selection between good and bad but rather of other operators (such as the legal/illegal binary described by Teubner)[42] and the idea that 'Justice . . . is the principle

39 Garapon, *Bien Juger*, p. 19. Professor Commaille considers that 'the "staging" of the exercise of the function of Justice is one of the manifestations of a traditional conception of representation as one of the embodiments of a power relying on the transcendence principle, which particularly requires to be represented: by an architecture, a work of art, rituals, etc.' Therefore, the *ars juris* would be 'one of these manifestations, one of these expressions in favour of a conception of society's structure from a certain legal regulation model'. Commaille, J., *L'Esprit Sociologique des Lois,* Paris: PUF, 1994, pp. 226–227: the 'mise en scène' de l'exercice de la fonction de Justice est une des manifestations d'une conception traditionnelle de la représentation comme une des incarnations d'un pouvoir s'appuyant sur le principe de la transcendance et, par là, qui exige particulièrement d'être représenté: par une architecture, par des oeuvres d'art, par des rites, etc.'.

40 Tambiah, S. J., 'The Magical Power of Words', *Man* 3 (2) New Series (June, 1968), pp. 175–208.

41 Heidegger, M., Introduction à la Métaphysique, Paris: Gallimard, 1967 (1935), p. 26.

42 Teubner, G., 'G Global Bukowina: Legal Pluralism in the World Society', in Teubner, G., (ed.), *Global Law Without a State*, Dartmouth: Aldershot, 1997, pp. 3–28.

of separation of good from bad'.[43] But the trial and the *procès* both start with the idea of dynamic process. The trial refers to the position of the parties before a judge, in a dispute. In order to facilitate the understanding of what underlies the resolution of a dispute, by using a legal institution able to separate good from bad, it seems interesting at this point to refer to Lyotard's definitions. First, a dispute is a conflict between two parties which cannot be resolved without a rule. Then, it may be a wrong which cannot be compensated, where the victim cannot assert his rights. Finally, it is a state where the language is ready to take its place, where 'something "needs" to be put into words/sentence, and suffers from the impossibility of being done at the moment'.[44] The word 'trial' itself carries the dynamic of the process, a scheduling of the words. In addition, according to Badiou, the event is the dimension of another process; that of the truth.[45] Then, it appears as a progression towards the legal truth, 'the judgment is the expression of a judicial truth, that is to say a truth whose source, development and finality are defined by the legal as it is realised in the trial'.[46] Indeed, the 'truth', moral truth, which differs from scientific or social truth, is supposedly and generally pronounced at the end of the legal procedure of the legal event, which makes this legal institution a sacred place which consecrates the judge's action.[47] Legal truth operates as a fiction which sanctifies the judicial function.

Consequently, it is important to analyse the symbolic position of the judge and to show that the legal event, in both common law and civil law, is a communication process where judges, lawyers, and parties interact, perhaps in different ways, through a monologue-dialogue system in a dialectical relationship.[48] The judge is

43 Garapon, *Bien Juger*, p. 28.

44 Lyotard, J. F., *Le Différend*, Paris: Éditions de Minuit, Critiques, 1983.

45 Badiou, A., 'The Problem of Evil' in Badiou, A., *Ethics: An Essay on the Understanding of Evil*, London & New York: Verso, 2001, p. 67.

46 Poncela, P., 'R Regard sur la Vérité Judiciaire', pp. 175–183, esp. p. 175, in *Dialogue, Dialectique en Philosophie et en Droit, Archive de Philosophie du Droit*, tome 29, Paris: Sirey, 1984, p. 175. See also Ravaz, B., 'Vérité Judiciaire et Vérité Religieuse', Champs libres n° 3, Paris: L'Harmattan 2002; 'Le Juge Judiciaire Gardien de la Vérité Historique ?', Champs libres n° 2, Paris: L'Harmattan 2002, pp. 225–245.

47 This happened thanks to the magical power of the words. As Professor Brunet highlights

> Thus we realise how applying the law means exercising a power: the power to decide on the meaning of the words. From this point of view, all judges would look like Humpty Dumpty who . . . pretended to be the master in the field.

Brunet, P., 'Approche Critique du Vocabulaire Juridique Européen: Le Pouvoir des Juges', Chronique de droit européen & comparé N° 17, Centre d'études juridiques européennes et comparées (CEJEC – Université Paris Ouest – Nanterre La Défense), Les Petites Affiches, August 2008, pp. 7–12, esp. p. 8.

48 This book is not an in-depth study of the different levels of justice or judges. It will be limited to the description of the legal event through general features. The kind of trial or *procès* which best fits with the described model is probably that of the criminal trial. With this in mind, I will not mention the differences between legal events with or without juries. It will nevertheless be taking into account as an element of the criminal justice structure in common law, although often used in civil law tradition. I will only consider that the presence or the absence of jury is without prejudice to the position of the judge as it is mentioned here.

related to the totem and to the Oedipus complex, and we will examine the differences between the number of totems and the elements which contribute to the positioning of the judge, in both legal traditions.

The judge as totem, the judge in the Oedipus complex

Psychoanalytic theory, and, in particular, the notions of totem and the Oedipus complex, may certainly be applied to the judge. More precisely, it is through the differences of quality and quantities of totemic position that the comparison may appear even more relevant.

The trial or the *procès* is an ambivalent legal event. This idea of ambivalence is present in Freud's works on the totem.[49] The totem, this object, this *thing* that holds a symbolic position for both the individual and for a group of individuals, is the foundation of a system of beliefs which creates a micro (social) organisation.

It is quite strange in a way to think that the totem is linked to the law.[50] But the totem is a *thing* which creates rules, and, in addition, which cannot violate the rules that it has itself created. Indeed, the taboos are linked with the sacredness of the totem. Freud explains that 'the clansmen are under the sacred obligation (subject to automatic sanctions) not to kill or destroy their totem and to avoid eating its flesh'.[51] Totemism results in 'instinctual renunciations': the worship of the totem, which includes a prohibition to hurt or kill the totem, the desire of the woman in the horde and brotherly alliance, and the restriction of 'the tendency to violent rivalry between [the members of the brotherhood Alliance]'.[52] The prohibitions, the taboos, revolve around the father, the first two on the father's side, and the last one on the father's contempt.[53] The totem is marked by the taboos that we will present here in a more detailed way, which are attached to it and constitute its heart: the members of the totem cannot kill the totem (the horror of patricide), while there is the absolute rule of the abstinence towards all the totem's women (the horror of incest).

The horror of patricide

This 'thing', the totem, is present in the legal framework. It is present in the normative rules.[54] If we compare this approach to the trial (or the *procès*), considering it as a characteristic of the legal, dynamic, event in the legal arena, we find similar characteristics. The 'legal' totem is a place where judges, lawyers and scholars 'exist'. They belong to it and know that they cannot violate the rules it created.

49 Freud, *Totem and Taboo*, pp. 1–17.
50 Ibid., p. 51
51 Ibid., p. 2
52 Freud, S., 'Moses and Monotheism: Three essays', *SE 23* (1939), pp. 1–138, esp. p. 118.
53 Ibid., p. 118.
54 Freud, *Totem and Taboo*, p. 51.

The particular totem, the legal totem, must be considered through the Oedipus complex, which evolves around the well-known triangular relationship between a child, the father and the mother.[55] In the Oedipus complex, the boy considers, at the same time, the mother as a 'subject of sexual investment' and identifies himself to the father as (ideal)[56] ego; ideal ego of the boy.[57] The main problem is that 'the little boy realises that his father is on the path leading to the mother'.[58] The son wants to be like the father because he loves the mother: thus it is necessary to kill the father. The desire of the mother becomes a desire that is forbidden, so it is taboo. This causes the development of the superego, the censorship of the ego which monitors and tries to define the heir of the Oedipus complex, the parental authority's internalisation.[59] It is there that the myth of the primitive horde, presented in Freud's *Totem and Taboo*, is connected with the politico-legal institution of the father, the symbolic Father that we will apply to the judge. All the pieces of this puzzle, the different elements of the Oedipus complex described by Lacan in many of his mathematical schemas, help the cartography of the complex.[60] He describes the complex by using the position of the subject S (Es), the division of the Ego a, and a' (the other, the mother), contributing in fact to the position of the father (or A) as the place of language, the authority, the law. This symbolic position in turn, may be filled in by other paternal figures.

This brings us to the story of the Corporal Lortie crime, narrated by Legendre. Lortie, a young corporal of the Canadian army, decided on 8 May 1984 to enter the building of the National Assembly of Quebec, with the intention of killing the government. He ran down the corridors using his automatic rifle against the people he met on his way, then, once arrived at the National Assembly Chamber, where nobody was present, because it was a day-off, he entered and sat on the president's chair, having killed three people and wounded eight. Commenting on his crime, Lortie claimed: 'the government of Quebec had the face of my father'.[61] For Legendre, what is important in this story is that in this ferocious attack, Lortie entered the building which hosted Quebec's institution to kill these specific institutions. What does the particular declaration of Lortie mean? In fact, political institutions may be considered as involved in the triangular relationship

55 The triangular relation judge-party A-party B.

56 According to Klein, the development of the superego depends for a boy or a girl. It differs although the result is actually the same. In this structure, the boy refers to the father as ideal image, whereas the girl goes to him to find the reproductive system lacking in the mother. Klein makes no difference between boys and girls. For the girls, the proximity with the mother is a long pre-Oedipal period, which changes during the phallic stage converging towards the penis that she doesn't have. Klein, M., *Le Complexe d'Oedipe*, Paris: Payot, 2001 (1945), pp. 138–145.

57 Chasseguet-Smirgel, J., *The Ego Ideal*, London: Free Association Books, 1985, p. 104.

58 Freud, S., 'Identification' in 'Group Psychology and the Analysis of the Ego', *SE* 28 (1921), pp. 105–110.

59 It is also possible to consider Freud's second topic. Id, ego/moi, super ego/surmoi.

60 Lacan, J., *Écrits* 1, Paris: Seuil, Point Essais, 1999 (1966), p. 53. Voir le 'Schéma L'.

61 Legendre, P., *Le Crime du Caporal Lortie, Traité sur le Père*, Paris: Flammarion, Champs, 1989, p. 74.

of the Oedipus complex. The father is, shall be, or will be killed, but because we are in the political sphere, where only the representation of a fiction exists, the killing may not be real; it is (always) symbolic.[62] We can conclude with two remarks: a) the father, or rather in this case the Father, represents, and therefore takes a symbolic position,[63] a position in the triangular relationship formed by the Oedipus complex; he is the authority, he is the law, and b) this shall be put in perspective with what Freud stated in *Civilisation and Its discontent*, that what begins in relation with the father ends with something which concerns the group.[64] We clearly see the social and cultural dimension of the superego, the Father representing the authority for a wider group than a family; the Law for society.[65]

One of the explanations for the French revolution is in line with this idea. The king of France himself was placed in a triangular oedipal position. The horde had to kill him. This 'real' murder by the Freudian horde can be put into perspective with the Lacanian symbolic order orchestrated in a democratic society through the elections. Because Lacan brings the 'not-the-father' [*non du pere*] closer to the 'name-of-the-father' [*nom du pere*], the symbolic position of the 'regulator-father' is a link to the authority. The judge is part of, and comes from, the *Curia Regis*. He relates to the king. Both have a paternal function of authority.[66] The Kings' traditional legitimacy and divine law 'pass', is transmitted to the judge, as an element of his court.

Even when the king is replaced by the elected elite (such as an elected head of state or an elected parliament[67]), the sacred aura of the judge is not only based on

62 It is possible to kill the staff of an institution, but not to kill the institution. See, for instance, what Derrida writes about architecture of political institutions buildings.

63 We may refer here to Lacanian topography SIR, Symbolic, Imaginary, Real.

64 Freud, S., *Civilisation and Its Discontents*, London: Penguin, 2002 (1930), p. 133.

65 This is linked to the society, to the group, and to its metaphors, as the idea of governing body, in the UK and that of 'separated' powers through the myth of the separation of powers. We could go beyond the scope of this book and comment here on the changes that have occurred in Canada and their impacts on Lortie. Indeed, 1982 is an important date for Canada which adopted a Constitution under the direction of Pierre Trudeau (The Constitution Act 1982) thus modifying the organisation of the country and getting 'freedoms' from London and in particular from the 'supreme' parliament of the United Kingdom (Westminster). Moreover, the strong figure himself, Trudeau, decided to quit his role of head of the government in early 1984.

66 The Curia Regis is an institution that could be found both in France and England as stated by Adams, G.B., in 'The Descendants of the Curia Regis', *American Historical Review* 13 (1) (Oct. 1907), pp. 11–15. See note 2 'Reference should also be made to the chart of the descent of French institutions'.

67 See Dicey:

> The authority of the state or the nation was during the earlier periods of our history represented by the power of the Crown. The King was the source of the law. . . . The royal supremacy has now passed into that sovereignty of Parliament.

Dicey, A.V., *Introduction to the Study of the Law of the Constitution*, London: Macmillan and Co., 1927, p. 279.

himself. The judge did not completely quit being sacred, remaining linked to the king and therefore to the divine. Let's take, for example, the *Conseil Supérieur de la Magistrature* (CSM) in France: this council is responsible for the appointment, the nomination and the discipline of judges. Under Article 64 of the Constitution of the Fifth Republic, the head of State is the guarantor of independence of the judiciary. Until the constitutional amendment of 2008, the CSM was thus presided over by the head of state himself (Article 65 of the Constitution).[68] This situation simultaneously contributed to favouring the autonomy of the judge and the maintenance of the sacred link 'God/Head of State/Judge'. We may find similar examples in common law countries. The Constitutional Reform Act 2005, chapter 4 s. 12 concerns the transfer of the appointment's functions to Her Majesty. In schedule 3, it provides indeed that 'Her Majesty, instead of the Lord Chancellor, shall appoint to certain functions'. Thus, the monarch is responsible for the nomination and revocation of judges, as the monarch-head of the State is the guarantor of the independence of the judges. This is also applicable to the president head of State.

So, what appears essential seems to be the symbolic position. This position creates authority and is related to what is sacred. It seems closely linked to its archaeology: the religion (God, the Father) and the tradition (the sovereign monarch), gathered through the vertical link 'God-judge'. The position of the judge depends on the horror of the patricide: the members of the totem cannot kill the totem. The 'totem judge' becomes sacred and takes a specific and fundamental position. The judge is also, in many respects, in an oedipal situation similar to that of the king as soon as he is in a totemic position himself, or by the presence of legality. We now need to examine further the second fundamental rule of the totem.

The horror of incest

In primitive societies, the rule of incest means that certain kinds of relationship – which Freud called customary rules – are prohibited. This rule was respected with religious rigour.[69] The rule can extend to real sex relations in the strict sense. In fact, in certain primitive societies, it is even forbidden for brothers and sisters to shake hands or even to talk, whereas in others, the father cannot stay at home alone with his daughters. However, the strict rule can be extended to the specific act of concealment. A girl can avoid her father by hiding when he passes, or a man needs to deliberately hide and refrain from looking towards his mother-in-law when she is passing.[70] The totem, sacred, cannot be looked at. It is so feared that even the optical connection shall be avoided. It is thus logical to link this to Bentham and his famous panopticon. The system described by Bentham is based on an optical relationship of power, which Foucault explores in his work,

68 This is similar in Italy. See Richard, P., *Introduction au Droit Italien: Institutions juridictionnelles et droit procédural*, Paris: L'Harmattan, 2004, p. 127.

69 Freud, *Totem and Taboo*, p. 10.

70 Ibid., p. 12.

emphasising the effects of the panoptical architecture: 'the major effect of the Panopticon: induces among the inmates a conscious and permanent feeling of visibility which assures the automatic functioning of power'.[71] In addition, it is clear for Foucault 'that the perfection of the power should tend to render its actual exercise unnecessary'.[72] The idea of the automatic functioning of power thus corresponds best to the unconscious than to the conscious: it is linked to the realisation of the symbolic position of the father and his authority. Bentham wanted a 'visible and unverifiable'[73] power. Obviously, the 'Panopticon is a machine to distinguish the couple seen-be seen'.[74] Individuals within the peripheral ring are always watched but never have the capacity to see; and the individuals (who have the power) in the middle, in the watchtower, can see everything without being seen. What is particularly interesting here, is the notion of appearance of power which shows an ideal form of power.[75] In a way, this point is similar to what Freud describes in *Totem and Taboo* and at the place of the A according to Lacan, the place of the 'symbolic Father'. We have here the power seen at its source, as a magical thing which is the paramount element of the basic organisation of the primitive society. Hiding, because of a magical belief, contributes to fear of the totem. The visual link becomes crucial. But this magic goes further than the conscious idea of its power: what becomes important is authority. The repressed thoughts imposed by the fear which is, in the case of primitive societies, the avoidance of any links with the totem, visual or optical, suppress the desire for the totem. What remains of the past in our present, is the unconscious fear of the power and the unconscious fear of the totem thanks to the Father and his authority. In the situation of the legal event, one can apprehend this second rule and, in particular, the optical connection. If the parties decide to go on trial or *procès*, this taboo emerges. Nevertheless, it can take different forms. In particular, it can operate as a deterrent, with the consequence of encouraging the individuals to stay in line and conform to the rules in order to avoid facing trial; but it also creates the fear of the legal event for the parties concerned. Lord Phillips' narration concerning his first client's behaviour illustrates this point perfectly: 'I met my client for the first time in the waiting room the day of the hearing. She was obviously very nervous. The first thing that she said to me was "I won't have to give evidence, will I?" ' His client was unable to face the judge and the case was resolved between the councils outside the court hearing. Lord Phillips concluded: 'she was relieved to miss her day in court, but I was very disappointed to miss mine'.[76] Lord Phillips' client's behaviour confirms what Lacan expresses, concerning the symbolic order,

71 Foucault, M., *Surveiller et Punir*, Paris: Gallimard, Tel, 1975, p. 234.
72 Ibid.
73 Ibid., p. 235
74 Ibid.
75 Ibid., p. 239.
76 Discours de Lord Phillips of Worth Matravers, Chief Justice of England and Wales, 'Alternative Dispute Resolution: An English Viewpoint', India 29 Mars 2008. http://www.judiciary.gov.uk/media/speeches/2008/speech-lord-phillips-lcj-29032008. www.judiciary.gov.uk/docs/speeches/lcj_adr_india_290308.pdf (accessed 15 November 2010).

which reminds us of Eliade and the myth of the medicines: it is one that cures. It's an individual cure, a personal one, but it is also a collective cure for the group. There are therefore mechanisms created that avoid trials. Let's limit ourselves to the story of Lord Phillips' client and how, in common law, very few disputes arrive at the stage of the legal event. Indeed, it is often enough to focus on the procedures which exist before the trial, the ADR, alternative dispute resolutions (such as arbitration or mediation) to avoid the occurrence of the legal event.[77]

To come back to Oedipus, we know that King Oedipus violated both taboos. He was both the incestuous rival of his father, and his murderer. For Lacan, the oedipal identification markers around the paternal totem were guilt, aggression, the murder of the father and the rivalry between the brothers, which structure the subject.[78] The father's position in the symbolic order is simple and clear: he is the place which founds human actions. The social pact created by the brothers' alliance, the moment after the murder, and the transcendence of aggression, concerns the symbol and, finally, the symbolic order. The system created is consciously revealed, while always present in our unconscious. The Oedipus complex links and is linked to the totem and its taboos. The judge collects all the aspects of the totem. But because of the articulation around the two rules, we can consider the case where the totem actually delimits a range of different situations based on the legal traditions' differences. This means that we are confronted by the quality and the quantities of totemic position.

Quality and quantity of totemic position

A strict division between the two legal traditions may be traced, thanks to the Lacano-Freudian ideas. The totemic organisation of the *procès* can be considered as a mono-totemic organisation; the organisation of the trial as a bi-totemic organisation. It is one important difference between the two major legal traditions. Both have the underlying and unconscious idea of a totem in their legal activities, but the functions differ and operate on different levels. Indeed, there is a second totem in common law legal events. In the *procès*, a second totem also exists but is situated outside the legal event: inside the legal organisation itself. These structures seem essential to distinguish the judge in common law from the judge in civil law traditions. The quality and the quantity of totems would then result from particular elements: the training of the judge, the speech of the judge, and the symbolic position, itself determined by other variables.

Training of the judge

The recruitment and the administrative, sociological and politico-legal aspects of the judiciary inform us not only of the origin of the judge but also how they are positioned in the myth of the separation of powers. In both legal traditions, the

77 See Marrani, D and Farah, Y, 'ADR in the Administrative Law: A Perspective from the United Kingdom', in *Alternative Dispute Resolution in European Administrative Law*, (Heidelberg: Springer 2014), pp. 259–279.

78 Lacan, J., 'L'agressivité en psychanalyse', in Lacan *Écrits* 1, pp. 100–123, esp. p. 116.

training of the judge is very important to the concept of the delivering of justice. For Guarnieri and Pederzoli, two basic models of legal recruitment exist; the bureaucratic one which corresponds to what happens in the civil law environment, and the professional model which corresponds to what happens in that of common law.[79] In common law, only experienced practitioners can become judges. Accordingly, it is a system of training mainly based on scientific knowledge, with universities as main suppliers offering the education of future judges.[80] So, graduates will have to become solicitors or barristers and practise for a reasonable number of years before being authorised to become a judge. At this stage, it is particularly important to note that the legal team involved in the trial, both judges and lawyers, is trained in the same way and speaks the same language. However, Woodhouse underlined that 'the appointment system of the judges in England and Wales has often been criticised because it is secret and discriminatory'.[81] There is no distinction between 'lawyers/counsels' and judges, except the move from an 'active' position (lawyers/counsels) to a 'passive' position (judges) of arbiter or referee. Just like a monarch or head of state in a parliamentary regime, the judge does not 'participate' in the adversarial system. He acts like an arbiter or referee and not like a captain. The judge represents and seems to be positioned as a totem. This is increased in a circulatory way to what the recruitment of the judges looks like: the judges come from the 'horde'.[82] Here, the judge is the father of the horde: the Father. The young want to take his place and kill him. The symbolic killing operates as a revolution, a situation which is similar to what Pareto describes as the circulation of elites.[83] The younger will take the place of the elder. If we refer to David's words, the judge is 'the practitioners' heir'; he acquires a symbolic position of the 'father-regulator', the law, the authority of A, the Father, in the Oedipus complex.

In common law, the training place is an experience of the bar, while, in the civil law tradition, judges are trained in specialised schools after being selected via competition among the academic graduates.[84] There is a divide between the legal actors who will be on the parties' side, the defence or not, and the legal actors who will be on the side of the State, the judge. Moreover, the judge is qualified as a public servant; it is obvious that he is there to serve the State, and basically the social structure, in accordance with his origin from the Curia Regis. The civil law judge does not seem to be a totem similar to that which we find in common law. The only link between the different actors of the legal team is their education. But

79 Guarnieri, C. and Pederzoli, P., *The Powers of Judges: A comparative study of courts and democracy*, Oxford: OUP, 2003, p. 20.

80 We can cite here the four discourses of Lacan and specifically the speech of the academic, 'le discours de l'universitaire', where the professor knows that the student does not know, where the 'sujet supposé savoir est une nécessité'.

81 Woodhouse, D., 'The Law and Politics: More power to the judge – and to the people?' *Parliamentary Affairs* 54 (2001), pp. 223–237, esp. p. 234.

82 Judges regularly met and dine with the 'horde'. We are faced with a collegiate ritual, that of the diners taking place in the 'Inns'. Legrand and Samuel, *Common Law*, p. 47.

83 Pareto, V., *The Rise and Fall of Elites: An Application of Theoretical Sociology*, New Jersey: Transaction Books, 1991.

84 Legrand and Samuel, *Common Law*, p. 47.

the way the career of the judges is organised, through its structured form and its public function, itself conditioned by the weight of the authority and the symbolic of public power, creates a strong move among the judges, from the low level (young people) to the upper level (the elderly).[85] In a way, the idea of circulation of elites and the totem reappear here, but in a separate bubble in the mechanism, though they will have less impact on the *procès* than in the case of the trial.

The training of the judge highlights the characteristics of the totem(s) in both legal events. In the trial, we can first consider the trial itself as totem, and then the judge. In the *procès*, only the latter is a totem. The judge does not have a second totemic position in the legal event, but has one, outside, in the public function and in others among the executive. This point may be demonstrated by the constantly renewed declaration that in England, the judiciary is (considered as) independent, while in France, there is a constant willingness of an independent judicial power, although qualified as authority, implying a lack of such independence, or at least a perception of this lack. As Lord Brown-Wilkinson stated in the *Re Pinochet* case,

> There is no room for fine distinctions if Lord Hewart's famous dictum is to be observed: it is 'of fundamental importance that justice should not only be done, but should manifestly and undoubtedly be seen to be done.' (see *Rex v. Sussex Justices, Ex parte McCarthy* [1924] K.B. 256, 259).[86]

See also the correlation with visual taboo and also the Chapter on cameras in courts for instance.

The table below incorporates the ideas developed above:

Table 2.1 Comparative totemic structure

Common law: **structure with double totem**	
Trial / Totem 1	
Judge / Totem 2	Parties
Solicitors / Barristers	

Civil law: **structure with single totem**	
Procès / Totem	
Parties / Counsels	Judge / Totem
	Young judges

85 Traditionally, young judges will work for lower courts after their initial training; they enter in a bureaucratic career and will be promoted on the basis of their merit and their experience. Article 64 of the Constitution of the Fifth Republic which enshrines the President of the Republic as guarantor of the judiciary Independence, provides, in addition that judges are appointed with security of tenure.

86 www.publications.parliament.uk/pa/ld199899/ldjudgmt/jd990115/pino01.htm (accessed 17 February 2017).

There are similar situations in both legal events – but with particularities linked to the quantities of totem. Moreover, the differences seem to increase when one analyses the judge's speech.

Speech of the judge

Derrida explains that the phenomenological space is open in and by the language, and more particularly that because of 'its legal value, the right to a distinction between the fact and the intentional law entirely depends on the language'.[87] The language conditions the distinction between the facts and law. In addition, it gives the legal event its articulation, limits it, and defines it – as it defines, according to Wittgenstein's famous formula, the world (or even all the worlds).[88] The judge is positioned through his speech which implements a language practice constituting a social link between the actors. The first actor (agent) supports a 'truth' which necessarily determines him every time he addresses the second actor (the other). The second one will only be able to react by producing something that depends on the truth that the first one has determined. However, this product cannot come back to the 'truth'. As Richard demonstrates, this perception structures the link between the two actors around four places.[89]

Table 2.2 The truth, four places of discourse

Agent				Other
		Impossible		
	Necessary		Contingent	
		Possible		
Truth				Production

On the basis of this schema and around these structural positions, four speeches may be organised depending on four factors which circulate around the first model to generate the next speech. Thus, a circuit is formed: the master's speech evolves towards the analyst's speech, including the hysteric's speech and the scholar's speech. Their production result from the position of the four terms, constitutive elements of the language: the meaning-master S1, S2 knowledge, the subject (barred) $ and the rest, what remains, the object that we also find in the Lacanian explanation of the Oedipus complex. These symbols mainly formed the master's speech; the fundamental structure base of all the other speeches. It is particularly important here to consider the master's speech and that of the analyst.

The master's speech obeys the following variables $ -> S1 -> S2 -> a. It is dominated by S1, the signified-master (here the agent). Lacan names it the Law.[90]

87 Derrida, J., *La Voix et le Phénomène*, Paris: PUF, Champs 3rd edn, 2005, p. 21.
88 'The limits of my language mean the limits of my world'. Para. 5. 6, Wittgenstein, L., *Tractatus Logico-philosophicus*, Paris: Gallimard, Tel, 1961, p. 86.
89 Richard, P., *Le Jeu de la Différence: Réflexions sur l'épistémologie du droit comparé*, Laval: PUL Dikè, 2007, pp. 114–116.
90 Lacan, J., *Le Séminaire XVII: L'Envers de la psychanalyse*, Paris: Seuil, Champs Freudien, 1991, p. 48.

The Law is the law. The law is authorised by justice, without ever being labelled justice. S1 as master-meaning, theoretical knowledge, imposes knowledge on S2 (here the other), and is the favourite ground of the slave. One can reasonably consider that the position of the judge in the trial/*procès* is situated at the master's speech level. In this schema, the judge *is* the Law. His position results from the 'truth' and the understanding that the other knows that he knows. The civil law judge, in a central powerful position, is seated above the other actors; he is the master. He is the 'mouth' which speaks or tells the law. When he speaks, his words are final. But he doesn't speak for himself, he speaks 'on behalf of'; through his authority he represents the society and what he says is not neutral. After a complete circuit, going through the hysteric's speech position, we are faced again with this set of variables: a-> $-> S1-> S2 and to that of the scholar S1->S2->a->$, after a revolution, the analyst's speech appears.

The analyst's speech is formulated as follows: S2 -> a -> $ -> S1. Object a represents here the substantial speech, resulting from the rejection of the speech. The agent's position in this case is that of neutrality. The other one is the object which looks like the neutral agent expressing the 'truth', because the agent knows from knowledge S2. We know that the analyst in psychoanalysis is a person in a neutral position. The subject is supposed to believe what the agent says, because the agent, here the analyst, is supposed to know.[91] This position also corresponds to that of the common law judge. In this context, the judge does not interfere. He is the totem and he is not the centre of the dialogical process which occurs in the legal event. Ultimately, the production is knowledge which goes through the previous memorised decisions and sentences, the judicial precedents. It is, in fact, 'through the accumulation of precedent', that 'a body of common experience' is created, through memory.[92] Oral becomes 'a word addressed to', having the 'function of a certain pact'.[93] The inversion of the saying *Verba Volant, scripta manent* finds its fullest expression: 'The *scripta* are *Volant*, whereas the words . . . remain'.[94] The truth, thanks to the trial, is built, following the stages of justice, with the law, while building the law. This is not without relation to the idea of 'chain novel' evoked by Dworkin. Each judge actually becomes a novelist, merely a participant who collaborates on a broader, more complex, but continuous work.[95] One party contradicts the other one to build a verbal joust constituting the real links of a chain.

This thesis confirms the idea of two opposite ontologies; that of the law – of the statute law, the norm voted by a legislature, a Parliament – and that of the case law, the norm emanating from judges. As Legrand explained 'the typical English judgment is the law and is as such regardless of any Act' and does not

91 Zizek, S., *How to Read Lacan*, London: Granta Books, 2006, p. 29.

92 Glenn, P., *Legal Traditions of the World*, Oxford: OUP 3rd edn, 2007, p. 125.

93 Lacan, J., *Le Séminaire II: Le moi dans la théorie de Freud et dans la technique de la psychanalyse*, Paris: Seuil, 1978, p. 233

94 Ibid., p. 232.

95 Dworkin, R., *Law's Empire*, Cambridge: Harvard University Press, 1986, pp. 228–238, esp. 229.

aspire to its statute. In France 'the decision intervenes as coming from the interior of the law . . . it intends to be the law'.[96] This contributes to a different positioning of the judge, depending on the place where we are, in the *procès* or the trial, which is also conditioned by several elements.

Conditioning elements of the symbolic position of the judge

There are four of them, including three specific (the judge's perception on his function; the idea of 'in the name of' and, finally, the important question of appearance) and one broader (the oral/written civilisation's issue).

The perception of the judge on his function

We may distinguish civil law from common law through the different perceptions of the function of judging. It is well known that in common law, judges are imagined as being responsible for the creation of the law, whereas in civil tradition, they are supposed to be only interpreters of the law. Indeed, for Dicey 'English law is in reality made by the judges'[97] whereas Cardozo developed the idea of 'the judge as legislator'.[98] But Dicey considers that judicial legislation is only a delegated or subordinated legislation,[99] whereas for Cardozo the judge-made-law has always been 'secondary and subordinated to the law made by the legislator'.[100] The common law is seen as made by the judges and it seems that at least one important part of what is considered as law comes from judges. In addition, judges proclaim what has always been in the *existence,* but has never been revealed before. When something is revealed, this 'thing' becomes a principle of common law. This vision merges with psychoanalytic theory. A legal principle is unconsciously present, but needs to be rediscovered. It has been repressed by the social structure. Yet this latter, one day, will need it because of a social affect, the advent of a specific time in history, or when a dispute opposes the members of society. Basically, there is no better solution than the one situated elsewhere . . . deeply rooted in history: it is the judge's role to bring it back into the light.[101] The 'psychoanalyst-judge', thanks to the use of transfer, extracts from the built truth of the parties what has always existed, unconsciously, as a legal principle.

According to Freud, the unconscious is the social, what Lacan considers, thanks to Lévi-Strauss, as the language, the language of the Other, which is also the language of the Father.[102] The repressed principle thus highlighted may be

96 Legrand, P., *Droit Comparé*, Paris: PUF, Que Sais Je, 2nd edn, 1999, p. 111.
97 Dicey, *Law of the Constitution*, p. 58.
98 Cardozo, B.N., *The Nature of the Judicial Process*, New Haven: Yale UP 1921, pp. 103–141.
99 Dicey, *Law of the Constitution*, p. 58.
100 Cardozo, *The Nature of the Judicial Process*, p. 14.
101 We can really see clearly here if history as to be considered as history of the society or as the personal history of the judge. That said, it may be the case that the two are in fact connected.
102 Chaumon, F., *Lacan, le Sujet et la Jouissance*, Paris: Michalon, Le Bien Commun, 2004, p. 18.

linked with the definition of the two psychoanalysts. The principle is the social. The common law has a social dimension that 'the law of Act', the legislative law, does not share. The practical aspect of one contrasts with the theoretical aspect of the other one. The language contributes to the expression of this principle. The judge, through the legal event, expresses what was hidden. In addition, as soon as a dispute is 'treated' at the highest level of a supreme court, it will become so powerful that its outcome will bind the future decisions.[103] Judicial precedents represent a work to a conscious level. The example of the *speeches* of the former supreme judges, the Law Lords, which are orally developed and exposed (opinions), illustrates well enough this point. The judge 'tells us', and so 'exposes the law'. The judge is the subject who is supposed to know. We believe that he knows the social truth and that he will announce it within the limit of the legal precedents. Dicey sums up this message:

> [our judges'] habit of deciding one case in accordance with the principle, or supposed principle, which governed a former case, leads inevitably to the gradual formation by the Courts of fixed rules for decision, which are in effect laws.[104]

In the civil law tradition, parliaments have the function of creating law. The judge cannot change or even 'touch' the law, because of its 'mythical' power. The French Revolution gave its foundation to the myth – this depoliticised speech[105] – through Article 6 of the Declaration of the Rights of Man and of Citizens of 1789 'Law is the expression of the general will' which implements Rousseau's ideas. Even if one can argue that judges have always been involved in the normative creation (especially in cases where legislation is silent or in specialised areas such as administrative law), the function of judges as legal actors is that of interpreting the law.[106] Judges work by using meta-languages, by interpreting the double semiotic relationship which creates the myth of the law.[107] Basically, this is verified in Article 5 of the French civil code through the idea that 'judges are forbidden to pronounce judgment by way of general and regulatory dispositions in cases that are referred to them'. Judges in civil law tradition thus are not in a symbolic position which may be considered as strong as the position of their common-law colleagues. The rules they applied have been decided before their action and they must respect them. Here the rules are conscious, although nothing discourages anyone to think that unconsciously, the legislator should respect these principles in his legislative work. The most important principle is undoubtedly the one

103 As this is compulsory to create such a memory, such an authority, in the exposing the (legal) principle.

104 Dicey, *Law of the Constitution*, p. 58.

105 Barthes, R., *Mythologies*, Paris: Seuil, Point Essais, 1957, p. 217.

106 Dicey, *Law of the Constitution*, pp. 378–380, esp. p. 380: 'It is true of this branch of French law as of the English constitution that it "has not been made but has grown"'.

107 Barthes, *Mythologies*, pp. 183–190.

108 Samuel considers that English judges were never constraint by a legal science and therefore

contained in Article 4 of the civil code; 'A judge who refuses to give judgment on the pretext of legislation being silent, obscure or insufficient, may be prosecuted for being guilty of a denial of justice'. Judges are bound by these guidelines, they have no other option but to interpret. This is a specific characteristic of the position of the judge in the civil law tradition. But here again, the judge does not participate to the same level of totemisation as his common-law counterpart. Moreover, the judge relies on another interpretative authority, positioned outside the totem of the *procès*; the doctrine, that Professor Samuel presents as an important body of professors, binds judges thanks to a science of the law they develop, influenced by the logic and mathematics.[108] The civil law judge interprets but is never supposed to create. He follows the principles established by the superego 'State' which, de facto, a member of society may, or must, accept to live in or may decide to leave. The judge must take into account that a member of society may not want to respect rules, placing him in a position of guilt whereas the State institutionalised the reparation of the wrong committed by non-complying with the law.

Appearance and protection

The appearance focuses on the court ceremony and how the 'accessories' of the judge's uniform and the place where justice is rendered are essential for the symbolic positioning of the judge. Moreover, appearance creates a distance which is, in a second time, protected.

Appearance and the creation of the distance

The parties can see the physical reality of the legal apparatus before them. It operates on at least two levels: the architecture of the building and the uniform of the actors. According to Garapon, 'the first act of justice is to delineate a place, to define a favourable space to its fulfilment'[109] while the uniform, the costume, the gown, this furred gown La Fontaine evoked 'covers a double body: the own body of the character who wears it and the invisible body of the social'.[110] The decorum and the ballet of the actors depict an impressive play for the layman. Is the process of justice good or beautiful? It is worth noting that what was considered as important in the decision of creation of the new Supreme Court in the United Kingdom was actually the creation of an independent court, physically separated from the House of Lords, where the most important court decisions, the final ones, had been delivered until then. Thus, what was essential in the choice was to create a specific place with its own building.[111] At every level, justice

there has never been a body of professors: Samuel, G., 'Epistemology and Comparative Law', in Van Hoecke, M., (ed.), *Epistemology and Methodology of Comparative Law*, Oxford: Hart, 2004, p. 72.

109 Garapon, *Bien Juger,* p. 23: '[l]e premier geste de justice est de délimiter un lieu, de circonscrire un espace propice à son accomplissement'.

110 Ibid. p. 83: 'couvre un double corps: le corps propre du personnage qui le porte et le corps invisible du social'.

must be seen to be delivered. The judge will give judgment in a place where he is identified as a symbolic figure, as the Father, the face of the law.[112] In both traditions, the judge in the space of the legal event holds an 'extra', elevated seat, designed to show his strength and to demonstrate his authority. In civil tradition, the judge is centred and becomes the axiological reference. The actors; the jury, the accused and the lawyers, are organised around the judge in a specific triangle. In common law, the judge is centred, but the actors are not organised around him. The judge does not appear as an axiological reference. The jury is to the side and the lawyers directly address the jury. As Garapon notes, two communication axes exist between the lawyers, the two parties and the witnesses, and between the lawyers and the jury.[113] That is mainly why very little 'goes through' the judge, whereas in France, for example, everything goes through the judge. If we reflect on this idea correlatively to that of the totem, the French judges, with more power and less representation, do not position themselves as totem whereas common law judges, with less power, but more representation, appear as totem. Let us not forget that the totem is to be feared. It creates obsessive prohibitions which prevent the individuals from doing certain things, starting with touching or looking at the totem.[114] From physical contact to eye contact, the physical position of the judge in a court stresses (or maybe at least should emphasise) the difference between the totemic positions: the common-law judge is in a position which forces the other actors of the legal event to avoid looking at him because he is the totem, and in short he is taboo. Symbolism of the building imposes the solemnity of the State, its strength, through the authority, which must be linked to the symbolism of the uniform of the judges.

The coloured gowns and the wigs are key elements of the judge's uniform.[115] The wigs are particularly 'considered as a powerful symbol which represents the long story of the British justice'.[116] The silk gowns with ermine, the royal fur, caricatured by that of the cat in the fables, and the gown of the first president of the French *Cour de cassation*, are also elements of the legal costume, similar to that of drama: 'its role is to be seen'.[117] Thus, distance is created through ceremony, the sublime. As Meltzer writes, 'the apprehension of beauty contains

111 The Constitutional Reform Act 2005. See also the commentary of Lord Falconer: '[t]he location and the setting for the UK Supreme Court should be a reflection of its importance and its place at the apex of the justice system, and the heart of the constitution': *Hansard* 1 March 2006: Column WS29.

112 Lacan, J., 'Fonction et Champ de la Parole et du Langage', in Lacan, *Écrits 1*, p. 276.

113 Garapon, *Bien Juger*, p. 153. See the commentaries of the American judges, pp. 149–174.

114 Freud, *Totem and Taboo*, p. 27.

115 Public Perceptions of Working Court Dress in England and Wales, October 2002, 1/3 p. 4 www.dca.gov.uk/consult/courtdress/orcreport.pdf (accessed 15 November 2010).

116 Ibid., p. 14. One of these comments seems closely related to the idea developed by La Fontaine on the 'chat fourrée'. 'Wigs', perruques, signify that justice has been served: 'the wig signifies that justice is being done'. We may compare this with what is said in *In Re Pinochet*.

117 Garapon, *Bien Juger*, p. 72.

in its very nature, the fear of the possibility of its destruction'.[118] This ceremony, this sublime element, makes us aware of an imposed and necessary majesty: Imposed by transcendence, necessary for social cohesion. The drama of justice contributes to the creation and the continuity of a necessary distance between the legal actors in the legal event. Ultimately, it contributes to the authority of the judge-Father. Indeed, 'the costume of the ritual made those who wear it representatives'.[119] Representation, because of the distance, accentuates the symbolic, as does the ability to represent. The judge's costume, though, is a decisive issue. The judge is the judge because he wears 'something' which distinguishes him from the others. The uniform enables the judge to be identified as such and to identify himself as a judge. He operates thanks to the legal event in a demonstration of the temporary superiority of the social among the individual.

If we come back to a comparison between the traditions we may say that in the common law the relationship between the architecture and the dress code – and therefore, also the symbolic role of the judge – includes, *ab initio* the idea that the judge is the character who symbolises the existence of the social structure. This seems to refer to the ideal notion of ego. A contrario within the civil law tradition, the judge is not considered as independent. It seems that in the shift from the king to the judge as source of justice after the French Revolution, the judge has become an element of the 'superego' in what became the 'new' State. In both cases, the parties unconsciously know that the judge is here to correct, to cure, and to remedy. The judge has an orthopaedic role, because he symbolises what must be.[120]

Protection against the failures of the appearance

One can consider that assaults against judges are related to the presence or the absence of a particular device, such as ceremonial aspects like the uniform. A judge who does not wear his gown does not represent society in the same way as one who does. In fact, we can say that he does not represent society at all: the lack of distance is signalled by the absence of symbolism and demonstrates a lack of authority. The totem is not protected from the horror of patricide. Lucien, who gathered impressive statistics on the issue in his research, indicates that the assaults against court judges constitute the negation of the symbolic of the judge.[121] In

118 Meltzer, D., 'The Apprehension of Beauty', in Meltzer, D., *The Apprehension of Beauty*, Strath Tay: Clunie Press, 1988, p. 6.

119 Garapon, *Bien Juger*, p. 94.

120 In common law, the parties are in an 'internal' dialogue which creates a monologue, a monolithic dogmatic truth with their legal teams. Both monologues are exposed to the judge. The judge will declare which truth is the best truth, after having confronted the monologues in a dialectical way. In the civil law tradition, the judge is here to create a truth in correlation with the State superego.

121 Lucien, A., *Médiation et modernité, Approche communicationnelle de l'institution judiciaire*, Toulon: USTV, Thèse, 2007, esp. p. 241.

order to promote the symbolic position of the judge, a special tool is needed, an additional protection.[122] In the United Kingdom, there is, for instance, contempt of court, which corresponds to the similar provisions of the French Penal code on the offences against the authority of justice (S. III). We note that a kind of contempt exists which is relevant to the idea of visual taboo in the totem: the one which concerns the taking of any photograph, the making of any portrait or any sketch of a judge or a witness, or a party to any proceedings before the court, either in court or in the precincts of the building (section 41, Criminal Justice Act 1925).[123] The most serious offences, the 'violation of the respect due to justice' as titles paragraph 1 of the section 3 of chapter V of the Penal code, are the abuses and contempt of court. Here, the criticisms against the judicial authority are considered as attacking the symbolic position of the judge. Moreover, the Penal code underlines the function of the 'additional protection'. Everything which is likely to undermine the authority of justice or to harm its independence must be fought. These are reminders of what is behind the judge, the 'power', the authority of society.[124]

When the offence is committed through the press or by broadcasting, the specific legal provisions governing those matters are applicable to define the persons who are responsible. Criminal proceedings are time-barred after three months from the day on which the offence defined by the present article was committed, if in the meantime no act of investigation or prosecution has taken place.

122 Addo, M.K., 'Are Judges beyond Criticism under Article 10 of the European Convention on Human Rights?', *ICLQ* 47 (2) (Apr., 1998), pp. 425–438, esp. p. 429.

123 www.legislation.gov.uk/ukpga/Geo5/15-16/86/contents (accessed 17 February 2017). Although there are many changes as described in Chapter 4.

124 Article 434–24: L'outrage par paroles, gestes ou menaces, par écrits ou images de toute nature non rendus publics ou par l'envoi d'objets quelconques adressé à un magistrat, un juré ou toute personne siégeant dans une formation juridictionnelle dans l'exercice de ses fonctions ou à l'occasion de cet exercice et tendant à porter atteinte à sa dignité ou au respect dû à la fonction dont il est investi est puni d'un an d'emprisonnement et de 15000 euros d'amende. Si l'outrage a lieu à l'audience d'une cour, d'un tribunal ou d'une formation juridictionnelle, la peine est portée à deux ans d'emprisonnement et à 30000 euros d'amende. Article 434–25:

Le fait de chercher à jeter le discrédit, publiquement par actes, paroles, écrits ou images de toute nature, sur un acte ou une décision juridictionnelle, dans des conditions de nature à porter atteinte à l'autorité de la justice ou à son indépendance est puni de six mois d'emprisonnement et de 7500 euros d'amende.

Les dispositions de l'alinéa précédent ne s'appliquent pas aux commentaires techniques ni aux actes, paroles, écrits ou images de toute nature tendant à la réformation, la cassation ou la révision d'une décision.

Lorsque l'infraction est commise par la voie de la presse écrite ou audiovisuelle, les dispositions particulières des lois qui régissent ces matières sont applicables en ce qui concerne la détermination des personnes responsables. https://www.legifrance.gouv.fr/affichCode.do;jsessionid=43B9DA993C2B8C02A1B620F63DC78996.tpdila15v_2?idSectionTA=LEGISCTA000006181767&cidTexte=LEGITEXT000006070719&dateTexte=20170822 (last accessed 15 August 2017).

Judging 'in the name of'

Justice is delivered 'in the name of' a sovereign, whether it is the people, a nation or a monarch.[125] There is a strong reference to the paternal figure of the judge, at the level of the symbolic Father, where the name of the father is declined in *non du pere*, the strict father. Indeed, here again, for Lacan, 'It's in the name of the father that we must recognise the support of the symbolic function which, since the beginning of historical times, identifies his person to the figure of the law'.[126] Legendre develops this point by examining the law of reason and the law of the father, explaining that these are two faces of the same notion, a fundamental reference to the big fundamental story whose function is 'to sort, to separate, to distinguish'.[127] Here we will simply relate that function to the main idea of the trial which is to separate, to sort. The use of the *name of* refers to the big Other, place of the significant, place of the language, where the subject 'receives' its own reversed message.[128] This takes place in the symbolic order where the big Other is located.[129] Actually, in *the name of* we find an operation, an action, the one of asking a third party, the reference, the authority, the law. It is something that the child will achieve when positioning himself in front of the mirror. The child will address the person who carries him, 'the act by which the child in the mirror, turning to the one who carries him, appeals by glance at the witness . . . the recognition of the image'.[130] In fact, 'it is enough to understand the mirror stage as an identification' which is, still according to Lacan, a transformation in the subject when he assumes his image after the intervention of the Father.[131] For the parties, the judge is in a position of identification of the ego ideal, the ideal model. He operates as a parent, in *loco parentis*.[132] Thus, the judge becomes the parent who punishes or rewards.[133]

125 We may wonder about the question of hierarchy between the three, but I will not discuss the question of legitimacy here. The issue is that of identification created by the 'in the name of'. As Richard analyses, Article 101.1 of the Italian Constitution evokes this idea of justice delivered in the name of the people, showing the importance of popular sovereignty whereas before justice was delivered in the name of the king. Richard, P., *Introduction au Droit Italien: Institutions juridictionnelles et droit procédural*, Paris: L'Harmattan, 2004, n96, p. 120. In France, justice was considered as the monopoly of the (sovereign) monarch and was delivered in his name. When the exercise of sovereignty 'shifted' to the (sovereign) people, justice was still delivered in the name of the sovereign, but the new one. Justice is then still delivered in the name of the sovereign.

126 Lacan, 'Fonction et Champ', p. 276.

127 Legendre, *Caporal Lortie*, p. 153.

128 See Zizek, S., 'The Big Other Doesn't Exist', *Journal of European Psychoanalysis*, Spring/Fall 1997.

129 Zizek, *How to Read Lacan*, p. 9.

130 Lacan, J., 'Remarque Sur le Rapport de Daniel Lagache', in Lacan, *Écrits 2*, Paris: Seuil, Points Essais, 1999 (1966), pp. 155–156.

131 Lacan, J., 'Le Stade du Mirroir Comme Formateur de la Fonction du Je', in Lacan, *Écrits 1*, pp. 92–100, esp. p. 93.

132 Schoenfeld, *Psychoanalysis and the Law*, p. 35.

133 Ibid., p. 93.

It even seems that certain judges identify themselves as their parents or the attorneys to their clients.[134] In civil law tradition, this identification takes place in the conscious. In the common law, the lower courts' judgments are implicitly in line with those of the upper courts. Therefore, they are 'mere' legislature committees acting in the 'name of'.[135] We must keep in mind that, in the United Kingdom, the separation between reality of the monarch and reality of the democracy is at its height. Justice is not delivered 'in the name' of the people but in the name of the monarch. Moreover, this judge representative is a facilitator enabling mankind, the parties, to be human. As Lacan underlines, 'if we have to define when the man becomes human . . . it is the moment where he enters in the symbolic relationship'.[136] Indeed, this judge positions himself as symbol, as a third party, 'element of mediation, who situates the two characters, puts them in another level, and modifies them'.[137] The judge, symbolic actor, 'in the name of' will allow the parties to be replaced in the social, in what Lacan calls the human environment which is the symbolic environment.[138] This brings us back to the issue of the language as well as some considerations on how legal traditions relate to a broader level to the written and oral traditions.

Civilisation of the oral tradition and civilisation of written tradition

Whether a culture uses spoken or written words, the way to express the judicial matter refers to the base and to the heart of its tradition. In the northern part of Europe, law originates from customary laws. This part of the world had to deal with oral transmission of knowledge, 'thanks to the accumulation of precedents', these memories of the law, giving birth to 'a body of shared experiences' through memory.[139] The core principle of the trial is oral. We find the idea of orality: evidence must be given orally and subject to cross examination, thus acting as a true counter power, a counterweight to the words of the other. In the south, the civil law tradition, rooted in the Talmudic and Chthonic traditions, as Professor Glenn explains, goes even further in the written roots than the Roman Empire, even though this latter had developed a written legal tradition which can be symbolised by the development of the Codex, the codification.[140] The consequences are manifold and evolve around the dialectical confrontation between secret and transparency.

134 Ibid., p. 97–99.

135 Indeed, in this regard, the appellate committee of the House of Lords had a similar function to that of the French and Italian constitutional courts. However, the creation of the new Supreme Court of the UK seems to modify this symbolic.

136 Lacan, J., *Le Séminaire I: Les écrits techniques de Freud*, Paris: Seuil, 1975, p. 178.

137 Ibid., p. 178.

138 Ibid., p. 180.

139 Glenn, *Legal Traditions*, p. 125. According to Glenn, there are two Torah, one written and one verbal which became written, pp. 238–239.

140 Ibid., p. 125.

First, we can consider the classical opposition between inquisitorial and adversarial (or contradictory) systems. According to Guarnieri and Pederzoli, 'while adversarial systems, contradictory, of common law are led by lawyers, continental systems are almost always led by the judge'.[141] In the common law, contradictory and adversarial mechanisms are characterised by a logic where 'each side is in charge of preparing its own brief'.[142] In the civil law tradition, inquisitorial mechanisms need a specific actor to lead the legal event, the investigating magistrate, the *juge d'instruction*. As Article 49 of the French code of criminal procedure states, 'The investigating judge is in charge of judicial investigations'. Therefore, he is the only person 'in charge of', under Article 81 of the code 'The investigating judge undertakes in accordance with the law any investigative step he deems useful for the discovery of the truth. He seeks out evidence of innocence as well as guilt'. Moreover, the investigating judge must determine the quality of the offence and the possibility of submitting it to the upcoming *procès*.[143] In fact, the beginning of the legal event depends on the investigating judge. If he agrees to open/initiate the *procès* he will lead the investigation. The investigating judge acts as a facilitator of the 'truth process' mentioned above and to which Badiou refers. He appears as a guarantor of independence. Indeed, there should supposedly be no pressure from one party to the other one because of the presence of the investigating judge in leading the investigation. In addition, he is the guarantor of the rule of law, as found in the same Article 81 of the code of criminal procedure, through the terms 'in accordance with the law'.

One can obviously comment on the inquisitorial nature of the procedure itself. The truth is built by an investigating judge whose function has been largely criticised.[144] It is well-known that in common law, the adversarial (or contradictory) nature of the procedure forced the parties and the advocates to build and reveal a

141 Guarnieri and Pederzoli, *The Power of Judges*, p. 129.

142 Eliot C. and Quinn, F., *English Legal System*, London: Pearson, 7th edn, 2006, p. 361.

143 Article 85: Toute personne qui se prétend lésée par un crime ou un délit peut en portant plainte se constituer partie civile devant le juge d'instruction compétent en application des dispositions des articles 52, 52-1 et 706-42. Article 86: Le juge d'instruction ordonne communication de la plainte au procureur de la République pour que ce magistrat prenne ses réquisitions.

144 The institution of the investigating magistrate has been under the spotlight for several years. Nicolas Sarkozy while President announced that he wanted to change the institution. M. Sarkozy Envisage de Supprimer le Juge d'Instruction, *Le Monde*, 6 February 2009, www.lemonde.fr/politique/article/2009/01/06/m-sarkozy-envisage-de-supprimer-le-juge-d-instruction_1138259_823448.html (accessed 15 November 2010.We will also refer to the report on the malfunction of the investigation in the Outreau case, 'Rapport de la Commission d'Enquête Chargée de Rechercher les Causes des Dysfonctionnements de la Justice dans l'Affaire dite d'Outreau et de Formuler des Propositions pour Éviter leur Renouvellement', www.assemblee-nationale.fr/12/rap-enq/r3125-t1.asp#P871_183359, 6 juin 2006 (accessed 17 February 2017). Besides, Germany and Italy transferred the investigating judge's powers to the prosecutor in order to avoid possible conflicts with the functions of investigation and judging. We may refer to her television series *Engrenages* [Spiral] and the incorruptible figure of the investigating judge, Roban.

partisan truth through an internal dialogue which occurs during the opinions. This truth becomes the judicial truth, a 'justice reality'. In the civil law tradition, the parties are deprived of this possibility. The function of the judge may be, as mentioned above, to create or to expose the law, to confirm or to 'tell' the truth or at least what the truth is. In the common law, the role of the judge is, from his symbolic position, his strength and his authority, to determine which truth, exposed by the parties, will become the reality of justice. In the civil law tradition, the judge must create the truth and expose it to the parties in accordance with the mono-totemic position. In addition, the trial in common law is (predominantly) a verbal exchange between the parties whereas the *procès* is (predominantly) a written exercise. The role of the judge is thus very different.

The judges' role in the adversarial system is in many ways more passive than that of the judge in inquisitorial systems, because in the first case, the judge acts as a major observer and a final arbitrator, and in the second case the judge acts as a more active researcher of the truth and a facilitator of the information.[145]

Basically, what separates the two legal traditions is supposed to reside in the presence of two resolution mechanisms which are in place, and in their relationships to either written or oral traditions. Thus, the trial differs from the *procès* mainly because of the procedure itself: a legal mechanism of exchanges. The reference point is the social structure. The adversarial or the inquisitorial system is defined by the way society wishes the operation to be carried out. In common law, society reflects on a mechanism providing actions, giving leeway to the parties. In the civil law tradition, society insists on the realisation of the operation, with something which connects to the inquisition, by limiting the liberty of the parties. It is certainly interesting to note, with Foucault, that '[i]n France, as in most European countries – except England – the whole criminal procedure, until the sentence, remains secret'.[146] As spotted by Foucault, there is an important exception: England. The case of England informs us on two main points. First, in the civil law tradition, where the organisation of the legal event is inquisitorial, the procedure is secret. It will condition and will be conditioned by the use of writing, because of 'the secret and written form of the procedure'.[147] Indeed, Article 11 of the French code of criminal procedure provides that 'except where the law provides otherwise and subject to the defendant's rights, the inquiry and investigation proceedings are secret'. Secret towards and from the public, in order to avoid 'trouble' inside and of the 'crowd' or of the people, and secret towards and from the accused, who is not aware of what is happening to him, until the final result, the conviction.[148] Before the French Revolution, the establishment of the truth was a royal prerogative and the king of France was the exclusive source of justice. After the French Revolution, judges became solely entitled to establish

145 Van Koppen, P. J. and Penrod, S., *Adversarial Versus Inquisitorial Justice: Psychological Perspectives on Criminal Justice Systems*, Berlin: Springer, 2003, p. 184.

146 Foucault, *Surveiller et Punir*, p. 44.

147 Ibid., p. 45.

148 Ibid., p. 44.

justice. During the 'inquisition', the examination, the judge has full authority to 'discover' (the truth). The truth wears the king's clothes (and somehow that of the State), the fur and the clothes underlined by La Fontaine: it is sacred. According to Foucault, in France, the investigation as 'the authoritarian research of an identified or certified truth' had clearly been imposed by the king, 'the sovereign power arrogating the right to establish the truth by a certain number of techniques'.[149] This was 'imposed by the old adversarial justice, but through a process coming from the top'.[150] The judge in civil law tradition makes all the decisions from the beginning to the end. There is never a real dialogue, but rather an intense monologue built on the examination of the parties. In that of common law, the judge does not really examine the parties. The trial is an event which gives a crucial place to orality. The judge relies on the counsels in common law, the judge must appear as a neutral operator, a referee,[151] or an analyst.[152] In fact, the parties are opposed in a dialectical relationship. They will present and expose their ideas in a confrontational way. One party will expose his own truth, and then the other one will do the same. Because the parties do not share the same technical language, and sometimes even speak two different foreign languages, they can only gain access to the level of internal dialogue with their lawyers.[153] They are in a stage of 'negotiation' according to Derrida,[154] which results in an internal dialogue among the parties, this transformation in partisan monologues, dialectically opposed, leaving a symbolic place for the father judge who 'represents', in psychoanalytic terms. The judge is the law when he shows the solemnity of justice's strength through his authority. Besides, in the common law tradition, where the organisation of the legal event is adversarial, the procedure is open and verbal. We are here in a dialectical relationship between two parties, in the middle of a confrontational relationship, a relationship with the opposition. The parties expose their views. The monologue truth A is exposed by a legal team and the same goes for the monologue truth B. From these monologues, and because the point is to find who is going to win, the relationship becomes a

149 Ibid., p. 262.

150 Ibid., p. 263.

151 Jauffret Spinosi, C., 'Comment Juge le Juge Anglais?' in *Droits, la fonction de juger*, Paris: PUF, 1989, p. 57.

152 He can or must also either disappear or withdraw himself from the situation like the narrator of the stolen letter does. (l'exclusion neutralisante du narrateur). Major, R., *Lacan avec Derrida*, Paris: Flammarion, Champs, 2001, p. 54.

153 This does not concern the legal team, because it is supposed to speak the same (legal) language. See also the Directive 2010/64/EU of the European Parliament and the Council of 20 October 2010, regarding the right to translation in criminal proceedings. Directive 2010/64/UE du Parlement Européen et du Conseil du 20 octobre 2010 relative au droit à l'interprétation et à la traduction dans le cadre des procédures pénales, *Journal officiel de l'Union européenne*, L 280/1 à /7.

154 Derrida, J. and Laboussiere, P. J., *Alterités*, Paris: Osiris, 1986, p. 85. The 'négociation' may be considered as a legal situation 'a-trial' that does not really (yet) exist in civil law tradition. ADR for instance, or pre-trial actions, bring a resolution of a *différend* prior to the trial totem. See also Lord Phillips' comments above.

dialectical one. He appears here as an arbitrator. He is in a neutral position and must not interfere. He observes and watches. He is present and absent at the same time.[155] The judge 'represents' and as a symbolic actor shows, in a precise ritual ceremonial, how solemnity is the strength of justice, in the name of the monarch (as indicated, in the United Kingdom, by the expression Her Majesty's Court Service).[156]

A softening of the dichotomy?

According to Levinas, '[the Hitlerian philosophy] questions the very principles of civilisation'.[157] After the Second World War, the idea was that of developing bridges between the countries which had been in conflict, not only between 1939 and 1945, but also during previous centuries. Several developments occurred in Europe, including one which was remarkable, the transnationalisation of the principles of the European Convention for the Protection of Human Rights and Fundamental Freedom (so, as Levinas stated, 'folding back' towards civilisation).[158] The European Convention is linked to what Levinas described as 'the spirit of freedom' or as 'a conception of human destiny'[159] and what Badiou considers a huge return to Kant,[160] with the assumption that human rights are harmless, non-evil rights.[161] The preamble to the European Convention presents us with the idea that governments in Europe are in a same state of mind, sharing both a common heritage and rights of the Universal Declaration of Human Rights of 1948.[162] These may be considered as illustration of the evolution towards 'non-evil':

> [The governments signatory hereto, being members of the Council of Europe], Being resolved, as the governments of European countries which are like-minded and have a common heritage of political traditions, ideals,

155 We can relate this to Freud's essay 'Beyond the Pleasure Principle', *SE* 18, (1920), pp. 14–15, as mentioned by Lacan in 'Fonction et Champ', p. 317. The little boy, Freud's nephew, plays with the ball while his mother is out. The presence and the absence of the object develops in another level, that of the language. It evolves in the symbolic order. See also Derrida, *Voix et Phénomène*, p. 9: 'le langage est bien le médium de ce jeu de la présence et de l'absence'.

156 Indeed, the crown, political body of the British Monarch, has been in charge of the judicial system for nearly 900 years.

157 Levinas, E., 'Reflections on the Philosophy of Hitlerism', 17 *Critical Enquiry* (autumn 1990), p. 64.

158 www.echr.coe.int/NR/rdonlyres/086519A8-B57A-40F4-9E22-3E27564DBE86/0/FRA_Conven.pdf (accessed 17 February 2017).

159 Levinas, 'Philosophy of Hitlerism'.

160 Badiou, A., 'The Problem of Evil', p. 8. Let us consider here this idea of the return to Kant, while Lacan proclaims the return to Freud.

161 Ibid., p. 9.

162 www.un.org/fr/documents/udhr/ (accessed 17 February 2017).

> freedom and the rule of law, to take the first steps for the collective enforcement of certain of the rights stated in the Universal Declaration.[163]

The move was widely recognised but must be considered as an ideal or a conciliatory objective of national dogmatic speeches. France and the UK were not only the founders of the European Council but also broadly contributed to drafting the European Convention. The hope of a community created by the two legal traditions was thus present in the 1950s. Although the 'non-evil' is present throughout the Convention, the rights, such as those protected by Article 6, are remarkably important for the legal event. It provides that 'in the determination of his civil rights and obligations or of any criminal charge against him, everyone is entitled to a fair and public hearing within a reasonable time by an independent and impartial tribunal established by law'. The transnational prescription develops a transnational enforcement which results in an imaginary abolition of the distance between the legal traditions. The resistance against the transnational by national visions was intense and still is. We can take, as example, the rate of ratification of the Convention: 24 years between the signature and the ratification in France, while the UK ratified it three years after the signature, but it was necessary to wait until the end of the twentieth century to see it fully operational.[164] Even recently, concerning the incorporation of the Convention in the UK thanks to the Human Rights Act 1998 (HRA 1998),[165] Lord Carnwath, as President of the Commission of the Laws, expressed that the inability to use the European Convention was the regret of his life as a lawyer. He stated that the HRA 1998 should have been adopted when the right of individual petition was accepted in 1965–1966. He commented that if not only the right of individual petition, but also the whole Convention had been adopter earlier, 'English judges and lawyers would have been able to influence more directly the development of the law of the Strasbourg Convention'.[166] This statement implies that although being the initiator of the Convention, the UK somehow left its operational side aside until 1998/2000.[167] Both legal traditions share common values, but are characterised by numerous differences. Basically, the preamble was prescriptive. A balance between the two traditions was to be found or, in a more 'violent' way, remove the idea or the belief of the dissolution of one tradition, giving way to the elements of the other one.

The creation of a *jus commune* associated with general principles of the law led, for example, French researchers to acknowledge, while writing about the Convention, that: 'with such methods of interpretation we are far from the

163 www.echr.coe.int/NR/rdonlyres/086519A8-B57A-40F4-9E22-3E27564DBE86/0/FRA_Conven.pdf, p. 2 (accessed 17 February 2017).

164 http://conventions.coe.int/Treaty/Commun/ChercheSig.asp?NT=005&CM=8&DF=&CL=ENG (accessed 17 February 2017).

165 www.opsi.gov.uk/acts/acts1998/ukpga_19980042_en_1 (accessed 17 February 2017).

166 Carnwath, R., 'ECHR Remedies from a Common Law Perspective', *ICLQ* 49 (3) (2000), pp. 517–528, esp. p. 527.

167 Most of the HRA 1998 came into force on 2 October 2000.

French traditional legal reasoning', because 'it is a pragmatic, Anglo-Saxon approach ... to which we have to get accustomed'.[168] Researchers and practitioners in both traditions seem to consider the European Convention as something very precious and important, but simultaneously as something which modifies their way of thinking and operating, so that each tradition fears a loss of influence, because it affects the heart of the national dogmatic speeches. Garapon and Allard explained that in Europe, the two legal traditions were mixed in the laboratory constituted by the European Convention.[169] They consider this point as a precise result of the general process of globalisation. The conclusion they reached seems to move towards the common law rather than civil law tradition. That is not therefore surprising that in the legal event, trial and *procès,* what 'disappears' seems to come from the side of the civil law tradition.[170] For example, during the *procès*, the hearing must be public in order to be in compliance with the Convention. We therefore sense how we move away from the inquisitorial system, from the importance of secrecy in the civil law tradition, and we note an evolution towards an organisation of the legal event which looks like that of the trial. Indeed, the hearing is, and it is perhaps a truism, given the etymology of the word (to hear), oral, a practice of communication which, according to Ricœur, has its ethics: *audi alteram partem*.[171] This would only be embryonic. In fact, in this tradition we find neither dialogue between the parties nor freedom of speech in the place of justice. The investigating judge is still, for the moment, the actor in charge of organising the necessary elements, and not the parties. These latter are not considered as adults.

The change of strategy in terms of protection of the rights brought by the European Convention may also be linked with what Meltzer states: '[the atrocities] of war were committed not by the rebels but by the representatives of law and order'.[172] There is here an element of social (re)-evolution to take into consideration. In these symbolic places of power, judges implement the respect of the law with in mind the notion of the rule of law.[173] But we may think that the

168 Guinchard, S., Brandac, M., Lagarde, X. and Douchy, M., *Droit Processuel, Droit commun du procès*, Paris: Dalloz Précis, 1st edn, 2001, p. 95. As highlighted by Strydom, Beck considered, as well, an European laboratory, but constituted by the 'other Europe', the European Union.

169 Since the end of the Second World War, the European legal space created by both the convention and the community made the European territory a European laboratory. We can particularly observe the transformation of multiple European societies into one European society. See again Strydom, P., *Risk, Environment and Society*, Buckingham: Open University Press, 1st edn, 2002, esp. p. 54.

170 Garapon, A. and Allard, J., *Les Juges dans la Mondialisation, la nouvelle révolution du droit*, Paris: Seuil, La République des Idées, 2005, pp. 35–56.

171 Ricœur, *Amour et Justice*, p. 27.

172 Meltzer, D., 'Tyranny', in Meltzer, D., *Sexual States of Mind*, London: Karnac, 1973, p. 144.

173 In its narrow definition, the rule of law organises a mechanism where subordinate rules have to conform to superior rules. This has to be seen sufficient by the judge to demonstrate the respect of the law.

law itself is the problem.[174] To come back to the idea of 'non-evil', Meltzer analyses tyranny as 'a social perversion in the defense against depressive anxieties'.[175] Anxieties result from unsustainable situations, such as what is discovered by Freud in the experience of the Rat Man. In one of the first analysis of Freud, the Rat Man demonstrates a certain degree of interaction, 'love and hate', towards his father, which evolves in certain aggressiveness. Freud explains that it is the result of fear; in fact repressed hope. A consequence of this unsustainable situation of the conscious love and the unconscious hate of the father is anxiety. The Rat Man had to make amends, to apologise, to repair. If we apply this to the European Convention, we can analyse it in the context of the repair process. It was designed as an ethical ambition to overcome the anxiety after tyranny: 'The operative virtue of the law was followed by an ethical ambition through the propagation of human rights'.[176] European society in the 1920–1930s consciously 'loved' (legal positivism, the respect of 'the rule of law' by Nazi Germany confirmed it) but, unconsciously 'hated'. Europe hated perhaps because of the fear (the repressed hope may be a simplistic explanation but a logical one of the ruin following the First World War in Germany and in Italy, the last links in the economical chain as Poulantzas remarked[177]). In the 1950s, it was time to repair, through a restorative process which in fact had two faces. On one hand, this transformation affected the judicial system through the myth of the separation of powers. It strengthened the judiciary, forcing and imposing its independence, in accordance with the belief of a totemisation of the legal event. It is, for example, exactly what happened in the UK. According to Woodhouse, the HRA 1998 (and then the European Convention) 'requires a sharper separation between the judiciary and the other branches of the government'.[178] Indeed, we keep in mind the prediction now achieved that 'in the long term, in order to protect their independence, the Law Lords would perhaps need to withdraw from the House of the Lords when it sat as a legislative chamber'.[179] The consequence was the creation of a new Supreme Court in the UK, physically separated from Westminster.

The cultural and social dimension of the judge after the restorative process, by the European Convention, also evolves towards a certain idea of democracy. However, nothing advocates the emergence of a convergence between the traditions, which would rather be an ideal goal, a promise of the European Convention, implemented by different evolutions. To a certain extent, it brought the two legal traditions closer; the judge representing society through the legal event. Moreover, the restoration, as ethical ambition, contributes to a cosmopolitan development. This cosmopolitan operation reminds us of the fifth

174 See Agamben, G., *State of Exception*, Chicago: University of Chicago Press, 2005.
175 Meltzer, 'Tyranny'.
176 Allard and Garapon, *Juges dans la Mondialisation*, p. 6.
177 Poulantzas, N., *Fascisme et Dictature*, Paris: Seuil, Point Essais, 1974, p. 24.
178 Woodhouse, 'More Power to the Judge', p. 235.
179 Ibid.

thesis of the Kantian idea from his *Idea for a Universal History from a Cosmopolitan Point of View:* 'The biggest problem for the human species, the one that nature forces it to resolve, is to reach a civil society administering universally the law'.[180] This is applicable both within and beyond Europe. The legal event would then contribute towards clarifying the issue of the social, of its 'law' and basically of structure. But we cannot be sure that the best solution is hidden behind universalism. Indeed, at the same time, and perhaps concurrently, the question of particularism, of pluralism, of the identity and the culture of the other one and its respect, may be evoked. This also relates to the idea of context from which derives the starting point of the variation ritual v. rituals.

Ritual(s), law, justice

It is perhaps crucial for our societies to remember what was, because what was is often essential for the understanding of what is and what will be. The function of the places of justice, as Garapon indicates and Commaille emphasises, is to tell a story, the story of mankind and its social life, using 'tricks; that are very similar to what is done in drama'. The actors of this judicial 'theatrical play' follow the law and operate on a stage, with one or more precise rituals. Therefore, we understand the importance of the link between places of justice, the individual, society and the law, a link which fully manifests in the stages of the (classic) ritual.

Place of justice, ritual(s) and structuring of society

Broadly speaking, according to Locke and maybe more to Hobbes, the state of nature, what Rousseau considers as the time before the celebration or without the experience of the *continuity*, is a terrible place. It is such a terrible place that human beings need to move to another state, the state of civilisation. That state corresponds to the time after the celebration, according to Rousseau, where one lives the experience of *discontinuity*.[181] Human beings become civilised when they succeed in containing, inside them, individually, but also for the group or society, the empire of the impulses: they become civilised when they can live together, or even when they can *hope* to live together. But behind the mask of the civilised man remains the urge of aggression towards his fellows. Thus, sometimes the mask of the civilised man falls to give way to his origin: the beast. Therefore, the civilised man needs to make lots of effort to contain his impulses, his desires. As ambivalent creatures, human beings are made of their desire for civilisation, but they also keep their desire for criminality. In the state of nature, humans could do anything they wanted, man could just *enjoy*. In fact, the crime in the state of civilisation is a mere occurrence of something archaic. Crime is committed because there is always someone else in front of us who stands as an obstacle to

180 Kant, E., *Idées d'une Histoire Universelle au Point de Vue Cosmopolitique*, Paris: Bordas, 2006 (1784), pp. 15–16.

181 Derrida, J., *De la Grammatologie*, Paris: Les Éditions de Minuits, 1967, p. 372.

our pleasure. The other 'type' is no other than the father. He is the paramount obstacle between the child and the mother, he hinders the child who wants the mother: for Freud, the criminal act number one, the crime *par excellence,* is the patricide. The father shall be killed because he strives to be or to appear as an obstacle to our pleasure. As we have seen in previous chapter, it is the starting point of *Totem and Taboo.*[182]

The totem is linked to the law.[183] But, as analysed previously, it is something which builds rules, and, moreover, which cannot violate the rules it created itself. We need to keep in mind that the taboos are linked to the sacredness of the totem. We recall that the prohibitions, the taboos, operate around the will of the father, either in accordance with it or against it.[184] Thus the totem is marked, as evoked previously, by the taboos which are attached to it and constitute its heart: the members of the totem cannot kill the totem (the horror of patricide), while there is the rule of the abstinence towards all women of the totem (the horror of incest).

Here, the myth of the primitive horde, the totem and the taboos, creates both a history of desire and of law.[185] The patricide takes place within the primitive horde. It shall be contained by the primitive law, the fundamental law, the simplest law of the state of civilisation: 'You shall not kill'. As soon as this law exists, society may pretend to be civilised. The myth operates as a pact, an alliance, between the brothers, members of the horde. They will not kill the father, because they are now civilised. However, if the crime *is* committed, a mechanism to resolve the wrongdoing is needed. Thus, there will be a specific legal event allowing redress of that wrongdoing, which is outlawed (outside the law), a *procès* or a trial. This event should be conceived as a staging repeating the original pact. This original pact, that Rousseau considers the act of birth of human society, therefore becomes a sacred act. According to Derrida: 'Only one institution is sacred to its view, only one fundamental convention: it is, as the *Social Contract* tells us, the social order itself, the law of the law, the convention which is the basis for all conventions'.[186] The brothers will be gathered in the *trial* and the crime will be a re-enactment of the primitive act of patricide, the original crime. As in theatre, both the actors and the public participate to this reconstitution, each participant identifying himself to the criminal and reliving the scene of the crime. In fact, in this short tale, we understand that the myth of the primitive horde and the murder of the Father demonstrate not only the way individuals and the group are intertwined, what basically becomes 'civilisation', but also what the

182 Freud, *Totem and Taboo*, pp. 1–17.

183 Ibid., p. 51. According to Freud, the first example of codification is linked to rules related to taboos: 'Qui ramène le droit à son fondement l'anéantit'.

184 Ibid.

185 Derrida, *Grammatologie*, p. 372. Freud wrote that laws are forbidding patricide and forbidding incest. This is at the time of the 'fair' '*la fête*' that incest becomes also a crime. Before that time, there is no incests, no crime, as there is no interdiction of incest, there is no society.

186 Ibid., p. 373.

mechanisms in place to protect this civilisation and in particular the importance of the legal event *are*, and, in turn, the importance of ritualisation in the judicial process.

According to Garapon, there can be no justice without a certain adaptation to a public space, enabling the public to 'see' this justice. In fact, it is necessary 'to reconsider justice not against ritual, but with it.' Indeed, for Garapon, the ritual is here as a memory; reminding us of the fundamental ambivalence of the legal event, place and time of the best forms of justice as well as the worst forms of injustice.[187] According to Peter Goodrich, the law itself in the twentieth century became 'a theatre of the competition and the incommensurable identities, a visible drama of justice and injustice'.[188] Thus behind the judicial ritual is above all hidden the religion and the magical structure linking time and space.[189]

The issue of time and space has always been a crucial issue: both for soft and 'hard' sciences of course. Plato already worked on the relationship between time and space.[190] In physics, the former 'natural philosophy',[191] the time and a shape of the space, the distance, are linked. The most basic expression of their relationship is probably that of the equation of speed: speed = distance/time. In a discourse regarding space and time, it is inevitable to mention Einstein and his space-time concept. He shows that the positioning of space is related, in many ways, to time. This is also true in human life, from the beginning of it, the first spatial positioning, the original position of the *locus* inside the mother, the first place of life, to its end, and the last place of rest, in the cemetery, the *loculus*. The issue of space and time is also present in philosophical works. For example, throughout Nietzsche's work, from birth (we especially find the birth in the title of his book *The Birth of Tragedy*), to death (the death of God, the end of God). Freud also considers space and time and develops the idea that their relationship is crucial for our world and for us as Jankélévitch underlines:

> Freud only said that Unconscious does not recognize the chronological time in which we settle the matters of our life and our death. But he never said that Unconscious does not have its own time which punctuates it in such a way that it is never the same, but pure otherness, finding stability only in the fantasy and the symptom.[192]

187 Garapon, A., 'What Should one Think of Judicial Ritual in Law?' in Ralph Lindgren, J. and Knaak, J., *Ritual and Semiotics*, New York: Lang, *Critic of Institutions* 14, 1997, pp. 23.51, esp. p. 29.

188 Goodrich, P., 'Europe in America: Grammatology, Legal Studies, and the Politics of Transmission', *Columbia Law Review* 101 (8), pp. 2033–2084, esp. p. 2079.

189 For a further study on what is a ritual, we can refer to the book of Reick, a student of Freud. Reik, T., *Ritual, Four Psychoanalytic Studies*, New York: Evergreen, 1962 (1946).

190 Sherover, C., (ed.), *The Human Experience of Time, The Development of Its Philosophic Meaning*, Evanston: Northwestern University Press, 2001, p. 15

191 See, for instance, *Principles of Natural Philosophy,* de Newtown.

192 Yankelevitch, H., 'Qu'est ce qu'un Concept en Psychanalyse', *Futur Antérieur* 10, February 1992, http://multitudes.samizdat.net/Qu-est-ce-qu-un-concept-en.html (accessed 17 February 2017).

Freud considered the unconscious as timeless (and detached from our sense of time), while the conscious was always linked to time (attached to our chronological sense of time).[193] The development, moving from the principle of pleasure (a kind of 'state of nature') to the principle of reality (a kind of 'state of civilisation'), in Freudian theory, implies an evolutionary change from a situation outside time to a situation 'with the time', the chronological social time, time where everything is done for, and by, acquisition and integration of social rules, code of conduct, of morale. Time is an element of the social which appears with otherness, the idea of the other.[194] In this unification of time and space, it seems that the logic of time regards the order of the story, whereas the logic of space creates a stage where events occur, including the legal event.[195]

Lacan merged Einstein's and Freud's ideas. He believed that the context of the analyst's work should exploit space and time. In the essay *Temps Logique*[196] he presented a refusal of all chronological aspects of time, according to Freud's original idea that the unconscious was timeless. This is basically what Lamizet mentions when he describes the idea of 'real event': the event has no duration; it is timeless, and belongs to a space where the subject is placed.[197] This event 'reaffirms' the subject and its relationship with the real. It is the satisfaction of our impossible instincts.[198] But 'impossible is not necessarily the contrary of the possible or, since the opposite of the possible is undoubtedly the real, we shall have to define the real as impossible'.[199] It is perhaps here the link with justice. For Derrida, deconstruction is impossible, and deconstruction is justice, a concept which is not 'deconstructable'.[200]

The particular characteristic of an event is obviously its movement. An event is something which comes from outside and affects what is inside. According to Lamizet, the event marks a limit between outside and inside.[201] The limit is a wall of separation between two spaces. This wall separates what is outside from what is inside. Transposed into legal terminology, we can consider that when one

193 Freud, S., 'The Unconscious', *SE* 14 (1905), pp. 160–215. Also Abraham, G., 'The Sense and the Concept of Time in Psychoanalysis', *The International Review of Psycho-Analysis* 3, (1976), p. 462.

194 As explained by Levinas, 'le temps n'est pas le fait d'un sujet isolé et seul mais [il] est la relation même du sujet avec autrui'. Levinas, E., *Le Temps et l'Autre*, Paris: PUF, 1983, p. 17.

195 Lamizet, B., *Sémiotique de l'Evénement*, Paris: Hermès, Lavoisier, 2006, pp. 41–48.

196 Lacan, J., 'Le Temps Logique et l'Assertion de Certitude Anticipée. Un nouveau sophisme', in Lacan, *Écrits 1*, pp. 195–211.

197 Lamizet, *Sémiotique de l'Evénement*, pp. 31–32.

198 Renucci, F., 'Les Voix pour le Dire', Actes du Colloque International 'l'Evénement dans l'Espace Euro-méditerranéen, Mémoire, Identité et Communication', pp. 27–39, esp. p. 29.

199 Lacan, J., 'les Fondements de la Psychanalyse', in Lacan, J., *Les Quatre Concepts Fondamentaux de la Psychanalyse*, Livre XI, Paris: Seuil, 1973 (1964) in Renucci op. cit.

200 Derrida, J., *Force de Loi, Le fondement mystique de l'autorité*, Paris: Galilée, 1994, p. 35.

201 Lamizet, B., *'Sémiotique de l'Evénement dans l'Espace Euro-méditerranéen', Actes du Colloque International 'l'Evénement dans l'Espace Euro-méditerranéen, Mémoire, Identité et Communication*, Toulon: USTV, 2006, pp. 17–26.

comes to a trial or *procès,* one moves from outside to inside, to the sacred place of justice, the courthouse or palace of justice. The walls of the palace or the court delimit, separate, but also define. The subject outside is always anonymous. When he comes inside the courthouse, it becomes 'defined', nominated, identified by a series of masks: the judge, the lawyer, the accused. After this, there is no more anonymity. This presence before a judge, following an eruption of the 'real' in the 'symbolic', is the language. That is what gives, for Derrida, the value of the distance between the facts and the law – which in our case defined the space of the legal phenomenon as legal event.[202] This also describes an event which is framed and orchestrated: there is a precise ritual which builds and structures the legal event and gives it its form. The idea of the event merges time and space through a theatrical ritual, that of tragedy, Greek tragedy mentioned by Nietzsche in *The birth of tragedy*. But this is also a ritual with a dramatic value, as highlighted by Goodrich.[203] Indeed, 'the Roman trial was explicitly a drama, played with actors or rhetoricians, who confronted through competitive versions of the real.'[204] The world is a theatre where human experiences occur, but on a gigantic scale, through a certain dramatisation. The courthouse may be transformed into a place of theatre where a play is performed, a ritual is occurring. All actors wear a certain costume, each performing his role, the role of his life (and sometimes of his death). Similarly, the Masonic Lodge opens to become 'a world' by specific rituals.[205] Of course this example is withdrawn from the Temple of Solomon, with its specific organisation, a movement, lighting and darkening effects, symbolising the reproduction of life and death. Each stage in the Temple is a sacred experience of life, in a movement from outside to inside, from the true external light to the symbolic internal light. As Duncan explains, 'we usually think of churches and temples as religious places, of a different nature from laic sites such as museums, courthouses or parliaments'.[206] But our 'supposedly secular culture is full of ritual situations and of events'.[207]

It is therefore not surprising that the typical architecture of judicial buildings is related to sacred places, temples (at least since the seventeenth century in France), where the sacred seems to link justice to God(s). In a truly Augustinian way, the temple of the God(s) has become the temple of the mortals, which imposes a sensational image: the Doric male, symbol of individual reason and willingness,

202 Derrida, *Voix et Phénomène*, p. 21.
203 Goodrich, 'Europe in America', p. 2078.
204 Ibid., p. 2081.
205 Wirth, O., *La Franc-Maconnerie Rendue Intelligible à Ses Adeptes, Volume II Le Compagnon*, Paris: Dervy, 1994. It is quite important to note here the links between free masons and the Republic. Wirth explains in *La Franc-Maconnerie Rendue Intelligible à Ses Adeptes, Volume III Le Maitre*, pp. 26–27 that freemasons are citizens of the Republic. *Res Publica* in fact belongs to them. See also pp. 160–161.
206 Duncan, C., 'Art Museums and the Ritual of Citizenship' in Karp, I. and Lavine, S.D. (eds), *Exhibiting Cultures: The Poetics and Politics of Museum Display*, Washington and London: The Smithsonian Institute, 1991, pp. 279–286, esp. p. 281.
207 Ibid.

the female ionic, symbol of imagination, and the feeling and intuition of the Corinthian columns.[208] We can be even more specific on the image of the temple. The Greek temple has always been put aside, isolated from the city, not only in a sacred enclosure, but also generally on a promontory, a citadel or an acropolis.[209] While 'the Roman temple, like some baroque churches, was a major element of the street, it had a façade with a large stairway leading to a richly carved Corinthian gantry'.[210] The place of justice, for the neoclassical architects, like in France for example, or Gothic revival in England, has always been the courthouse, 'speaking through allegorical and metaphorical forms', playing with the natural movement of the Earth and the Sun, days and nights, life and death, light and darkness, opposing the 'temple illuminated by justice with dark places dedicated to crime'.[211] We feel here the idea of separation, of a strong dichotomy, between white and black so dominant in the word of the legal event in the common law tradition, the trial.[212] Klein's works lead us to consider this idea of black and white through bad and good. For different reasons, the child uses the separation of the good (object) from the bad (object).[213] The judicial ritual in a public building which looks like a temple contributes to this junction between justice and human development. This reminds us of one of the reasons temples were used as a means of justice for many centuries, in the development of the so-called post-primitive societies.

The place where justice shall be delivered is a sacred place, enlightened by the light of the truth, in contrast with the darkness of criminal places. [214] As with Derrida, we may think that the calling into question of the very idea of building (especially public) is correlative to protesting the institutional authority.[215] All the instruments involved in even the 'creation' of the authority are thus fundamental, the ceremonial being one of the key elements of the ritual, which, according to Moore, would be commutable terms.[216] As Chase and Bruner explain,[217]

208 Wirth, *Le Compagnon*, p. 193. Doric is linked to the apprentice, Ionic to the *compagnon* and Corinthian to the master.

209 Furneaux Jordan, R., *Western Architecture: A Concise History*, London: Thames & Hudson, 1993, p. 28.

210 Ibid., pp. 46–47.

211 Markus, T., *Buildings and Power, Freedom and Control in the Origin of Modern Building Types*, London: Routledge, 1993, pp. 34–35.

212 We find this in the ritual of the common law trial. As explained earlier, the trial is an operation of separation of the good from the bad, a triage.

213 Klein, M., 'L'amour, la culpabilité et le besoin de réparation' in Klein, M., *L'Amour et la Haine*, Paris Payot 2001 (1937), pp. 87–88.

214 We may, with Lacan, consider that 'Truth begins to be established only once language exists'. Lacan, J., *My Teaching*, London: Verso, 2008, p. 29.

215 Wigley, M., *Architecture of Deconstruction: Derrida's Haunt*, Cambridge, MIT Press, 1995, p. 47.

216 Chase, O. and Bruner, J., *Law, Culture and Ritual: Disputing Systems in Cross-Cultural Context*, New York, NYU Press, 2005, p. 134.

217 Ibid., p. 131.

> challenging the institutions (the courts)[218] require the use of ritual practices in the service of legitimacy. In order for this to work, the *borrowed* ceremonies shall resound through the symbolic association with other institutions which are themselves worshipped (religious ritual).[219]

Regarding judicial architecture, it is worthy to note the presence of a specific ritual which mingles with architecture. A complex system of values exists which connects to the speaking architecture, when the building, which imposes the solemnity of the political institutions, of the State, enlightens, in turn, its authority. It is related here too to the Masonic initiation and to the perfect architecture of a lodge: 'a holy ground', a 'temple'.[220] It is the scene of the initiation, the place where ritualisation occurs, where the reception or acceptance rite of the new member takes place. It is a space where the time is organised, through rites, to create a symbolic system of morality. Time, space, the ritual and the moral are here linked. The passage through the initiation allows growth, to mature, thanks to a certain dynamic event. It allows passing from the darkness to the light of the morality system. At the same time, this operates as it does for life, like education, the one provided by the parents, and reiterates an initiatory path, from a beginning to its end, from a start, a new start, and almost a rebirth. This idea is very similar to what Lacan considers in his theory at the end of the psychoanalysis; the cure.[221] The end of the cure is the opening to something else. *Analysus* is the time when the subject knows something different, differently. In the world, or in a palace of justice, a courthouse, experiences of the human development replayed, from the time of birth to a time not of death literally, but of the death of *something*, a renewal, a transformation into something else. This is asserted and confirmed by a very strong link existing between the myth of birth and re-birth and the rituals attached to puberty.[222] All these rituals go beyond the sole individual experience. They are related to social organisation. They operate as guides in timelessness, similarly to the parenting in human experience.

Psychoanalysis is often presented as something like parental education, *de facto,* a chronological succession of events from the birth to the re-birth, from birth to death. The analyst's room becomes a temple. Here, the time, which punctuates the speech of the unconscious, in a specific space, creates, as in the case of the Masonic lodge, a symbolic space. It is a space, an arena between two actors rather than a 'specific' construction: the space of the analyst's room is also a space created by the binome analyst/analysand. In contrast with the unconscious'

218 My emphasis.

219 My emphasis.

220 Wilmshurst, W.L., in Masonic initiation explains what the perfect architecture of the lodge is: a 'holy ground', a 'temple'. The initiation of the Freemason is a ritual of reception, of acceptance of the new member in the lodge, masonry being a moral system. http://masoniclibrary.com/books/The%20Masonic%20initiation%20-%20W.%20L.%20Wilmshurst.pdf

221 Lacan, 'Temps Logique', pp. 195–211

222 Reik, *Ritual*, pp. 91–166, esp. p. 156.

timelessness aspect, the analysis is ritualised: time and space are shaped and reshaped continuously, together. That is why, in *Temps Logique*, Lacan modulates the time in three periods: the moment of the gaze, the moment of understanding and the moment of concluding.[223] Each period has a repercussion in the analysis work, from the beginning of the analysis until its end, and acts as help in the movement from pleasure to reality. We may consider that something like the act of judging is playing here; something which looks like parental education. Thus, it is possible to link the space of the legal event and the time of the legal event to space and time of psychoanalytic theory.

Thus, this is not unrelated to the idea of ritual as transformation, which reproduces the general scheme of the passage or transition rites that Moore, van Gennep, Turner and, of course, Garapon describe as the ritual of justice.[224] The courthouse, the palace, the place where justice seems to be delivered, becomes a space framed by rituals. These places are similar to the *locus*. The architecture of the place of justice, as Garapon mentions, is built on the initiation rites, or passage rites, which revolve around three phases reflecting, more-or-less, the chronology of the Lacanian time.[225] In the discovery of the function of the building, the ritual appears as the link between the construction and the meaning. Meaning for the individual, meaning for the group of individuals, what is ultimately considered as *society*. As Badiou underlined, 'a universal singularity is not of the order of the being but of the order of the *emergence*. . . . Any universal originates in an event'.[226] This may be applied to the legal event. The idea of ritual also concerns the function which metamorphoses a transition 'of the quotidian life of a different context in which the quotidian is transformed'.[227] The ritual has a 'power of transformation' which is not without interest in the process of justice.[228] It is necessary, in the judicial process, to push all resistance forces to society to disintegrate; that is to say, what goes against a fluid functioning of a society, of the possibility or the necessity for a group to work in harmony. Therefore, the courts must orchestrate this harmony by means of a ritual, which 're-establishes order in the world by the sacrifice, the hardship or the enlightenment'.[229] For Eliade, myth and ritual are connected.[230] The ritual abolishes the profane time, the chronological time, and retrieves the sacred time of the myth.[231] The sacred time meets the sacred place in the legal ritual: both define the way the staging of

223 Lacan, 'Temps Logique', pp. 195–211.

224 Chase and Bruner, *Law, Culture and Ritual*, p. 134.

225 Garapon, *Bien Juger*, pp. 45–49.

226 www.lacan.com/badeight.htm (accessed 17 February 2017).

227 Bowie, F., *The Anthropology of Religion*, London: Blackwell Publishing, 2000, Excerpts from Chapter 7 'Ritual Theory, Rites of Passage, and Ritual Violence', pp. 151–168, citing Alexander, B., esp. p. 139

228 Ibid.

229 Duncan, 'Art Museum', p. 281.

230 This is particularly true for Eliade who considers that the myth is alive, dynamic, a role model giving meaning and value to the human being. Eliade, *Aspects du Mythe*, p. 10.

231 Ibid., p. 172.

the representation is hinged. When we consider what occurs abstractly in the building, the ritual, this spatiotemporal 'thing', institutes justice and makes a certain appearance of the place of justice necessary and specific: 'Both inside and outside the hearing court, everyone feels something about the rule and its application'.[232]

The three phases of the (classic) ritual

As Duncan explained, 'In all places of rituals, a certain kind of performance takes place'.[233] This occurs in three phases which link the legal ritual to the psychoanalytic experience.

Time of the gaze and the first phase of the legal ritual

The beginning of the analysis is the time to look at something or someone, the time of the gaze.[234] It constitutes a brief moment, a 'time zero' similar to 'birth' and divided in two sub-periods: the face-to-face and the lying on the couch. It is also a time where something appears in front of us, such as the courthouse, which appears in front of us before we enter it. The face-to-face is a characteristic situation of the classic medical visit. It is the moment where the patient, 'subject supposed to believe', is going to be confronted with the 'subject supposed to know'.[235] The psychoanalyst knows because 'once the patient is involved in the treatment, he has the absolute certainty that the analyst knows his secret'.[236] In front of the courts, the subject is also put in a position of belief. The most important subject is the patient, the one who is supposed to believe. The courts show the authority of the State and oblige the subject supposed to believe to see justice presents here and now. The patient must quickly abandon the 'facing the analyst' stage to be left alone. The face-to-face style of the medical visit must transform and the patient will lie on the couch. Therefore, the conversation with the analyst will be very different. This change contributes to a situation where the patient needs to face anything but himself, lying on the couch with his back to his analyst. Then, begins the second sub-period which shall lead to the opening of the unconscious. It is the time where the two protagonists, analyst and patient, stand at the foot of the language wall and begin to climb it together.[237] This second period is really a transition between the time zero and the true start of the analysis. Thus, we are in the opening time of the analysis, the opening of the 'Time to Understand', time which will last until the end of the analysis. When he enters the courthouse, the subject will also be confronted with himself.

232 Goodrich, 'Europe in America', p. 2077.
233 Duncan, 'Art Museum', p. 281.
234 Lacan, 'Temps Logique'.
235 Zizek, *How to Read Lacan*, p. 29.
236 Ibid.,p. 26.
237 Lacan, 'Fonction et Champ', p. 314.

The first stage of the judicial ritual looks like the time of the analysis. Garapon calls it the preliminary ritual of separation. It is, in itself, a transitional phase between the outside and the inside of the building, separating 'before' and 'during' the event, the time of 'creation' of the legal event while the two other phases are internal to the building, are part of the event, *are* the event. Those who prepare to enter a courthouse or palace of justice, are individuals equal before this majestic façade, but they will become the accused, witnesses, lawyers, judges, after having passed the threshold of the entrance, they will be separated by a dynamic process. The accused will have to go to the dock; the witnesses will be identified as witnesses; the gown or the wig in the case of the common law trial, will allow the lawyers and the judges to be distinguished from the other protagonists. The separation of the individual from a fixed point in the social structure, according to Turner, is the factor helping the actors of the legal event to move from anonymous to non-anonymous.[238] It is also understood that some may not regain their anonymous status after the legal event. This phase is 'before', it is a preliminary stage, a pre-threshold per its Latin etymology (*prae+limen*).

The second period is that of the transition between time zero and the start of the analysis, the movement from outside to inside, where the event is created. It is the time to get inside, by entering the building and starting the second phase of the judicial ritual.[239] The analysis really starts and here comes the time to understand, which will last until the end of the analysis, the end of the legal event.

The time to understand and the second phase of the legal ritual

During the time to understand, the patient's thinking occurs in a particular place, where the staging is essential. In Lacanian clinical situations, the staging takes place in the analyst's room and depends on the time of the session, which allows the articulation of time and space. The timing of the session is imagined to thwart the resistance of the subject, to disconcert him due to the particular times; what Lacan calls 'our short sessions'.[240] The stop and go, the suspension of the session, operates like the punctuation in the language, and contributes to the definition of a particular space and to the opening of the unconscious, an unconscious considered as 'guilty', which hides behind its alibi.[241] Punctuation not only fixes the meaning, but also transforms the physical space of the analyst's room into

238 Chase and Bruner, *Law, Culture and Ritual*, p. 134.

239 This shall be compared to the non du père/nom du pere (no of the father/name of the Father). As Lacan indicates, the symbolic function of the 'naming' positions the subject. Lacan, 'Fonction et Champ', p. 276.

240 Ibid., p. 313.

241 Ibid. Moreover, it is worth remembering here that for Lacan, the unconscious is structured as language.
Ibid., esp. p. 267. See also Lacan, J., 'The Insistence of the Letter', *Yale French Studies, Structuralism*, 36/37 (1996), pp. 112–147.

something more 'integrating' for the subject.[242] Similarly, the freemasonic lodge built on the model of the Solomon temple, may be a gathering of men, as well as a manmade construction, a building. The assembly of freemasons becomes, symbolically, the lodge itself. In the same way, the second preliminary phase of the legal event, the rite of confinement or reclusion or of transition, defines a stage which is not only physical. Individuals enter the courthouse and wait in corridors, vestibules, in the waiting room. It is a time of transition between two spaces, a time of reflexion. Traditionally in France these spaces are dark, and contrast with the hearing rooms, which are bright. It is not only an anteroom, but also a place which connects in bodily anatomy; the uterus, the vestibule (*vestibulo*). It is also the entry, a court, a, more-or-less, closed space in front of the main entry of a Greek or Roman house or of a building. In fact, the liminal space is not limited. It is a grey area situated between two clearly defined areas (the 'outside' and the 'inside').

Finally, the analyst involved in the 'time to understand' becomes the master. When he decides to stop the session, it is time to do it, in sequence, until this moment where the patient is ready to go 'free', after having refocused his mind in reality. In a certain way, the free subject can now take his responsibility as an adult. Parental education will end in the trial, by a dynamic of birth and re-birth: the sentence will make the subject a new one, an adult, a responsible subject, someone able to be integrated or reintegrated into society. The ritual will have operated as a transformation tool. To finish, there is the 'time to conclude' and the last phase of the legal ritual.

As Lacan's XXVth Seminar title, the time to conclude is the third time of the *Temps Logique*.[243] It is time to finish, to cast off. The analysed is in a hurry. He wants to finish the analytical process as quickly as possible. In a way, this relates and is comparable to the notion of reasonable time of a hearing, contained in the right to a fair trial guaranteed in Article 6 of the European Convention.[244] Lacan calls the '*psychological I*' the time when I becomes linked to the other, thus integrating the social time as Levinas underlines, interacts, links his truth to the others' truth. The time of the end of the analysis is the time where the patient releases himself.[245] This is also when he understands that death is his unique master, allowing him to understand, in turn, that life is his friend.[246] The treatment, the cure, is the extended action of helping the patient, a help which guides him to climb the wall of the unconscious. The analysand, thanks to this process, reaches a level of understanding of his unconscious which is attached to the language. This does not mean that he understands everything, but rather that

242 Lacan, 'Fonction et Champ', p. 312. It worth noting that the surrealists Breton, Aragon, Prévert, and Eluard decided to use *free verse* characterised by the lack of punctuation with aim to accentuate automatic writing, closer to the unconscious according to them.

243 Lacan, 'Temps Logique'.

244 www.echr.coe.int/NR/rdonlyres/086519A8-B57A-40F4-9E22-3E27564DBE86/0/FRA_Conven.pdf (accessed 17 February 2017).

245 Lacan, 'Temps Logique'.

246 Lacan, J., 'Variantes de la Cure-Type', in Lacan, *Écrits 1*, p. 347.

he knows now what will enable him to live closer to something, to his life, rather than close to a fantasy world where he was living. The time to conclude is the time when the patient decides that he is experienced enough to consider himself as an adult. Let remind us of the meaning of *analysus.* The patient feels free, enabling him to act as himself rather than acting as if he was himself. To conclude is a conclusion, the conclusion of a chapter, a slice of time, which opens to another one. Regarding *Temps Logique*, concluding is also deducing. It is the final moment of the psychoanalysis, where the patient deduces from what he knows now that he can be a bit freer, that he can live. Thus, the patient can allow himself to live.

He will live as a responsible subject. This is what will happen after the third phase of the legal ritual, the post introductory aggregation rite or (re-)constitution. This phase comes 'after'. This is the end of the legal event, just as the time to conclude is the end of the analysis. Etymologically, *post+limen*, positions the moment to put an ending after the threshold. It is moving towards the light, towards the 'truth',[247] towards the solution that will be given. From dark to light, here the sacred nature of the legal event is strengthened, punctuated by the three phases. During this phase, every actor is dressed in their costume and not only do we know who is who, but also who is doing what. Normally the judge will judge, in presence of the public. The public attends as representative of the society, as representative of the primitive horde replaying, from the start, the patricide, and helping express the truth. The ritual generally implies the performance (truth being expressed by the judge),[248] which implies the presence of the public.[249] This place is where the judge is identified as a symbolic figure, where the superposition of the judge and the symbolic father of the Oedipus complex is playing.[250]

Justice must be considered delivered. The symbolic attachment to the building of the palace of justice or the courthouse imposes a vision of political power, of its authority. Representation, because of the distance, brings the symbolic as the capacity to represent the signified justice within the signifier courthouse. This is done in a place of light, where the symbol is the sun. Justice becomes symbolic light. It is a similar moment to the end of the analysis because the ritual takes the form of a re-birth.[251] By becoming adult, after having recognised the responsibility of a wrongdoing, the subject can be born again and can now be integrated again in civilisation, his 'brothers' attending to this rebirth and witnessing. The ritual entails an overtaking of the individual and brings back order. As Eliade said: 'All we have to do is to repeat the cosmological ritual, and the unknown territory (the "Chaos") transforms into "Cosmos", becomes a *imago mundi*, a "ritually legitimised home" '.[252]

247 See what Lord Denning says on the subject of truth in Jones v National Coal Board [1957] 2 All E.R. 155, CA.

248 My emphasis.

249 Chase and Bruner, *Law, Culture, Ritual*, p. 132.

250 Lacan, 'Fonction et Champ', p. 276.

251 See Eliade, M., *Rites and Symbols of Initiation: The Mysteries of Birth and Rebirth,* Putnam: Spring Publication, 2009.

252 Eliade, *Aspect du Mythe*, p. 173.

From this link between space and time, we may thus also consider another dimension, linking the two to social life. Each event is indeed a dialectical experience. According to Lamizet, the representation of an event is a dialectic between the singular experience and the collective representation logic.[253] Thus, the meaning of the legal event is something which expresses both singularity and collective. The singular time and the social time create a symbolic mediation of temporality.[254] The singularity of the space and the public space also creates a particular geography, which may be called the symbolic mediation of social geography.[255] But this is not absolutely exact. The wait of the patient, suffering subject, is then transformed into the integration of what he may be, in accordance with the civilisation in which he is situated. Eventually, what is learnt in psychoanalysis and in justice, is only integration, the 'how to be part of' society. But, basically, it is not the end but the beginning of something else. As Zizek expounds, 'Moral is never only a question of individual consciousness'.[256] Nietzsche's self, as well as the Freudian id, have a social dimension. Stage by stage, the 'private' experience of morality becomes the experience of the group. Genealogy describes the process of a dual development. The intimate experience transmutes in a wider dimension. Self-morality develops like the Big Bang universe in a vast and intense world of experience. This basically gives a full meaning to what Levinas says: 'time condition is in the relationship between humans or in history'.[257] The ritual contributes to a necessary sacrifice, a relived sacrifice which transforms and civilises us, helping us in the movement from pleasure to reality.

Conclusion

We can understand that the (positioning of the) judge depends on a series of factors, or of more-or-less organised and more-or-less developed variables, following one or several historical, political, social . . . contexts. Thanks to this ritualised construction, the judge and justice organise, articulate, live. Thus, the event arises as a novelty but also as a witness of a mythical past, which is told in the places of justice. As Levinas writes, 'An event happens to us without a priori having absolutely anything, without having a slightest project, as it is said today'.[258] In the ritualistic dynamic of justice, the project is dual. It concerns a process of communication, where the totem and the Oedipus complex play, especially in the two European legal traditions. This project allows the restoration of order, firstly by resolving the dispute very close to the heart of the individual, the subject. But because of the symbolic position of the judge, the project becomes one of social cohesion. It contributes to the diminution of the latent

253 Lamizet, *Sémiotique*, p. 305.
254 Ibid., p. 306.
255 Ibid.
256 Zizek, S., (2007), 'Knight of the Living Dead', *New York Times* OP-ED Saturday, 24 March 2007.
257 Levinas, *Temps et Autre*, p. 69.
258 Levinas, *Temps et Autre*, p. 62.

aggression present in the civilisation as underlined by Freud. It concerns both the individual and society.

Some significant and striking differences of ritual in the two European legal traditions, or elsewhere, help to illustrate how in a 'classical' way, we oppose the other of the civil law to the other of the common law. This is probably unconsciously rooted in our minds. The two former, major, imperial powers, those which controlled the pre-modern and modern world, France on one side and Great Britain on the other one, shaped the law and the vision of justice of most of the regions of the world. The development of many legal families was linked to these empires, contributing to the constitution of blocks of countries following either the French or English prototypes. But beyond the oppositions which are presented to us, we discover two ways of seeing and understanding the world and thus the law. In the European regional context, in a post-World War II situation that some call postmodern, the transnational development of human rights dominates. Through an exchange and increasing permeability between the two legal traditions, the legal event and the judge, by one or several rituals, reassure us on the civilisation, reproducing archaic acts which 'speak' to us and tell us a past story that is, in fact, so present. With Hegel, we can consider that the things which have a different aspect are, in reality, the same, and with Wittgenstein, we can consider that the things which are similar are, in fact, different.

Pierre Bourdieu subtly examined the substitution of the memory by an image. He analyses family photo albums and their function of past trophies, past events. These operate like identification benchmarks. Thanks to them, the family receives confirmation of its unity of the time by the sight of its past. Besides, the album of the family's photos reassures them of a unique experience giving to the individual memories a common past. These photos act as an exorcism of the past, remembering it and acting here as a ritual similar to the funeral ritual. [259]

If we build an argument on Bourdieu's idea, by analogy, the representation of justice reconfirms a social identity and merges the individual and the group.[260] Moreover, according to Freud, we do not know if our childhood's memories are attached or not to our childhood or if they are recreated memories by recent events which recall our childhood memories. Those memories do not emerge but are shaped at the time where we think of them. They do not have any consideration for historical accuracy, from the process of their formation, and even concerning

259 Bourdieu, P., 'The Cult of Unity and Cultivated Differences', in Bourdieu, P., *Photography: A Middle-Brow Art*, Cambridge, Polity Press, 1990, p. 31.

260 There are here evident similarities between this theory and that of the mirror in Lacan, in particular the idea of ignorance and unawareness, where the child identifies himself with his image even though it is his external appearance (how s/he sees him/herself) rather than what he feels inside. See 'The Mirror Stage as formative of the function of the I as revealed in psychoanalytic experience', delivered at the International Congress of Psychoanalysis in 1949, in Lacan, J., *Écrits: A Selection* (Alan Sheridan trans.), London: Norton, 2004, pp. 1–7.

the selection of the memories themselves.[261] When myths emerge in our modern lives, ceremony becomes a crucial element of the representation of justice. As in the case of the family album, we have a crystallisation of individual memories into collective memories (common memory), through the spatiotemporal relationship that the places of justice communicate to us. Thanks to them, the memories of the myth of the creation of the world, of the horde, of the patricide, of the struggle against aggressiveness and the advent of the 'you shall not kill', make sense.

The recent development of transparent places of justice, detaching from the traditional judicial architecture, evokes the idea of a democratic and opened justice. Nevertheless, the place and the time of justice coexist. It shows a vision of an egalitarian and non-hierarchical order, which tends to erase the past. In fact, it fails twice, because not only does it not erase it, it also strengthens its ideological dimension.[262] If the architecture of the places of justice is a language which is spoken following one, or even several, time(s), according to the idea of one, or several, ritual(s), then, as any language, it cannot be innocent. The values and the intentions of each author and each participant are present in each second, each stone, according to a speech which represents by its silence something absent.[263] The questioning of 'brutal' architectures of the 'sacred place' courthouses, where rituals are performed again and again, showing a play which encompasses the past, much alike the album of family photos, has a risk: the questioning of the whole conception of the structure of the world. The microcosm which plays in justice goes well beyond the mere resolution of the dispute. It recreates a macrocosm and fully gives back to humans the place they always had as being in the world. We cannot help but refer to Heidegger.[264] The presence of the Dasein in his world is strengthened by a unitary phenomenon that Heidegger describes. We are here in a basic state of the Dasein,[265] in its essential structure,[266] basically its understanding: 'the [act of] understanding is an original determination of the Dasein's existence'.[267] The world is, and exercises, a fascination on the being.[268] Dasein is the world and the world is an element of Dasein. Being-in-the-world belongs to the basic constitution of the being that is in each case mine, that at each time I myself am. Self and world belong together; they belong to the unity

261 Freud, S., 'Screen memories', *SE 3* (1899), pp. 299–322, esp. p. 322.
262 The use of a classical language does not require knowledge of architecture from the subject. The courthouse perhaps is not always simple but it 'speaks'. On another hand, an office building, which share similar designs that a few recent courthouses is easier to understand, more accessible for contemporary subjects of a capitalist, liberal and democratic society. But this one does not speak, or more precisely does evoke neither justice, majesty, nor authority.
263 Markus, *Buildings and Power*, p. 4.
264 Heidegger, M., *Being and Time*, Oxford: Blackwell, 2007 (1927), p. 78.
265 Ibid., p. 86.
266 Ibid., p. 83.
267 Heidegger, M., *The Basic Problems of Phenomenology*, Bloomington: Indiana University Press, 1988 (1927), pp. 275–276.
268 Heidegger, *Being and Time*, p. 88.

of the constitution of the Dasein and, with equal originality, they determine the 'subject'.[269] Without this macrocosmic dimension, there are no individuals. But it is not certain that the individual is absolutely aware of it. This fascinates us and the result is a certain vision of the world.

As with Merleau-Ponty, we understand then that: 'It is true . . . that the world is what we see' and 'that we need to learn to see it'.[270] The space and the time of justice, through the ritual(s), leads us to interpret the world. We see it as this large 'thing' that contains us. This vision helps us as an integral moment.[271] The relationship between oneself and the world is interactive. The ritual(s) help this interaction between the being and the world, and the being and its interpretation of the world, making us what we are, positioning us in time and in space, enabling us to understand this membership.[272] The world is a playground for the Dasein, a dynamic space where it evolves, from the past to the present, from the present to the future. The being in the world is a spatiotemporal thing. The world, as ontological structure of the Dasein, evolves.[273] As with Bettelheim,[274] we may think that mythical explanations of the eternal problems of life give way to more rational explanations as soon as man feels safe. Then we reject, repress, forget, or pretend to forget the essential, by creating soft and sweet places of justice, rational and friendly spaces. At the same time, by doing so we erase the origin of civilisation, with rejection of aggressiveness and the patricide as core element of the socialisation. The fundamental character of interaction with the cosmos shall therefore be a continuous research that only the ritual(s) enable it to relive.

269 Heidegger, *Basic Problems*, p. 298.

270 Merleau-Ponty, M., *Le Visible et l'Invisible*, Paris: Gallimard, Tel, 1964, p. 18.

271 Overgaard, S., *Husserl and Heidegger on Being in the World*, Dordrecht: Kluwer Academic Publishers, 2004, p. 12

272 Heidegger, *Being and Time*, p. 118.

273 Heidegger, M., *The Metaphysical Foundations of Logic*, Bloomington, Indiana University Press, 1984 (1928), p. 170.

274 Bettelheim, B., *Psychanalyse des Contes de Fées*, Paris: Pocket Lafont, 1976, p. 82.

3 Contemporary spaces of justice

Use and abuse of transparency*

In this chapter, I will further analyse the question of spaces of justice. This chapter reiterates some of the arguments already made in the previous ones, but focuses more on the contemporary development. Empirical evidence suggests that there is a link between the architecture of courts of justice and respect for the law. Court architecture may influence the efficiency of the law in terms of individual case resolution, which has an impact on the cohesion of society. Law courts operate like a microcosm of the social organisation, where rituals of birth and re-birth take place, alongside the re-creation of the original transgression that marked the first step towards society. Courthouse design is important because courts a) constitute long-term investments that will be used for many years,[1] and b) convey a specific message of authority. Courthouses are spaces where the law is 'spoken' and where 'divine justice' results. In the past, the original myth of authority was represented by neo-classical (in civil law countries such as France) or Gothic revival architecture (in common law countries such as the UK) in 'palaces of justice'. In more recent years, we have witnessed a radical shift in courthouse design. The representation of authority through judicial architecture has now been replaced by a contemporary 'post-modern' approach that seems to modify the original myth. This article examines the use of transparency, or what is termed here the new opacity, as an integral aspect of contemporary courthouse design.

* A version of this chapter was presented at the University of Coimbra and subsequently published in Portuguese as 'A evolução pós-moderna dos espaços da justiça: O uso e abuso da transparência', in Patrícia Branco (ed.) *Sociologia do(s) Espaço(s) da Justiça: diálogos interdisciplinares* (Coimbra: Ces/Almedina, 2013). Another version was presented as Judicial Architecture on Trial: From Opacity to Transparency? A Comparative Perspective on the Evolution of Places and Palaces of Justice at the annual conference of the Law and Society Association in 2011 and published as Post-Modern Evolution of Places of Justice: The Use and Abuse of Transparency' in *Objectvity in Legal Discourse. The Comparative Perspective*, Breda & Rodak (eds.) (Peter Lang International, Dia-Logos Series, Studies in Philosophy and Social Sciences 2015), pp. 183–209.

1 HM Treasury, 'Green Book', 2003, pp. 69–72.

Introduction

A post-modern approach to places of justice has seen judicial architecture moving away from more traditional designs, which has had the effect of 'deconstructing' these palaces of justice. The key question would seem to be: does this affect the importance of the concept of justice and, in particular, the idea that justice has to be 'seen to be done'. As Krier notes, 'All great human institutions are to this day symbolised by classical monuments: St Peter's in Rome, the Capitol in Washington, Westminster in London',[2] and we should add to this list all the great palaces of justice. In fact, 'The dignity, authority and self-respect of such bodies [including the palaces of justice][3] are made visible in the majesty of their architecture'.[4] The risk with post-modern courthouse design, however, is that there is no recognition of such aspects: the new Civil Justice Centre in Manchester provides a useful example here. As observed by Mulcahy in her account of an exchange about the building between Stephen Quinlan and an architectural historian, 'the new Manchester centre [is] not recognisable as a courthouse'.[5] This statement mirrors the results of interviews conducted on the other side of the Channel by Lecourtois about the new Caen courthouse in Normandy. Lecourtois notes that the design triggered a range of public reaction: 'From the exterior it is not as representative of justice as the old courthouse', or 'In the former one, there were the columns, and that is more Roman. . . . Viewed from the exterior one cannot know that it is a courthouse'.[6] Furthermore, in relation to the issue of recognition of a building, we need to assess carefully the perceptions, or lack of perceptions, that derive from a building that is unrecognisable.

For centuries, 'traditional' courthouse architecture has clearly 'shown' its judicial authority.[7] Post-modern designs seem to remove clarity from this message conveyed by the buildings, however. Classical judicial architecture has always shown a certain transcendence, something vertical in the design features that express, make visible, the links between God–Monarch–Judge; traditional design suggests something 'sacred', then, that perhaps conflicts with the immanence, the horizontality, of contemporary democracy. If we assume that the signified 'justice' is immutable and the signifier 'place of justice' is not, we must look carefully at the representation of justice in a postmodern democratic environment in which 'horizontality' rather than 'verticality' is supposed to be the defining trait, and in which courthouses have left the sacred in order to enter the capitalist market. As stressed by Resnik and Curtis, 'Most of the new courthouses, often clad in glass to make justice's transparency, celebrate courts without

2 Krier, L., *Architecture: Choice or Fate,* Winterbourne: Papadakis Publisher, 2007, esp. p. 177
3 My emphasis.
4 Krier, *Architecture,* p. 177.
5 Mulcahy, L., *Legal Architecture,* London: Routledge, 2011, p. 14.
6 Lecourtois, C., 'Perception Architecturale et Image', *Colloque International 'Images et citadinité',* Alger, 2005. pp. 1–10, esp. p. 5.
7 Markus, T., *Buildings and Power: Freedom and Control in the Origin of Modern Building Types,* London: Routledge, 1993, pp. 34–35

reflecting on the problem of access, injustice, opacity, and the complexity of rendering a judgement.'[8]

Some philological remarks

We may have forgotten in the contemporary era that to apply the law is to exercise a power – the power to decide on the meaning of words. From this perspective, we are all like Humpty Dumpty, who pretended to be a master of this game.[9] Thus, I will open this enquiry by looking at the words 'palace' and 'justice', which are connected in the English phrase 'palace of justice' (as it is used in the *Oxford English Dictionary*) or in French, '*palais de justice*'.

'Palace'

The dictionary definition of a palace of justice is as follows: 'In France and French-speaking countries: a building housing a court of law; a law court'.[10] But courts of law, law courts, or courts of justice are, rather, an assembly of judges or other persons legally appointed and acting as a tribunal to hear and determine any cause – civil, ecclesiastical, military, or naval. The palace of justice is a law court, a place where law has, or founds, its space, similar to the 'vast and luxurious residence belonging to or having belonged to an important person, a royal residence'. The word palace or *palais* comes etymologically from the classical Latin word *Palatium*, which was the name of one of the seven hills of Rome (also called *Mons Palatinus*).[11] It refers to the imperial residence or temple located on the Palatine Hill, imperial or royal residences in general, and in post-classical Latin, it also refers to (*palatium*) the emperor (fourth century), royal officials (seventh century), the bishop's palace (ninth century), the prince's manor (eleventh century), and a town hall (twelfth century). Justice is so intangible, so noble, so sacred, that it needs a strong signifier: it needs to be hosted in a place similar to one devoted to other incarnations of power (emperors, kings and bishops).

'Justice'

According to the *Oxford English Dictionary*, there are three definitions of justice.[12] It is primarily the quality of being just. It also means the administration of the law (linked to the idea of the court and the king) and, finally, it refers to the person administering justice (which is also linked to the court and the king). If these

8 Resnik, J., Curtis, D., *Representing Justice: Invention, Controversy, and Rights in City-States and Democratic Courtrooms,* Yale: Yale Law Library Series in Legal History and Reference, 2011, esp. p. xv.

9 Brunet, P., 'Humpty Dumpty a Babel? Les juges et le vocabulaire juridique', *Chronique de Droit Européen et Comparé* (Les Petites Affiches) 17 (2008): pp. 1–9, esp. p. 2.

10 Dictionary, Oxford. 2011.

11 Ibid. Although it is likely that palaces were a Greek 'invention'. See, for example, C. F. Macdonald, 'The Palaces of Minos at Knossos', *Athena Review* 3 (30) (2003): Minoan Crete. www.athenapub.com/11knoss.htm

12 Ibid.

three definitions appear *prima facie* to be naturally connected, the connection occurs, in my opinion, at different levels. If we respect moral values, or divine laws, as 'just' (in the first definition) then there is no need to go further, and no need for the other two definitions. We may reasonably assume that this form of justice can only exist in some sort of ideal society. The organisation of a 'normal' society requires a system that implements respect for the rules of that society, perhaps by way of sanctions, as it is generally agreed that there is a distance between the theoretical vision of contractarian theories and their application. Moving from a state of nature to a state of civilisation should be something that is desired by those involved, so that the rules they give themselves should be automatically respected. The place of justice that is the palace of justice becomes such an important space, such a central element of the 'real' existence of the law, that this is where it takes its full signification: it is a social dimension in which the administration, and the administrator, of the law are positioned. It illustrates perfectly the idea that the function of a building and the look of the building are intertwined, and in the case of palaces of justice, the perception of the building conditions the process of justice. Justice, Derrida notes, is the impossible. Indeed, '*La justice en elle-même, si quelque chose de tel existe, hors ou au-delà du droit n'est pas deconstructible*'.[13] The signified 'justice' is not subject to any deconstruction and is therefore immutable; however, its representation – the signifier 'justice' – is.

This hypothesis, which mixes Derrida's definition and semiotics, leaves us with a signified (justice) and a signifier (the place of justice): the signified cannot be deconstructed and is immutable, but the signifier, a representation of this concept through buildings, is subject to evolution, fashion and trends. The following section will discuss the evolution in courthouse design, from a traditional architecture used in the main representatives of common and civil law legal traditions (in England and France) to a post-modern architecture that claims to be 'transparent'. I will then consider the dilemmas posed by such post-modern courthouse design, and the differences between notions of opacity and theories of transparency.

Evolution of places of justice: From traditional (opaque) to post-modern (transparent) law courts

In matters of law court design, according to Lecourtois,

> *Trois principes programmatiques paraissent inviter à la mise en œuvre d'une échelle symbolique formelle. Ces principes se présentent sous forme de propositions par lesquelles les architectes sont invités à penser de manière spécifique certains éléments d'architecture. Ces éléments sont: 1) la monumentalité qui doit passer par un vocabulaire architectural spécifique (colonnes, frontons, emmarchement,*

13 Derrida, J., *Force de Loi, Le 'fondement mystique de l'autorité'*, Paris: Galilée, 1994, p. 35.

> *statuaire); 2) l'ouverture à penser relativement à un traitement de la transparence et 3) la théâtralité ou pédagogie qui doit être mise en scène relativement aux temporalités de la justice.*[14]

Justice has to be 'seen to be done': thus its signifier, the place of justice, combines monumentality, a particular use of transparency and theatricality. The place where this occurs plays an important role in the administration of the signified (justice) and for its administrator. Traditional courthouse architecture is an example of the secularisation of the religious architecture of England and France, which I will compare here; it has been questioned recently in discussions among architects about the necessary transparency of post-modern design.

Comparing the traditional architecture of places of justice in France and England

For traditional architects, the place of justice was a palace of justice in which a complex system of values and ritual(s) were connected to the *architecture parlante*, (speaking or talking architecture). The monumental building opens up the mind through its theatricality, imposing upon the viewer the solemnity of the state and of authority.

The typical architecture of judicial buildings relates to sacred places – temples or churches; in this way, the link to holiness appears to link justice to god(s). In a truly Augustinian way, the temple of the god(s) has here become the temple of the mortal, which imposes a sensational image. Interestingly, the Greek temple 'was always set apart from the town, not only being put in a sacred enclosure, but usually also upon a headland, a citadel or acropolis',[15] while '[t]he Roman temple, like some Baroque church, was a feature in the street; it had a façade with a great flight of steps leading to a richly carved Corinthian portico'.[16] It is no surprise, then, that an architect such as Krier notes that the kinds of buildings discussed here are classical in origin:

> Classical: from Latin classical, of highest class . . . make[s] [with the vernacular] distinctions of rank at different levels, between private and public, between individual and collective, between urban fabric and monument, between house and palace . . . It is concerned with symbolic language, with the construction and decoration of public structures, with buildings . . . and monumental features in general.[17]

14 Lecourtois, C., ' "Espace de la conception" d'architectures judiciaires: les nouveaux palais de justice (Caen, Melun, Nantes, Grenoble et Pontoise)', *Diagonale Phi. n°4, Université Lyon 3*, 2010, pp. 31–52, esp. p. 38.

15 Furneaux Jordan, R., *Western Architecture: A Concise History*, London: Thames & Hudson, 1993, p. 28.

16 Ibid., pp. 46–47.

17 Krier, *Architecture*, p. 53.

For neo-classical architects, the place of justice was a palace, 'speaking through allegorical and metaphorical forms', which played with the natural movement of the Earth and the Sun, days and nights, life and death, light and darkness, contrasting the 'temple illuminated by justice' and the 'dark places devoted to crime'.[18] We might sense here the idea of a separation, of a dichotomy, a black and white vision of life and of the world.[19] The place where justice must be rendered is a sacred place because it is illuminated by justice and the light of the truth, which contrasts with the dark places devoted to crime.[20] We may, like Derrida, think that 'questioning . . . the very idea of building is aligned with a questioning of institutional authority'.[21] All the apparatus involved in the 'creation' of authority is therefore fundamental. In the case of judicial architecture, what is interesting is the presence of specific judicial ritual(s) that mix with the architecture.

Rather than the neo-classical, architects in England have traditionally used a different type of signifier: the gothic revival. This term (sometimes referred to as Victorian gothic or secular gothic) usually refers to the period of architecture practised in the second half of the nineteenth century (around 1830 to 1870). Eastlake observes,

> The renewal . . . of a taste for Mediaeval architecture, and the reapplication of those principles which regulate its design, represent one of the most remarkable phases in the history of art.[22]

Eastlake traces the Gothic to the sixteenth and seventeenth centuries, while also examining its re-appropriation in the Victorian era. It is another type of sacred design, as demonstrated by the 'Monasticon Anglicanum'.[23] The 1818 Church Building Act emphasised that Gothic was to be the ecclesiastical style. The commissioners responsible for the financial side of things essentially discovered that a Gothic church cost less to build than a neoclassical one. However, Eastlake notes that the design was adopted for civic buildings when the government decided that the new Houses of Parliament should be Gothic.[24] This was reinforced by an acknowledgment of the versatility of the style and its obvious possible

18 Markus, T., *Buildings and Power, Freedom and Control in the Origin of Modern Building Types*, London: Routledge, 1993, esp. pp. 34–35.

19 We find this in the ritual of the trial itself, which is, in fact, the act of separating the good from the bad, the *triage*.

20 We may agree with Lacan that 'Truth begins to be established only once language exists'. Lacan J., *My Teaching*, Verso 2008, p. 29 Hence, the notion of jurisdiction, *juris diction*, the place where the law is said.

21 Wigley, M., *The Architecture of Deconstruction: Derrida's Haunt*, Cambridge: MIT Press, 1995, p. 47.

22 Eastlake, C. L., *A History of the Gothic Revival*, London: Longmans, Green and Co, 1872, p. 1.

23 Ibid., p. 2.

24 Ibid., p. 187.

secularisation: 'the revival of the Gothic as a versatile style with secular application was the reconstruction of the Palace of Westminster'.[25] Pugin and Barry's design, which won the 1835 competition to redesign the Palace of Westminster after its destruction in a fire in 1834, employs the perpendicular Gothic style both inside and out.

The Royal Courts of Justice (the Law Courts) was probably the most successful Gothic public building after the St Pancras railway station. A restricted competition involving major architects of the day, including Barry, Waterhouse, Scott and Street (among 11 entries) was held in 1866.[26] The judges made no award at first but after much confusion selected Barry's plan and Street's elevation. In 1868, however, the contract was given to Street alone.[27] The main frontage was a multi-element stone design in a thirteenth century French style. The Gothic hall leading from the entrance was supposed to be similar to that found in the ritual of justice in France, a *salle des pas perdus*, with dimensions of 70m by 15m by 25m, like Lincoln Cathedral – another demonstration of the connection with the sacred.[28]

The Gothic Revival seemed to give a form to a particular feeling for the spiritual and for tradition, which were already associated with the monarchy and traditional English conservatism; neo-classical style, on the other hand, seems to voice the rational and the radical that is associated with the republicanism of France and the USA. It was therefore a nationalist or even a dogmatic nationalist discourse of 'speaking architecture' that developed in the nineteenth century. We should add that for Krier,

> In traditional cultures, invention, innovation and discovery are the means to modernise time-honoured and practical systems of thinking, planning, building, representing, communicating in the arts, philosophy, architecture, language, the sciences, industry and agriculture. . . . They are the means to an end. . . . Fundamental aesthetic and ethical principles are deemed to have universal values which transcend time and space, climate and civilisation. In modernist cultures, invention, innovation and discovery are ends in themselves. . . . There are no longer any universal ethical and aesthetic categories.[29]

25 Sutcliffe, A., *Architectural History of London,* New Haven: Yale University Press, 2006, p. 100.

26 In appendix 283, he explains that St Pancras was a Venetian Gothic design, the 'first instance of the adaptation of medieval design for such a purpose in London'.

27 Eastlake, *Gothic Revival,* p. 128.

28 Sutcliffe, *Architectural History of London,* pp. 106–107. Pugin was strongly influenced by Lincoln Cathedral. See for illustration Pugin: God's Own Architect, www.bbc.co.uk/programmes/p00n58pm (accessed 15 March 2015).

29 Krier, *Architecture,* p. 51.

Figure 3.1 Palais de Justice, Nice, France.

Figure 3.2 Royal Courts of Justice, London, UK.

Questioning what is here

The design of law courts matters. It matters particularly because recent years have seen the construction of radically different designs of courthouse buildings. I believe this should be questioned, and that we need to analyse how this new trend in courthouse design affects public understanding of the places and spaces where justice is done. One of the problems encountered in the representation of justice is that palaces of justice have imitated temples and churches, which has connected them with the religious and the spiritual.[30] According to Latour, 'Now that the modernity of our world is coming to a close, we understand that it was no more secular than any other'.[31] The divide between religious/secular seems to vanish, or to have vanished. As a space where the ritual of justice develops, the place of justice is a microcosm that evidences the vanishing of this divide. As Duncan notes, 'A ritual site of any kind is a place programmed for the enactment of something. It is a place designed for some kind of performance', where 'participants perform or witness a drama – enacting a real or symbolic sacrifice'.[32] Could we apply this statement to 'post-modern' courthouses? For centuries, the traditional architecture of courts has clearly demonstrated authority;[33] modernism seemed to follow the same trend, but post-modern designs seem to be removing the clarity from the message conveyed by the buildings. For Jencks, 'Modern architecture died in 1972';[34] postmodern architecture emerged as a critique of modernism. It is 'committed to pluralism, the heterogeneity of our cities and global culture, and acknowledge[s] the variety of tastes, cultures and visual codes of the users';[35] it employs 'curves, blobs, folds, crinkles, twits or scattered patterns', and 'sends complex messages, ones that often carry ironic, dissenting or critical meaning, those that challenge the status quo'.[36] This statement goes to the heart of the main issue: the function of the building and its design are connected, linking the appearance and the institution. For Heidegger, 'to appear' is what is in front of us; what 'appears', as in ancient Greek 'what is instituted', always meant what was left in front of us[37]. It could therefore be the case that as the signified justice is immutable, its signifier should not depart too much from the traditional way of representing it, otherwise the meaning of the complex messages given out could

30 This has also been the case for museums, as explained by Duncan, 'The Art Museum as Ritual', in C. Duncan, *Civilising Rituals, Inside Public Art Museum*, London: Routledge, 1995, pp. 7–20, esp. p. 7

31 Latour, B., 'Visualisation and Social Reproduction: opening one eye while closing the other . . . a note on some religious paintings', in *Picturing Power: Visual Depiction and Social Relations*, edited by G Fyfe and J Law, London: Routledge, Sociological Review Monograph 35, 1988, pp. 15–38, esp. p. 34.

32 Duncan, 'The Art Museum as Ritual', esp. p. 12

33 Markus, *Buildings and Power*, pp. 34–35.

34 Jencks, C., *The New Paradigm in Architecture: The Language of Postmodernism*, Cambridge: Yale University Press, 2008, p. 9.

35 Ibid., p. 2.

36 Ibid.

37 Heidegger, M., *Qu'appele t'On Penser?* 3rd edn. Paris: PUF, 1959, p. 189.

be lost. In other words, we cannot play with the architecture of the courts of justice as we may play with other types of buildings, even those of other political institutions, without facing the risk of justice losing meaning.

We must question judicial architecture because, as explained by Derrida, 'the questioning of the very idea of building is aligned with a questioning of institutional authority'.[38] It is indeed the case that the design of public buildings resounds throughout the society of which they are supposed to be a part. Primarily, as previously mentioned, they represent a huge and long-term investment.[39] In fact, 'institutions are understood as buildings that can be displaced only by rethinking architecture'.[40] For Derrida, therefore, the rethinking of institutional politics turns out to be architectural.[41] What we see, what is put in front of us, what appears, is thus of significance. What is re-*presented* becomes a necessity in the buildings of political institutions, as 'we have delegated to hundreds of non-human lieutenants the task of disciplining, making, and moving other humans or other non-humans'; we thus have 'instruments [that] bring faraway places, objects and times to us which are thus represented – this is presented again – for our inspection'.[42] These public buildings are in fact the only proof, the sole evidence, of political power, its main and only representation, its main and only signifier: they give *soul* to the political through the eyes of whoever looks at them. Let us not forget that there is a crucial difference in law between the natural person and the legal person (artificial): in the case of a natural person, we have a real person; in the case of a legal person, we have a fiction. In consequence, one 'exists' while the other does not; one is 'alive', the other is not. Krier considers this issue when he writes, 'the value of ancient monuments does not reside in their material age but essentially in the quality of the ideas that they embody'.[43] These buildings are the signifier of signified ideas: they give them a 'body'. This is particularly true for ideas such as justice and the law. Legal persons, including public persons, like corporations or states, need something, perhaps like a magician's trick, to give us the feeling that they are what they are, because '[t]he language of institution is that of buildings'[44] and, of course, because 'there is no institution without representation'.[45] An institution is supposed to create the presence of a fiction (a legal person) that is absent. Representation is the presence of the absent. In this sense, representation gives life to the institution, and 'institutionalises' it.

38 Wigley, *Architecture of Deconstruction*, p. 47.

39 See HM Treasury, pp. 69–72. Also www.ogc.gov.uk/documents/CP0067AEGuide7.pdf. In addition, 'The long lifespan of the existing building stock means the majority of it will still be in use between 50 and 100 years' time', at www.rics.org/site/download_feed.aspx?fileID=2162&fileExtension=PDF

40 Wigley, *Architecture of Deconstruction*, p. 47.

41 Ibid., p. 48.

42 Latour, 'Visualisation and Social Reproduction', p. 15.

43 Krier, *Architecture,* p. 73.

44 Wigley, *Architecture of Deconstruction*, p. 51.

45 Ibid., p. 51.

We could apply here, by analogy, Derrida's considerations on representation in his comments on Rousseau. He states that the signified 'sovereign people' are represented by 'the assembly', and therefore they are the representative signifier.[46] The institution will rule for, and on the behalf of, the sovereign. The representation follows a primitive presence and brings a final presence, and occurs when the signified is absent – as in the present case of justice. Derrida goes on to demonstrate that the representative is not the represented (the signifier is not the signified) but is only the representative of the represented (only the signifier, in fact). As representative, it is not simply the other of the represented.[47] This re-presentation brings the absent into the moment. It focuses on the signifier by giving it the function of representing the absent signified. Justice, our signified, is represented by the palaces of justice – its signifier. It brings us the impossible, the absent, and of course, the design that is adopted matters: depending on the radical nature or even the brutality of the design, it will give different representations of what justice is (or is supposed to be). From those designs, we may feel or perceive the authority of political power, what it wants to say about itself and about us, about individuals and society. It seems significant then that in our contemporary world all is being done to 'dismantle' traditional representation. While 'in democracy popular taste continues to have easier access to aristocratic than democratic high art',[48] signifiers of the places of justice are becoming transparent and architects claim to be in a process of opening up the old opaque courthouses.

Discourses of transparency

It seems extraordinary to witness the almost constant use of (the argument of) transparency by architects involved in the design of new courts. It seems obvious for contemporary designs to be using glass and steel or aluminium. But if these are used for private dwellings and commercial buildings, does it mean we should or could use these materials everywhere, in all cases? We know that a legal person needs representation, and that a legal person encompasses public and private entities. But does applying the same treatment to the design of a commercial office block and to a public building make sense? What about in courthouses? To illustrate this point, I will use the case of the new Bronx courthouse designed by Uruguayan architect Viñoly. Viñoly is well known for designing commercial buildings that use a lot of glass. His design was a typical example of a post-modern courthouse, which opened in 2007. The façade of the courthouse is a great example of the use and abuse of glass and aluminium. But there is something more interesting here than the use of specific materials: the discourse supporting this use. Given the frequent use of glass, it is perhaps unsurprising that we find a systematic use by the architect of 'transparency' in the justifications for, and explanations of, his design:

46 Derrida, J., *De la Grammatologie,* Paris: Editions de Minuit, 1994, p. 418.
47 Ibid., p. 419.
48 Krier, *Architecture*, p. 21.

> Rafael Viñoly, architect of the Bronx courthouse, sought a design that would give the judicial system an image of openness and transparency, rather than the opaque, closed feeling of the traditional courthouse. 'What interested me was transforming the public's perception that the building . . . represented an institution that was seen as closed and in need of protection from the community'. . . . The [new] building speaks to the participatory and the democratic nature of the judicial system and its fundamental and constructive mission in our society.[49]

Womack-Weidner goes on to note,

> The feeling of transparency and openness permeates the building. The courtrooms, jury deliberation rooms and robing rooms, all of which are in the interior of the building, have natural light from clerestory windows that 'borrow' daylight from the corridors between the courtrooms.

A non-exhaustive selection of articles in specialist and non-specialist publications brings further clarity to the argument, in which transparency is everywhere:

> This is achieved [transparency][50] by not concealing the building functions behind a representational face, but by allowing the buildings' program, structure and circulation to be viewed, providing a literal and metaphoric transparency of the judicial process.[51]
>
> The Bronx Criminal Court Complex, through its form and transparency, will redefine the relationship of the courthouse with the surrounding community. Glass is used to convey a sense of openness that stands in sharp contrast to traditional courthouse design.[52]
>
> The architects believe that this facades system gives the building an open and unintimidating appearance – all of its functions remain on public view, providing literal and metaphoric transparency to the judicial process.[53]

Its project director, Fred Wilmers, called the courthouse 'a metaphor for the transparency of the judicial system, the openness of government'.[54]

49 Womack-Weidner, A., 'New York Opens Second Mega-Courthouse', *Benchmark, Journal of the New York State Unified Court System* 2, no. 3 (fall 2006), pp. 1–2.
50 The author's emphasis.
51 *Bronx County Hall of Justice*. 2011. http://archiypesource.com/projects/61-bronx-county-hall-of-justice/description (accessed 15 March 2015).
52 *The Bronx Criminal Court Complex*. 2001 http://wirednewyork.com/forum/showthread.php?t=3685&page=1. (accessed 15 March 2015).
53 *Open curtain wall gives transparency to the judicial process*. 2011. http://archrecord.construction.com/projects/bts/archives/civic/07_bronxhall/default.asp (accessed 15 March 2015).
54 Hilferty, R., *Jury Beauty*. 26 February 2008. www.nysun.com/arts/jury-beauty/71877/ (accessed 15 March 2015).

> Located on 161st and 162nd Streets between Sherman and Morris Avenues, the Hall of Justice is a visually dynamic glass building where judicial transparency is not only a metaphor but also quite literal. With forty-seven courtrooms, seven grand jury rooms, the Department of Corrections, the Department of Probation, and the Bronx District Attorney's office, it is one of the largest courthouses in the country.[55]

Sometimes, a critical but rather isolated view is expressed:

> But just as we recognize the protective value of transparency in government, and in the justice system, literal transparency can be a security feature, too. In the eighteenth century, the philosopher Jeremy Bentham envisioned a prison – the Panopticon – in which inmates could be under constant, surreptitious observation. Viñoly's courthouse is a compassionate Panopticon: It allows everyone to observe everyone else. This doesn't obviate the need for cameras or guards, but it limits the possibility of nasty surprises.'[56]

It is perhaps logical to have such a glass building and the many resulting statements about transparency in this context, but we should carefully consider this discourse about the use of glass/transparency because it collides with notions of openness and democratic processes. In fact, 'an equation of glass and access to justice is simplistic'.[57] Transparency has been used by architects to push certain post-modern designs, certain representations of buildings, of legal persons, and they have not differentiated between public and private functions in so doing. It does not mean the design is actively wanted by the decision makers, as a true choice, but rather that the decision makers have followed the statements made by those who are supposed to know about buildings – the experts – the architects.[58]

According to Supreme Court Justice Felix Frankfurter, 'Justice must satisfy the appearance of justice'.[59] We could interpret this idea of the appearance of justice in many ways. Notably, I could drag this idea to the extreme end of the spectrum of 'appearance'. Here, the notion that justice has to be 'seen' to be done is fully translated by a glass building – a building so transparent that anyone can see inside it. For Mulcahy, 'Transparency is seen as undermining mystique and inviting public participation by rendering surprises less likely'.[60] The place where justice is (or is supposed to be) done should be 'opened' through the use of glass

55 ' 'Viñoly in the Bronx' Opens in Art Gallery', *Lehman College E News*. Vol. 3. NY, 2009.

56 Davidson, J., *Bronx Clear, How a courthouse polices us through the glass*. 4 February 2008. http://nymag.com/news/intelligencer/43599/ (accessed 15 March 2015).

57 Resnik, Curtis, *Representing Justice*, p. 341.

58 We should keep in mind the Lacanian 'subject supposed to know', the analyst, who is thought by the 'subject supposed to believe', the patient, to know everything, including his secret. Zizek, S., *How to Read Lacan*, London: Grant Books, 2006, pp. 28–29.

59 Bruner, J.S., *Law, Culture and Ritual: Disputing Systems in Cross-Cultural Context*, NY: NYU Press, 2005, p. xi.

60 Mulcahy, *Legal Architecture*, p. 152.

in post-modern court buildings. A new myth, a new great narrative, seems to emerge and to be based on a new paradigm: transparency. It is as if we were taking the affirmation that justice must be seen to be done a step further. Indeed, what is better than a transparent process, delivered in a transparent building? We are facing a new dilemma of post-modernity, of post-modern architecture: we want a transparent process in a transparent building, but are we certain that a transparent building is the way forward for conveying this new transparent process?

The dilemma of post-modern courthouse design: Transparency v. Opacity/Opacity v. Transparency

This section will further develop the discussion of transparency put forward by the architects. As mentioned, courthouse architects should operate on a symbolic scale. They should implement elements such as monumentality to demonstrate power and authority, together with a certain amount of transparency to open minds and theatricality for pedagogical purposes.[61] Lecourtois refers here to a certain level of transparency, not to full transparency, and she also notes that it merely concerns any demonstration of democratic values.

Transparency is fashionable in general architecture. We can walk the streets of many cities around the world and see clear examples of 'transparent' architecture, where buildings have a considerable amount of glass on their façades. But if perhaps it seems unimportant to question transparency in commercial buildings, this 'fashion' in architecture overspills into public building design and, more crucially, to the design of courthouses. To question this, we will next consider transparency in architecture and in psychoanalysis, and analyse how opacity is in fact the true transparency: the use of 'transparency' is more concerned with power. Finally, the next section will 'gaze', with Lacan, at (or through) a transparent building.

Transparency: architecture and psychoanalysis

If, using transparency, I completely deconstruct the opaque, old fashioned court of justice (or rather what we are told is an opaque, old fashioned design), I cannot really 'see' the place of justice as a palace anymore, because it does not seem to suit the historical and human context of the 'liberal democratic/capitalist' era. The word 'transparent' comes from Medieval Latin, *transpārēnt-em*, and is a present participle of *transpārēre*, composed of the prefix *trans* and the verb *pārēre*, to appear, to be visible. It also relates to *transpicio*, to see through. In addition, transparency relates to parenting: trans-parent. We therefore have a word that tells us the story of something that moves from one side to another and opens something.

61 Lecourtois, C., "Espace de la conception' d'architectures judiciaires: les nouveaux palais de justice (Caen, Melun, Nantes, Grenoble et Pontoise).' *Diagonale Phi. n°4, Université Lyon 3*, 2010, pp. 31–52, esp. p. 38.

'Trans' comes to us with the sense of coming 'across, through, over, to or on the other side of, beyond, outside of, from one place, person, thing, or state to another', but also 'across, crossing', or 'beyond, on the other side of', and finally, 'beyond, surpassing, transcending'. The trans-parent is, accordingly, something that goes beyond, or on the other side of the parents (both parents), that gives access to the parents. What more is needed to convince us that transparency is about hierarchy and verticality, about power and control, rather than about openness and democracy?

It should be noted that there are many discussion of parenting in psychoanalysis, and we find the notion of transparency in psychoanalysis, particularly its loss; indeed, 'while Freud preached the loss of transparency, the Enlightenment philosophers emphasised the gain of transparency'.[62] If transparency appears important, it is through its loss that psychoanalysis considers it. Transparency is not new. Resnik notes its political roots in the philosophy of Rousseau.[63] For Bessire, transparency has been around since at least the nineteenth century, moving from the aesthetic into every field of study;[64] it is therefore not surprising to see transparency in fields such as architecture and law. However, we should consider the relationship between the two, in light of new court design as it relates to 'justice', and should keep in mind that psychoanalysis could provide some useful insights here. But first we should return to architecture, and to do so I will refer to Rowe and Slutzky's 1963 article on transparency both literal and phenomenal.[65] Rowe and Slutzky demonstrate the polysemy of the word transparency as follows:

> According to the dictionary definition, the quality, or state, of being transparent is both a material condition – that of being pervious to light and air – and the result of an intellectual imperative, of our inherent demand for that which should be easily detected, perfectly evident, and free of dissimulation. Thus the adjective transparent, by defining a purely physical significance, by functioning as a critical honorific, and in being dignified with far from disagreeable moral overtones, becomes a word which from the first is richly loaded with the possibilities of both meaning and misunderstanding.[66]

This striking statement shows *prima facie* the difficulties we face: the many possible meanings of the term and, of course, the potential for misunderstanding. It is also critical, I believe, to any study on court buildings. If the possibilities for diverse meanings and misunderstandings are vast, then the use of 'transparency' in court

62 Friedel, W., 'Sigmund Freud: the loss of transparency', in *Copernicus, Darwin and Freud: Revolutions in the History and Philosophy of Science*, 185–270, London: Wiley-Blackwell, 2008, p. 188.

63 Resnik, Curtis, *Representing Justice,* p. 342.

64 Bessire, D., ' Transparency: a two-way mirror?' in *30 years of IJSE: Festschrift in honour of Professor John O'Brien*, edited by D. Pettman, Bradford: Emerald Group Publishing, 2005, pp. 424–438, esp. p. 425.

65 Rowe, C. and Slutzky, R., 'Transparency: Literal and phenomenal', *Perspecta* 8 (1963), pp. 45–54.

66 Ibid.

buildings carries these diverse meanings and misunderstandings, although the signified 'justice' remains unchanged. For Rowe and Slutzky, 'Transparency means a simultaneous perception of different spatial locations'.[67] Transparency not only abolishes distance but also produces immediacy: there is nothing to mediate, no 'protection'. Rowe and Slutzky open their enquiry by defining transparency in relation to painting, then move to architecture, in a process reminiscent of what Lacan did when he introduced architecture to the discussion of 'anamorphism . . . in a discussion of the role and function of projection' again emphasising the connection between architecture and psychoanalysis.[68] Rowe and Slutzky consider two types of transparency: 'Transparency may be an inherent quality of substance, as in a glass curtain wall; or it may be an inherent quality of organisation. One can, for this reason, distinguish between a literal and a phenomenal transparency'.[69] Literal transparency here means the use of materials that make a building transparent (the glass walls and open floor plates of Gropius's Dessau Bauhaus, for example, while phenomenal transparency refers to an effect, a perception of what is created by a particular organisation of 'things' (the facades and interior spaces of Le Corbusier's Villa Stein at Garches, for instance).[70] Rowe and Slutzky observe:

> Literal transparency . . . tends to be associated with the *trompe l'oeil* effect of a translucent object in a deep, naturalistic space; while phenomenal transparency seems to be found when a painter seeks the articulated presentation of frontally displayed objects in a shallow, abstracted space.[71]

They add:

> Provided with the reality rather than the counterfeit of three dimensions, in architecture literal transparency can become a physical fact. However, phenomenal transparency will, for this reason, be more difficult to achieve; and it is indeed so difficult to discuss that generally critics have been willing to associate transparency in architecture exclusively with a transparency of materials.[72]

As summarised by Holm, 'Colin Rowe and Robert Slutzky define phenomenal transparency as a conceptual effect of modern spatial configurations, to be distinguished from properties of glass and other materials that allow for the penetration of the vision'.[73] Phenomenal and literal transparency are related to

67 Ibid.
68 Holm, L., 'What Lacan Said re: Architecture', *Critical Quarterly* 42 (2000), pp. 29–64, esp. p. 31.
69 Ibid., esp. p. 46.
70 Ibid.
71 Rowe, Slutzky, *Transparency*, p. 48.
72 Ibid., p. 49.
73 Holm, L., 'The New Yorkers', *Architectural Theory Review* 12, no. 2 (2007), pp. 104–120, esp. p. 115.

architectural *trompe l'oeuil*, one being the opposite of *trompe l'oeil*, while the other is linked to *trompe l'oeil*,[74] creating a (literal) transparency that has as its corollary a (phenomenal) opacity. [75]

'Transparency' is therefore not as simple as it seems, and we can, therefore, understand why decision makers might rely too much on 'those who are supposed to know': architects are supposed to know how complex these issues are. Another issue it seems relevant to question is the reason for using transparency, or the reason for using opacity. What are we hiding, and what do we want to show? Looking at (primitive) architecture, Holm observes that it is 'organised around emptiness', and 'enters the symbolic order by a process of "primitive sublimation"';[76] it thus relates to Freud's *Das Ding* 'the Freudian Thing'.[77] This emptiness appears as 'the presence of a hollow, a void, which can be occupied by any object and whose agency we know only on the form of the lost object, the *petit a*.' *Petit a* in Lacanian theory is that which is lacking; as Zizek states,[78] it is something that will never be, 'except by circumnavigating the eternally lacking object'.[79] Architecture therefore both encloses emptiness and circulates around the lost object: the transparent quality of a building might correspond to the search for what is lacking. The opacity of traditional court buildings shows something that is present, while transparency shows us something absent that *should be* present: transparent court houses show us the entrance to the void. However, 'the signifier (symbolic order) screens us from the real'[80] and the opacity of the building appears to be crucial in the mechanism of mediation, creating distance and authority. That said, Holm goes on to state, 'Architecture is an empty temple awaiting the entry of God in a "lightning-flash of individuality"'.[81] This is a clear statement on the quality of the signifier, the building, and the link between the 'temple' (the sacred signifier) and individuality, or even subjectivity, which is instrumental in the perception of courthouses. To paraphrase Holm, architecture evolves and becomes not only something that encloses emptiness, but that represents it: it represents the absence of what is represented.[82] We arrive at the postulate that 'an architecture which represents itself . . . might appear behind its representation. [This would be an architecture that] signif[ies] the presence of an absence'. In the case of post-modern design, we do have the feeling of a complete absence.[83] The signifier has 'opened' its facade in order to 'show' what is inside but there is nothing there – nothing but the '*objet a*, the absent object

74 Holm, *What Lacan Said*, p. 47.
75 Holm, 'The New Yorkers', p. 15.
76 Holm, *What Lacan Said*, p. 29.
77 Ibid.
78 Zizek, S., *The Fragile Absolute: Or, Why is the Christian Legacy Worth Fighting For?* London: Verso, 2000, pp. 145–146.
79 Holm, *What Lacan Said*, p. 33.
80 Ibid., p. 34
81 Ibid., p. 36.
82 See also Derrida here. Derrida, *Grammatologie,* p. 418. Holm, *What Lacan Said*, p. 43.
83 Holm, *What Lacan Said*, p. 44

which is the cause of desire, but which never satisfies desire'.[84] The void is authority, in my opinion, and the interaction between opacity and transparency highlights the true misrepresentation designed by the expert architects.

Transparency as the true opacity, opacity as the real transparency

Because I am analysing buildings, and perhaps because of the pertinence of psychoanalytic theory to this analysis, this section looks at the setting of the first psychoanalytic place: Freud's office. Freud's study in Vienna creates a space that is specifically organised for the then-new technique of analysis. In his papers on technique, Freud indicates that 'the doctor should be opaque for his patients and, like a mirror, should show them nothing but what is shown to him'.[85] What is important is the specific space created, which will foster the dynamic between the analyst and the analysand; the positions of the actors are, to Freud, adequate for the purpose. The location of the patient at initial contact is the classical doctor-patient face-to-face situation. The patient faces the doctor, but with a twist. He is central, but is facing a mirror placed on a window. The patient sits and faces his own image. What he sees is his reflection in the mirror. When Freud sits, he blocks the view of the mirror.[86] The mirror functions simultaneously as a window, as do the mirrors in Etruscan tombs, assisting the passage to the other world. Lacan's analysis of the mirror instructs us to 'think of the mirror as a pane of glass. You'll see yourself in the glass and you'll see objects beyond it'.[87] He dislocates the opposition between transparency/reflexivity, as with the position of the mirror on the window in Freud's study. The relationship between opacity and transparency in psychoanalytic theory is, therefore, as in architecture theory, not as straightforward as we might think. In the building, the bricks or concrete block the view from outside to the inside. They elaborate a psychic image of what is inside, because the facade (face), and hence the importance of its design, creates a specific feeling when 'it appears'; it is put in front of us, as Heidegger observes.[88] In a building made mostly from glass, there is no separation, no distance, because of its transparency. There could be an elaboration of an image but this image would be of another type of building: a shopping mall, an office block. The brick or concrete wall operates like the mirror that reflects an image of authority while a transparent glass wall cannot foster that psychic image.

The image|screen of the linear perspective found in Lacan's diagram is 'both transparent (image) and opaque (screen). Any image is both a transparent window onto the world (Alberti, the perspectivist's metaphor) and a solid surface that

84 Ibid., p. 44.
85 Fuss, D., and J. Sanders, 'Bergasse 19: Inside Freud's Office', in *Stud: Architectures of Masculinity*, edited by J. Sanders, Princeton: Princeton Architectural Press, 1998, pp. 112–139, esp. p. 120.
86 Ibid., p. 120–121.
87 Ibid., p. 121.
88 Heidegger, *Qu'appele t'On Penser?*

reflects light'.[89] It is 'the negotiated locus of identity and desire'[90] but also, and more importantly for our case, it provides a view of the world.[91] However, the view of the world appears to be different for a subject facing one type of court and a subject facing another type. The notion of the view of the world is therefore primordial to this essay as it refers to an additional process, that follows vision, the one of interpretation, which connects with the symbolic order found in lacanian theory. According to Holm, 'A plane reminded us that a twin tower is a symbol',[92] and if we transpose this point to courthouses, we find that a building that hosts the process of justice may be a 'real' building but it hosts one of the fundamental institutions – justice (and is therefore also 'symbolic').

In order to look further at the transparency of the building, we need to return to our earlier questions: transparency – to what end? Opacity – for what purpose? What are we hiding and what do we want to show? The functions of the building and its face/façade are connected. According to Lacan, the interior is present in the exterior. In addition, Miller notes, 'the most interior – this is how the dictionary defines "intimate" (*l'intime*) has, in the analytic experience, a quality of exteriority'.[93] Thus, the façade of a building explains the inside. What appears in front of us tells us what is behind. The term 'interior' is connected to the term *intimus.* It helps us to reach the deepest point in the interior: 'the most intimate is at the same time the most hidden'.[94] The point made by Miller about Lacan's work in this regard is that 'the most intimate is not a point of transparency but rather a point of opacity'.[95] The argument many architects make about transparency can therefore be read through Lacanian theory: the idea that being able to see through a building will tell us the story of the process of justice being done inside, according to a democratic ideal, makes a transparent design of a building obvious. However, the notion that one may show the interior of the building through use of literal transparency (glass, windows) as a means to show its intimate mechanisms, to reach deep inside the process of justice, is false; one has to be able *not* to see through, even though this may seem prima facie to be contradictory. These things have to be hidden, as it is through opacity rather than through transparency that the most intimate level is reached. Psychoanalytic theory tells us that transparency does not give us access to the inside. A transparent palace of justice does not bring so much as a glimpse of the democratic process inside, for instance, or show that a fair trial has taken place.

89 Holm, 'The New Yorkers', p. 109.
90 Ibid.
91 Ibid., p. 110.
92 Ibid., p. 114.
93 Miller, J.A., 'Extrémité', in *Lacanian Theory of Discourse: Subject, Structure, and Society*, edited by M. Bracher, F. Massardier-Kennedy, M.W. Alcorn and R.J. Corthell, NY: NYU Press, 1997, pp. 74–87, esp. p. 76.
94 Ibid. Miller also describes the notion of extimacy, a Lacanian neologism created to explain that what is intimate is something or somewhere else. Interestingly, Lacan considers that extimacy is related to the Other of the Other of the signifier, the Other of the law, the Other that lays down the law to the Other, the Law as absolute, a metalanguage, see ibid., p. 78.
95 Ibid.

Figure 3.3 Manchester Civil Justice Centre, Manchester, UK.

Figure 3.4 City of Justice, Barcelona and L'Hospitalet de Llobregat, Barcelona, Spain.

Figure 3.5 New Amsterdam Court House, Amsterdam, The Netherlands.

For Holm, 'It is a dual paradox of the transparency of vision and the opacity of representation that seeing them *as if* they get smaller is to see them *as* the same size'.[96] Indeed, the 'visual field is composed not only of what I see, but what you see – this latter is usually more important – in so far as what you see is communicated to me by words, pictures, and other media, all of which constitutes what Lacan calls the field of the Other'.[97] What becomes important, then, is what you see: 'I do not see your view, but I frequently know what you see, especially if I am in it'.[98] The gaze becomes another key variable here. It is the presence of the Other: the subject is viewed not only as subject but also as the internalised presence of significant others.[99]

I gaze at a transparent building . . .

We should now consider what happens when we gaze.[100] After all, the building I consider, like any building, is positioned or located in front of me; it appears to me, as Heidegger puts it. I need to recognise it, to perceive it. It is a normal activity for me to look at it, and I gaze at it. I refer to Lacan here and his essay 'What is a picture?' in *The Four Fundamental Concepts of Psycho-Analysis.*[101] Of course, a building is not a picture; however, two observations are useful here. First, with the increase of web browsing and digital photography, what we have most of the time is a series of (2D) pictures of (3D) buildings.[102] Furthermore, architects start with a 2D representation of future 3D buildings, so they conceptualise the building on plan before its construction. Second, the process of representation and the ways in which it is instituted – through pictures of a façade, or through the façade itself – is similar enough to art for us to use what Lacan describes in this essay on the picture. I suspect that post-modern buildings operate as what Lacan calls *trompe-l'œuil* ('deceive the eye'). Lacan narrates the story of a competition between two ancient painters, Zeuxis and Parrhasios.[103] Zeuxis receives acclaim for painting grapes so life-like that even the birds that try to peck at them are fooled. In his pride, Zeuxis then goes to look at the work of Parrhasios. But Zeuxis sees only a veil, and so he asks to see the painting that Parrhasios has hidden behind the veil. Well, Parrhasios' painting *was* the veil, so well done that it fooled even the master of deceptive painting. Lacan points out, 'it is clear that if one wishes to deceive a man, what one presents to him is a painting of a veil,

96 Holm, 'The New Yorkers', p. 106.
97 Ibid., p. 108.
98 Ibid.
99 Ibid..
100 Some readers may consider that I am biased here, using only Lacan to analyse the notion of the gaze. For more, see Krips, H., 'The Politics of the Gaze: Foucault, Lacan and Zizek', *Culture Unbound* 2 (2010), pp. 91–102.
101 Lacan, J., *The Four Fundamental Concepts of Psycho-Analysis,* edited by J.A. Miller. London: Vintage, 1998, pp. 105–123.
102 This might change of course. Technology will allow for 3D presentations. But they will remain presentation on a 2D screen.
103 Lacan, *The Four Fundamental Concepts of Psycho-Analysis*, pp. 111–112.

that is to say, something that incites him to ask what is behind it'.[104] This is the purpose of the *trompe-l'œuil*:

> What is it that attracts and satisfies us in *trompe-l'œuil*? When is it that it captures our attention and delights us? At the moment when, by a mere shift of our gaze, we are able to realize that the representation does not move with the gaze and that it is merely a *trompe-l'œuil*. For it appears at that moment as something other than it seemed, or rather it now seems to be that something else.[105]

In a way, like Lacan, I consider that palaces of justice (like icons, or Holms' symbols) hold us under their gaze. But what makes evident the 'value' of the building is that whatever it represents (again, like icons), it has to do with God, and with the fact that God is also looking at it. Behind the building stands the social pact, articulated by the Name-of-the-Father.[106] Freud, says Lacan, was led irresistibly

> to link the appearance of the signifier of the Father, as the author of the Law, to death, even to the murder of the Father, thus showing that although this murder is the fruitful moment of the debt through which the subject binds himself for life to the Law, the symbolic Father, in so far as he signifies this Law, is certainly the dead Father.[107]

We know that the building is the signifier but we also know that it must always relate to a signified. Indeed, 'the peculiarity of the signifier [is] the fact that it is unable to signify itself.'[108] When I gaze at the building hosting the courts of law, then, where the work of justice takes place, I should immediately interpret (recognise) that it is a place where justice is going to be done. Subjectivity plays a strong part here: multiple subjectivities, of course. I understand immediately what I face, what I gaze at, when a *Palais de Justice* looks like a *Palais de Justice*. I realise that this is a partisan assumption because if I consider a 'vertical' building, showing and expressing the transcendence of God/King/Judge, I refer to a certain type of society. But when I consider a post-modern 'transparent' building, it brings another type of society to mind, because it is merely a *trompe-l'œuil*.[109]

104 Ibid., p. 112.

105 Ibid.

106 'Parce que Lacan rapproche le non-du-Père au nom-du-Père, la position symbolique du "père-régulateur" est un lieu de l'autorité'. See the connection made by Lacan between the 'no of the father' and the 'name of the father'.

107 Lacan, J., *Écrits: A Selection,* translated by A. Sheridant London: Routledge, 2005, p. 152.

108 Lacan, *The Four Fundamental Concepts of Psycho-Analysis,* p. 249.

109 On another level, it could well be the case that as a legal academic, I am 'educated' to understand what is in front of me, while this is perhaps not the case for everyone.

Figure 3.6 Sydney West Trial Courts, Parramatta, Australia.

Perhaps we need to turn to Benjamin here, and consider what is actually socially at stake with the use of glass. In Benjamin's work, the role of glass in architecture is aligned with the exposure of bourgeois hypocrisy and the negation of commodity fetishism.[110] Glass lacks aura and is the enemy of the secret: 'Like the camera, the function of glass is to liquidate cultural tradition, reshaping the entrenched social relations of domestic space'.[111] There is a feeling of revolution behind Benjamin's consideration: he advocates the use of glass not in order to create a 'wall of windows', like the modernist architecture of Le Corbusier,[112] but to destroy the

110 McQuire, S., 'From Glass architecture to Big Brother: Scenes from a cultural history of transparency', *Cultural Studies Review* 9, no. 2 (2003), pp. 103–123, esp. p. 106.

111 Ibid.

112 Ibid., p. 107.

Figure 3.7 Colchester Magistrates' Court, Colchester, UK.

Figure 3.8 Court house, Santa Coloma de Gramenet, Spain.

established order, not to open the interior onto the exterior, but to make the interior permanently available to the exterior. As 'opened', transparency equates here to openness: 'Faith in openness and transparency forms one of the pillars of architectural modernism'.[113] A close connection therefore exists between 'the

113 Ibid., p108.

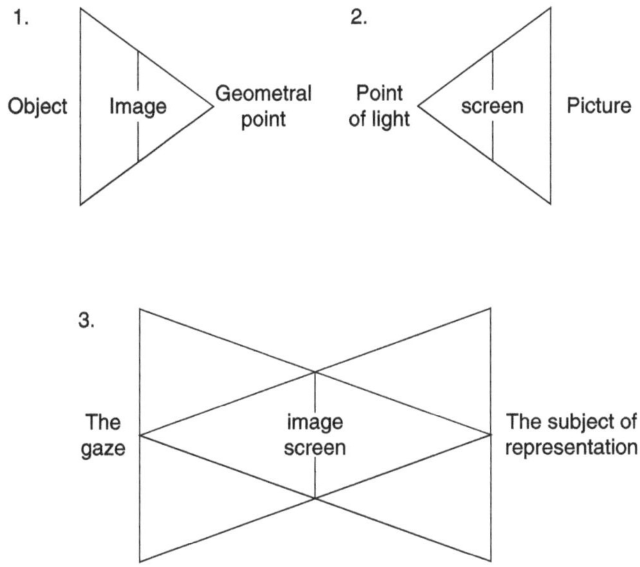

Figure 3.9 Lacan's analysis of the mirror.

aesthetic of the new architecture and the emergence of a more general 'openness' in society'.[114]

What we arrive at is the replacement of one signifier by another. According to Lacan, this replacement takes place 'along the vertical substitutive axis of language'.[115] The signifier 'justice' thus moves from one type to another. The glass building becomes a metaphoric interpretation of Justice that builds its meaning in accordance with a new ideology for which the architect acts as the voice.

What society seems to want (we are told) is accountability, feedback, self-reflexivity. This trend towards the self-reflective seems to be pro-active (again, we are told). If I want to be certain of what is going on somewhere, I need to be able to see, to *see through*. And it seems obvious that I may gaze better if the wall I face is not a brick wall but a glass wall.[116] As such, transparency has become the true deconstructed architecture. Its physical expression is the use of glass in buildings, creating clear constructions that have an affinity with other contemporary products – such as the cosmetics of Neutrogena: transparent products are equated with a 'guaranteed purity'.[117] 'Purity guaranteed' underlays the design of Foster

114 Ibid., p108.
115 Holm, *What Lacan Said*, p. 56.
116 I am still considering something that separates – some kind of wall, but one that is transparent; I imagine an open space, like an open-plan contemporary office space.
117 Bessire, ' Transparency: a two-way mirror?', p. 425.

and Partners, the firm that won the 1992 commission to transform the Reichstag into the new home for the unified Germany's parliament. Foster's team focused on making the processes of government more transparent: 'not every part of the Reichstag can be open to the public but we have ensured that where possible it is transparent and its activities are on view'.[118] Here, too, definitions across disciplines collapse and end up blurring the meaning of words.

Conclusion

Transparent public buildings are seen as buildings without secrets. Foucault believes that transparency gives power: 'If Bentham's project [the Panopticon] aroused interest, this was because it provided a formula applicable to many domains, the formula of "power through transparency" '.[119] What lies beneath transparency, then, is an insidious capturing of power: power through transparency. We know by the observations made in relation to courts that transparency has now replaced opacity in court design. The old opacity was not the result of secrecy, however, but had a purpose: it was intended to contribute to the process of justice, which – via a specific ritual ('the hearing') taking place behind the wall, inside the building, including the use of light and shadow – symbolised the 'truth'.

One of the main problems of transparency is the abolition of distance, which is an essential element of the ritual of justice, so necessary to create authority and to render justice 'correctly'. The concern of transparency is immediacy: as in capitalism, what is important is immediate profit. But 'immediate' also means the abolition of the mediating process, in a situation where there is nothing in between – without mediation. According to Bud on Silverstone, a medium such as television may be described as a 'mythic phenomenon'. Silverstone's point is that 'we of the profane world have access to something which in its unmediated state and by its very distance is sacred'. Bud, by analogy, recognises 'the mythic role of the museum in providing a specially authentic, intense, or direct contact with the "sacred" subject', which 'acts to reduce fear and provide "understanding" of the special phenomenon'.[120] I will, in turn, apply this idea to court buildings, for this is, in essence, what happens in post-modern designs of places of justice: the mediation is removed (transparency), and we end up in contact with the 'sacred'. The *Palais de Justice* has become a glass palace. Contemporary office

118 Ascher Barntones, D., *The Transparent State: Architecture and Politics in Postwar Germany,* London: Routledge, 2005, p. 201. Glass was also used in the German Federal Constitutional Court to 'create actual and metaphorical transparency in the aftermath of the horrors of the Third Reich. Mulcahy, *Legal Architecture*, p. 152.

119 Foucault, M., 'The Eye of Power', in *Power/Knowledge: Selected Interviews and Other Writings, 1972–1977*, edited by C. Gordon, NY: Pantheon Books, 1980, pp. 146–165, esp. p. 156.

120 Bud, R., *On the Social Production of Visual Difference, the Myth and the Machine: Seeing Science through Museum Eyes*, in *Picturing Power: Visual Depiction and Social Relations*, edited by Fyfe, G. and Law, J., London: Routledge, 1988, p. 134.

buildings are made of steel and glass that can easily be seen through. Transparent office buildings signify something of the transparency of capitalism and democracy, and something of the emptiness of the ideas that surround them.[121] But behind this permanent opening is concealed a permanent facilitation of surveillance and control.[122] The gaze is everywhere, on everything. There is a totalitarian aspect to this transparency that leaves the signifier 'justice' empty. We seem to be moving towards what is presented to us as democratic: a transparent democracy. However, we should remember that '[d]emocracy is defined by the insurmountable boundary that prevents the political subject from becoming consubstantial with power',[123] and that this particularity 'means that [in the language of psychoanalysis] the place of authority is "a purely symbolic construction" that cannot be occupied by any "real" political official'.[124] In other words, immediacy is not consistent with democracy.

We should not forget that transparency points to a generalised surveillance, which has always constituted the favourite means of dictatorships. Zizek explains that in a democratic society, the monarch (and I extend this to any figure of authority, such as heads of state or judges) guarantees the non-closure of the social.[125] Medieval jurists were aware of this when they designed fictions to help the 'uninterrupted line of royal bodies natural, with the permanency of the body politic represented by the head together with the members, and with immortality of the office, that is of the head alone'.[126] While the medieval monarchy found a solution to the problem of interrex, the permanence of inter regnum in democratic society takes as its source the fact that the throne is empty: a general sense of emptiness is very present in democracy. This is perhaps why Laclau believes that the logic of totalitarianism has the same source as democracy.[127] Here, emptiness and full transparency are interrelated, and I assume that they are similar things. As a major *trompe-l'œuil* or fascinating *tromperie*, the glass city of the *Wizard of Oz* reaffirms the sweet and subtle feeling of both *tromperie* and totalitarism. Dorothy feels safe in the Emerald City that is also a glass city: 'I am sure we are in no danger',[128] she says, as '[t]he houses of the city were all made of glass, so clear and transparent that one could look through the walls as easily as through a window'.[129] I have a feeling

121 Even the use of glass in stadium seems to voice the link between transparency and democracy. Resnik, Curtis, *Representing Justice*, p. 341.

122 As noted here, transparency has invaded most discourses. Bessire, 'Transparency: a two-way mirror?', p. 426.

123 Breger, C., 'The Leader's Two Bodies, Slavoj Zizek's postmodern political theology', *Diacritics* 31, no. 1 (2001), pp. 73–90, esp. p. 78–79.

124 Ibid., p. 79.

125 Ibid.

126 Kantorowicz, E. H., *The King's Two Bodies, a Study in Mediaeval Political Theology*, Princeton: PUP, 1997, p. 316.

127 Laclau, E. and C. Mouffe, *Hegemony and Socialist Strategy: Towards a radical democratic politics*, London: Verso, 2001, p. 186.

128 Baum, F., *Dorothy and the Wizard of Oz*, Boston: MobileReference, 1908 (2008), p. 10.

129 Ibid., p. 11.

that the new myth built on the contemporary paradigm of transparency aims to suppress everything that is of the neo-classical era, or part of the Gothic revival – such as the temple design – which signified 'be careful when you enter here'; the intention has been to replace it with a post-modern office design that signals 'don't worry'. In conclusion, we could simply apply here what we learnt from the Wizard of Oz: the city may be transparent and may feel safe, but the powerful wizard turns out to be a fraud – an ordinary man hiding behind a curtain operating a giant console of buttons and levers, manipulating people and things.[130] Even in the glass city, then, great danger can be revealed. The glass walls, the transparent houses, did not prevent the *trompe-l'œuil* of the fake wizard, and it seems likely that transparency in courthouse design will result in little more than some version of Orwell's vision: Big Brother will watch us here, too.

130 See D. Willis on the Wizard in 'The Emerald City' in D. Willis, *The Emerald City and Other Essays on the Architectural Imagination*, Princeton Architectural Press 1999, pp. 87–98, esp. pp. 96–97.

4 The abolition of the judicial walls

Cameras in courts and the reshaping of judicial spaces*

> It is not merely of some importance but is of fundamental importance that justice should not only be done, but should manifestly and undoubtedly be seen to be done.[1]

My intention in this chapter is to show that the use of cameras in courts is not as innocent, or rather neutral, and positive, as we may have been told it is, not only by one-sided government officials but also by some of our eminent colleagues such as Professor Stepniak.[2] Indeed, what I will refer to as 'visual technology' creates and redefines limits, pushes borders to the extent that there is, in the case of courts, a specific space of justice, a specific legal space that is created, a space that is centred on the judge and its representation on screen. I would like here to make a short preliminary remark on the fact that both cinema and TV are, by analogy, creating similar spaces. The scene and the actors in a trial, the scene and the actors in a play, and the scene and the actors on a screen, seem to affect the settings of the space therefore created in a very similar fashion. That said, my brief remark should trigger some additional thoughts, that are connected to recent developments in the virtual (judicial) world, such as the idea of filming and broadcasting courts (and I want to focus on the UK here because of what has been happening recently in that jurisdiction), but also the variation of scale between a theatrical representation and a televised representation. Indeed, filming and broadcasting the administration of justice is not the same as watching any kind of fiction. Yet, at the same time, filming and broadcasting implies the idea of mass media, something that touches many more

* A version of this chapter was presented at 'Judges on screen: A comparative perspective' at the Law and Society Conference 2012, Honolulu. Another version was presented as 'Judges on Screen: From Fiction to Reality', in 2012, at ENS Cachan, France, amended and presented as 'Spaces of justice on screen: A comparative perspective', RCSL Toulouse, 2013. The final version was presented as 'Cameras in Courts: between reality, fiction and voyeurism' at Law and Society Conference 2014, Minneapolis, 2015, Seattle, and 2016, New Orleans.

1 *R* v *Sussex Justices, ex parte McCarthy* [1924] 1 KB 256 at 259.

2 Daniel Stepniak, 'Technology and Public Access to Audio Visual Coverage and Recordings of Court Proceedings: Implications for Common Law Jurisdictions', *William & Mary Bill of Rights Journal* 12 (2004), pp. 791–823.

people than the audience at a trial or even at a play. How the legal space is defined is one question that has been answered by many colleagues such as Professor Linda Mulcahy.[3] But how this space is affected when the walls are erased because of the introduction of cameras in courts? How is that space redefined by images and the self-reflection of fiction and reality of what is seen? Let us just reflect on the fiction and reality for a moment. If what is going on in a court room is not seen, if the audience is very limited, which is often the case as spotted by Katy Mack in her review of Professor Mulcahy's book; 'a lack of effective public engagement with modern legal process',[4] then the only 'idea' we may have of a court room has to come from fictional representation in TV series and movies. That said, according to Professor Moran, the judge occupies the place of a marginal figure in 'legal cinema' and in related scholarship.[5] Occupying a marginal figure is an interesting point. For instance, it does not mean the representation of this figure is marginal but rather that the place of judges on screen is marginal. I believe this highlights one of the interesting elements of the judge: its relation to totem.[6] It is then not surprising to find mechanisms or objects similar to taboos in many countries when it comes to representing judges on screen: everything is done to avoid showing what happens in the court room, or at least to limit opening the courts to the parties and the audience. Indeed, in many jurisdictions, filming and broadcasting in courts has been banned: the judge is truly considered as a totem, as previously mentioned.[7] If we cannot see the 'true' or the 'real' work of justice being done, then we are left only with one way to 'see' it, with the only way to show justice and the judge: via a fictional representation of what may have occurred, 'simply', on screens. But then again, as I touched upon above, the effects of that representation on screen, a representation that is in fact a double representation, a representation of a representation, create a space that defines and redefines where justice is done through the notion that it has to be seen to be done.

As mentioned, this chapter will merely use the case of the UK (or more specifically England and Wales[8]) as example, as it was until recently forbidden to

3 Linda Mulcahy, *Legal Architecture: Justice, Due Process and the Place of Law*, London: Routledge 2011.

4 Mack, K., '*Legal Architecture: Justice, Due Process and the Place of Law* by Linda Mulcahy: *Representing Justice: Invention, Controversy, and Rights in City-States and Democratic Courtrooms* by Judith Resnik and Dennis Curtis', *Journal of Law and Society* 39 (2) (2012), pp. 317–325.

5 Leslie Moran, 'Every Picture Speaks a Thousand Words: Visualizing Judicial Authority in the Press', in Priska Gisler, Sara Steinert Borella, Caroline Wiedmer (eds), *Intersections of Law and Culture*, Palgrave, 2012, pp. 31–49, esp. p. 6.

6 David Marrani, Confronting the Symbolic Position of the Judge in Western European Legal Traditions: A Comparative Essay', 3 *European Journal of Legal Studies* 1 (2010), pp. 47–77.

7 Ibid.

8 In Northern Ireland, section 29 of the Criminal Justice (Northern Ireland) Act 1945 applies similar limitation to recording images and sounds than England and Wales prior to 2013 while there are no restriction in Scotland. See Ministry of Justice, Proposals to allow the broadcasting, filming, and recording of selected court proceedings, 2012, https://www.gov.uk/government/uploads/system/uploads/attachment_data/file/217307/broadcasting-filming-recording-courts.pdf, esp. p. 9.

film and broadcast court proceedings, while others, such as the USA, Australia and New Zealand, diverted from that interdiction.[9] Until recently, there were only two solutions to 'see' justice being done: you had go to court or to watch a movie in the cinema or on TV. The only experience of justice for many has been the representation of the judge in 'legal cinema'. What was known about justice was an image, the only image known of the judge 'acting' as a judge. It is therefore only through representation of judges and justice in cinema and TV programs that the perception of the figure of the judge but also of the justice system itself is created.[10] A game of images, images of the judge, images of how the whole scene works, although orchestrated by directors, contributes to what is known about justice. As stressed by Feigenson and Spiesel, 'the ostensible credibility of pictures that seem to present reality directly and unmediated . . . combined with people's growing dependence on those pictures for their knowledge of the real, has multiplied the possibilities for managing people's impressions of the world'.[11] That point summarises the difficulties that face the use of camera in courts.

I will start by presenting the Crime and Courts Act 2013 and the relation between open justice and transparency, before considering how work on voyeurism, simulacra, and third meaning are relevant to the introduction on cameras in courts.[12]

Crime and Courts Act 2013: cameras in courts, open justice and transparency

The fictional representation of justice has been the only way to massively 'see' justice being done in part of the UK, although things were actually slightly modified in 2012, to give a full transposition to fear that reality would become fiction and fiction would become reality. This was organised through the Crime and Courts Act 2013, which legally transposes the way to tackle, we have been told, the distorted view of reality brought by TV dramas and has apparently increased transparency. The fiction/reality of a court hearing become combined, in self-reflexive ways, and have to be analysed together with the voyeurism; the pleasure of looking. One may want to look at the genealogy of the Crime and Courts Acts 2013 for a start: the 2012 Queen's Speech and the 2012 Crime and Courts

9 In France, article 308 of the criminal procedure code prescribes that 'As soon as the hearing has begun, the use of any recording or sound broadcasting equipment, television or cine cameras, or photographic equipment is prohibited under penalty of a €18,000 fine'.

10 As a comparative lawyer, but also as a legal academic who decided to use contemporary techniques of teaching, I have used cinema and TV to show the differences between civil law and common law, between inquisitorial and adversarial systems through the specific representation made on the screens, between on the one hand the 'active' judges and on the other the 'passive' judges. One may want to remember movies such as *Giovanni Falcone* (Placido 1993) or *Le Juge Fayard* (Dewaere 1977) movies, but also movies with more or less 'absent' judge like *12 Angry Men* (Fonda 1957) or *To Kill a Mockingbird* (Peck 1962) or even the absent or redefined space created on screen by the movie *Erin Brockovich* (Roberts 2000).

11 Neal Feigenson and Christina Spiesel, *Law on Display*, New York: NYU Press 2009, pp. 16–17.

12 http://www.legislation.gov.uk/ukpga/2013/22/introduction/enacted (accessed 17 February 2017).

Bill.[13] I particularly would like to focus on the intentions, express and hidden, behind the spirit rather than the letter of the bill. In her speech, the Queen declared:

> My government is committed to reducing and preventing crime. A Bill will be introduced to establish the National Crime Agency to tackle the most serious and organised crime and strengthen border security. The courts and tribunals service will be reformed to increase efficiency, transparency and judicial diversity.

If we may not comment on the idea of increased efficiency or judicial diversity it is certainly interesting to comment on transparency. When the Queen presented the programme of her government, she refers to the need of transparency. As we discussed in the previous chapter, transparency appears to have become the new paradigm in justice architecture and it is not surprising to find it also present in the question of filming and broadcasting in courts.[14] But as it was developed in literature, transparency is not a notion that is as simple as it seems. For instance, according to Pingeot, what should be carefully analysed is what side of transparent we are referring to. Are we considering 'transparent' as *invisible* or 'transparent' as *visible*?[15] Indeed, someone 'transparent' is someone quite invisible, while it is, also, an object that lets light through. The meaning of transparency oscillates between appearing and disappearing. That new paradigm in the case of architecture was linked, as discussed, to literal and phenomenal transparency, and the attempt made by architects to push glass as a transparent material to show justice and/or democracy, equating both to transparency. In the case of cameras in courts, we are witnessing the birth of a new equation: transparency equals open justice. Indeed, what is more transparent than the abolition of walls by glass as we have witnessed in many court houses, but even more, the total disappearance of the meaning of walls, via the cameras? That is how the door to filming the process of justice was opened. The point of transparency in the British government programme has been addressed by the Crime and Courts Act 2013, which relaxed the rules on filming and broadcasting court proceedings. Let us first consider what the rules were prior to 2013.

Prior to 2013, ban on filming in courts

In 1925, the British legislator decided to ban recording and broadcasting arguing, as the only interest the members of the press had was to take advantage of the sensational nature of the event and to make money.[16] In addition, it also considered that:

13 https://www.gov.uk/government/speeches/the-queen-s-speech-2012 (accessed 17 March 2017).

14 See the previous chapter on the question of transparency.

15 Pingeot, Mazarine, *La Dictature de la Transparence,* Nouvelles mythologies, Laffont, Paris, 2016, esp. p. 182 and pp. 13–20.

16 Stephen Mason, Cameras in the courts: why the prohibition occurred in the UK?, *Amicus Curiae,* Issue 91 Autumn 2012, pp. 22–27, esp. p. 25, http://sas-space.sas.ac.uk/5769/1/2095-3056-1-SM.pdf

> The alarm expressed by authorities at the growing level of public interest in media reports of gruesome or salacious cases – a trend apparently fuelled by the newly introduced publication of courtroom photographs and sketches to accompany press reports of proceedings.[17]

Recording and broadcasting images and sounds in courts were considered as offences. Taking pictures in court and broadcasting them was prohibited by s.41 of the Criminal Justice Act 1925.[18] The 1925 Act made it an offence (while recording sound in courts unless permitted by the court was banned by s.9 of the Contempt of Court Act 1981[19]). By extension, filming was also prohibited by case law.[20] The general ban was relaxed by s. 47 of the Constitutional Reform Act 2005 which dis-applied these restrictions to the UK Supreme Court.[21] That said, most courts are open to the public (this is the idea of open court) and journalists have been able to be present inside and to report from courts, subject to reporting restrictions. The legal system of Scotland has long been ahead of England and Wales on this issue; since 1992, some filming in court proceedings has been allowed in Scotland, following a practice note by the Lord President, Lord Hope.[22] In April 2012, the sentencing of David Gilroy for murder was televised.

17 Daniel Stepniak, 'British justice: not suitable for public viewing?' in Paul Masons (ed.), *Criminal Visions*, London: Routledge 2012, Ch. 13.

18 www.legislation.gov.uk/ukpga/Geo5/15-16/86/enacted (accessed 17 February 2017):

> 41 Prohibition on taking photographs, &c, in court
>
> (1) No person shall—
>
> (a) take or attempt to take in any court any photograph, or with a view to publication make or attempt to make in any court any portrait or sketch, of any person, being a judge of the court or a juror or a witness in or a party to any proceedings before the court, whether civil or criminal; or
>
> (b) publish any photograph, portrait or sketch taken or made in contravention of the foregoing provisions of this section or any reproduction thereof;
>
> and if any person acts in contravention of this section he shall, on summary conviction, he liable in respect of each offence to a fine not exceeding fifty pounds.
>
> (2) For the purposes of this section—
>
> (a) the expression 'court' means any court of justice, including the court of a coroner:
>
> (b) the expression 'judge' includes recorder, registrar, magistrate, justice and coroner:
>
> (c) a photograph, portrait or sketch shall be deemed to be a photograph, portrait or sketch taken or made in court if it is taken or made in the court-room or in the building or in the precincts of the building in which the court is held, or if it is a photograph, portrait or sketch taken or made of the person while he is entering or leaving the court-room or any such building or precincts as aforesaid.

19 www.legislation.gov.uk/ukpga/1981/49 (accessed 17 February 2017).

20 *J Barber & Sons v Lloyd's Underwriters* [1987] 1 QB 103; *R v Loveridge, Lee and Loveridge* [2001] 2 Cr App R 29, CA.

21 www.legislation.gov.uk/ukpga/2005/4 (accessed 17 February 2017). Proceedings of the UK Supreme Court are routinely filmed, recorded and broadcasted, and are streamed live on the Sky News website, http://news.sky.com/home/supreme-court.

22 www.gov.uk/government/uploads/system/uploads/attachment_data/file/217307/broadcasting-filming-recording-courts.pdf (accessed 17 February 2017).

A documentary showing the full murder trial of Nat Fraser in Edinburgh was broadcasted by Channel 4 on July the same year.[23]

What are the changes brought by the 2013 Act?

The 2013 Act

When TV cameras were allowed in courts, it became possible to have recordings of Court of Appeal hearings, with the BBC, ITN, Sky News and the Press Association cooperating on the project. In-court video-journalists have been hired. They were supposed to recommend the most interesting cases to be recorded and broadcasted. This commenced on the 31 October 2013 on Sky News. The 2013 Act was complemented by the Court of Appeal (Recording and Broadcasting) Order 2013 made under its section 32(1).[24] The Order applies to the recording and broadcasting of hearings in the Court of Appeal, in open court and before a full court. It means that from 2013, the Criminal Justice Act 1925 s. 41 and the Contempt of Court Act 1981 s. 9 remain in force but the Lord Chancellor (with the concurrence of the Lord Chief Justice) has the ability to make an Order dis-applying those sections in specific circumstances. The court retains a right to reapply any dis-applied provision in the interests of justice or in order that a person is not unduly prejudiced.

It is quite interesting to read the precise definition given by the order in Art. 2. For instance, 'broadcast' means the transmission to members of the public of a recording of a hearing of the court, which fits the idea of the right for the public to be present in court (even if that is virtually). Meanwhile, 'recording' means a visual or sound recording on any medium from which a single image, a moving image or any sound may be produced or reproduced, or the making of any such recording, and 'record' and 'recorded' shall be construed accordingly. Finally, 'legal representative' means a representative who is an authorised person entitled to exercise a right of audience before the court within the meaning of Part 2 of the Legal Services Act 2007(b) and who is acting on behalf of a party to the proceedings to which a hearing relates.[25] The Order also divides the operation of recording and broadcasting. Some limits have been introduced, such as the one on space of justice and the ones on recording. The only space of justice concerned is the 'court': the Court of Appeal, and only open courts before full courts (Art. 3). Recording is allowed, and therefore the 1925 Act and 1981 Act are dis-applied (Art. 5 to 7 Order), only of the following:

23 Available at https://youtu.be/RVtiu6diut0 (accessed 17 February 2017).

24 www.legislation.gov.uk/ukdsi/2013/9780111101100/contents (accessed 17 February 2017).

25 A 'right of audience' means the right to appear before and address a court, including the right to call and examine witnesses. See Legal Services Act 2007 Schedule 2. Persons authorised to exercise the right of audience, are those who authorised by a listed body: The Law Society, The General Council of the Bar, The Chartered, Institute of Patent Attorneys, The Institute of Trade Mark Attorneys, The Association of Law Costs Draftsmen and, under certain limitations, The Institute of Legal Executives. Legal Services Act 2007 Schedule 5. www.legislation.gov.uk/ukpga/2007/29/contents (accessed 17 February 2017).

- Appeal or an application for permission to appeal or refer,[26]
- an AG reference on review of sentencing (s. 36 of the Criminal Justice Act 1988),
- an application by a prosecutor concerning retrial for serious offences (Part 10 of the Criminal Justice Act 2003).

But then the Order goes deeper and details several limits for the recording. It distinguishes the presence, or not, of legal representatives for instance. If there are legal representatives, the recording is limited to the submissions of a legal representative, their exchanges with the court and the judgment. Without legal representatives, only the judgment will be recorded. It then specifies who can record. It has to be a person who (a) is permitted in writing by the Lord Chancellor to record hearings in court; and (b) assigns any copyright in the recording of a hearing to the Lord Chancellor, for and on behalf of the Crown.

Filming proceedings does not mean broadcasting the footage. Indeed, as mentioned, there is a separation of the two operations. According to articles 8 to 11, broadcasting is allowed if recordings are made according to articles 5 to 7. Articles 8 to 11 set out when the recording of a hearing can be broadcasted and what content is permitted in a broadcast. The permission has to be given, according to article 9, by the court to broadcast a criminal conviction appeal (unless the court does not order a retrial), or for an application for permission to appeal against conviction or an application by a prosecutor under Part 10 of the Criminal Justice Act 2003, otherwise recordings may be broadcasted with no permission.

The Order laid down some interesting substantive condition. According to article 11, a report or presentation of proceedings that includes a broadcast of a hearing must be fair and accurate having regard to the overall content of the report or presentation and the context in which the broadcast is presented. In addition, no recording may be broadcasted for the following aims: a party political broadcast; advertisement or promotion, except where such advertisement or promotion relates to a report or presentation of proceedings that includes a broadcast; light entertainment; and satire.

To sum up, there are many conditions and limits attached to the permission to filming and broadcasting in courts. However, we have witnessed quite recently an attempt to decrease those limits, which may trigger a qualitative and quantitative increase. On the 20 March 2016 it was announced by the Justice Minister that Crown Courts will test, for 3 months, filming, but not broadcasting, trials.[27] Eight courts in England and Wales (Central Criminal Court and in the Crown Court at Southwark, Manchester (Crown Square), Birmingham, Bristol, Liverpool, Leeds

26 Except against verdict of not guilty by reason of insanity (s. 12), appeal against finding of disability (s.15) and a hospital order, interim hospital order or supervision order (s.16A of the Criminal Appeal Act 1968); or a decision in family proceedings as defined in section 75(3) of the Courts Act 2003.

27 www.gov.uk/government/news/crown-courts-to-pilot-filming-for-the-first-time (accessed 17 February 2017).

and Cardiff) were chosen as the locations for the pilot and only judges' sentencing remarks were selected to be filmed. A statutory instrument was introduced on 21 May 2016, determining the timescale for the test. The current Court of Appeal broadcaster has agreed to support the pilot period at no cost to the public purse, which was strangely stated and highlighted even though it was also explained the process would be managed under the existing *commercial arrangements* in place for the Court of Appeal.

What was said to convince us . . .

Until 2013, as mentioned above, what has been seen by the public/masses, the audience, of the inside machinery of the justice process, the intimate process, came from movies and TV series. This was considered negative by government officials. That is, for instance, stated in many exchanges during the legislative debate in this abstract taken from the second reading of the Bill at the House of Lords on the 28 May 2012.[28]

> Lastly, this part also contains an important provision that will help to increase public understanding of the justice system. Most members of the public have no direct personal experience of what goes on inside a courtroom. Their perceptions will be derived from TV dramas that more often than not give a distorted view of reality. Allowing the broadcasting of judicial proceedings will help to demystify the workings of the justice system and increase public confidence. Of course, there is a balance to be struck between increased transparency and the safeguarding of the proper administration of justice. To this end, we want to start by allowing the broadcasting of advocates' arguments and judgments in the Court of Appeal before extending this to sentencing remarks in the Crown Court. However, I can assure the House that there is no question of victims, witnesses, defendants or jurors being filmed.

The assumption is that the public/masses only know courts (and therefore justice) from TV. That is a question that the British government considered an extremely important one to be addressed in order to increase transparency and to safeguard the proper administration of justice. The text was very critical of the dramatization of what is going on in court. Indeed, the view expressed during the debates was that a reality that derives from the fiction (TV series, cinema) creates 'a distorted view of reality'.

One may understand how the argument unfolded logically. In fact, we were pushed to believe that in order to have a good and undistorted view of the reality of the operation of justice, the public/masses needed to have access to that reality without any mediation. Therefore, we had to consider the introduction of cameras

28 www.publications.parliament.uk/pa/ld201213/ldhansrd/text/120528-0001.htm#1205282000384 (accessed 17 February 2017).

in courts, filming and broadcasting, to help resolve the previous question. Cameras were supposed to abolish mediation, to give the public an unmediated access to courts. In consequence, what was underlying here was something similar to the argument used by architects in post-modern courts, when they were offering to use glass: unmediated aspect of the mechanism, of any mechanisms, is crucial to the (appearance of) transparency. This time we have a movement that goes further than glass walls to demonstrate transparency. We have cameras in court for transparency. The argument triggers two remarks. The first one concerns the question of mediation and the second one the quite tight connected question of transparency. Unmediated access to the court appears to be the solution for transparency, as we are told. But does the presence of cameras, lenses and the need of a screen equate 'unmediated' or does it simply replace one type of mediation with another one, a 'technological' one? Indeed, 'the screen has an ambivalence that it shares with transparency, of blurring at the same time as showing. To screen signifies to hide, not to show'.[29] Furthermore, transparency, as we have seen, may also have a reverse effect to the one expected, an effect that brings more opacity than transparency.[30] An image is in fact not transparent at all, but proposes a fantasy of truth, proof. Showing something is contrary to hide something. But this hyper transparency, the result of a *sursaturation*, an 'over-saturation', of images, is obscene; an obscenity that sees around it the constitution of rituals of transparency.[31]

Let us consider here the comment made in another official document.[32]

> The Government is committed to improving transparency and public understanding of the courts system, and allowing broadcasting from court is part of this work. Television has a role in opening up the courts to the public, demystifying the criminal justice process and increasing understanding of sentencing.

Here, the argument goes a little further. Not only is transparency placed at the apex of the argument, but the place of TV is considered crucial. TV is clearly recognised here as the educational medium. This point has been relayed by newspapers and other prestigious commentators such as Kenneth Clarke, the Justice Secretary at the time, who declared that 'The Government and judiciary are determined to improve transparency and public understanding of court through allowing court broadcasting'.[33] It is rather true that in a democracy, education is certainly one of the key elements for the functioning of a complex

29 Pingeot, *Dictature de la Transparence*, esp. p. 150: 'L'ecran a cette ambivalence qu'il partage avec la transparence, de masquer en meme temps qu'il montre. Faire ecran signifie "cacher", pas "devoiler" '.

30 See previous chapter on transparency.

31 Pingeot, *Dictature de la Transparence*, pp. 154–156, citing Baudrillard.

32 www.gov.uk/government/uploads/system/uploads/attachment_data/file/98438/fs-cj-films.pdf Point 7 (accessed 17 February 2017).

33 www.telegraph.co.uk/news/uknews/law-and-order/9170589/TV-cameras-to-be-allowed-in-court.html (accessed 17 February 2017).

political system. But one should be concerned with the ambivalent two-sided view one may have about the TV. This was spotted, for instance, by the Attorney General of the time Dominic Grieve who voiced a slightly different opinion:[34]

> The issue that then arises is, is this going to help public understanding or might it contribute to the whole thing being turned into a piece of theatre, which might also be undesirable? Clearly filming people actually being sentenced is likely to be undesirable as it would probably encourage theatricals.

In fact, TV channels have been showing fictional representation of reality 'justice' for years and have therefore 'trained' the mind of the public. The perception, rightly, of administration of justice has been linked to what has been on screen. What is on offer now is, we seem to be told, to use TV to show the real justice, not a representation of justice. Therefore, we are told we should be using TV not to re-present, but to educate. This argument is echoed by authors. Indeed, according to Stepniak,

> The lack of public confidence in the judiciary often reflects a low level of public understanding of the role of courts and the judicial process. This has led to calls for courts to take an active role in promoting or facilitating public education and awareness.[35]

Again, what may collide here is the expectation of the public that will watch what is on screen. That consideration should not be disconnected, in my opinion, from Plato's analysis of reality and appearance (and indeed, I believe, disappearance). But even then, that point is something quite different from things as they appear to be, as phenomena.[36] Justice is, as we all know, something very complex to grasp, with definitions, such as Derrida's, considering that, in fact, justice is impossible.[37] Justice is one of these Freudian 'things' that need something else, an agent, to represent it. The agent may be a judge or it may be a building. We need, for the 'signified justice', a 'signifier' to appear to us and show us what it is. When we are told that, through transparency, we are touching the reality of justice, we may be concerned and critically analyse that point rather than accepting or rejecting, ***prima facie***, the argument. In fact it is slightly more complicated than this: we are touching something that we should not really touch, something that may burn us. It may, in fact, be even worse than this. What the entry of cameras in court produces is not as neutral as we may think. It is also a re-representation, one that goes wild because it triggers a sort of double representation of what justice really is. And the point of the 'entry of cameras' in courts introduces another angle and

34 Ibid.

35 Stepniak, 'Technology and Public Access to Audio Visual Coverage and Recordings of Court Proceedings: Implications for Common Law Jurisdictions', esp. p. 806.

36 Harold Pritchard, 'Appearances and Reality', *Mind*, 15 (58): 223–229.

37 See chapter on transparency.

new actors: actors of the cameras, the broadcasters. When we read further into this document, at points 8 and 9, we have that issue explained.[38]

> The technical and operational issues around court broadcasting will be covered in guidelines issued by the judiciary and agreed with the Ministry of Justice, Her Majesty's Courts and Tribunals Service, and the broadcasters. Such issues would include the procedures for operating cameras, the process by which a judge might suspend filming or refuse permission to broadcast footage, and limitations on positioning of cameras and camera angles. Use of the footage will be restricted to news, current affairs and educational purposes only, so that it is not used in light entertainment, satirical programmes, advertising or promotion. Similar agreements are already in place governing broadcasting of the proceedings of the Supreme Court and Parliament.

The issue of 'All costs from broadcasting in courts – including installation of the technical equipment and on-going maintenance – will be funded by the broadcasters' seems to be quite attractive, but it is also quite worrying to have a partnership between HMCS and the major broadcasters.

It is quite easy to realise that fiction and reality are in fact intertwined here. In fact, it is quite obvious for voluntary or involuntary reasons. The Crime and Courts Act is partly the result of a very carefully orchestrated lobbying activity on the part of TV channels. The major broadcasters have operated here as the architects operating in the matter of court architecture. They collapsed the meaning of transparency with other ideas such as democracy and (open) justice and imposed a specific outcome. The initiative of TV broadcasting in court, strongly supported by David Cameron, followed lobbying by the BBC, ITN and Sky News. In a 2012 joint letter the main UK broadcasters argued that: 'The ability to witness justice in action, in the public gallery, is a fundamental freedom. Television will make the public gallery open to all'. Broadcasters became human rights legislators. The letter signed by John Ryley, head of Sky News, Helen Boaden, director of BBC News and John Hardie, ITN CEO clearly referred to topical issues that have been part of the legislative debate, such as improving public understanding of the justice system, bringing transparency to courts and the collapse between transparency, democracy and justice.[39]

Here is the letter in full:

> Last September the Government announced its intention to change the law to allow the limited televising of courtrooms, in order to improve public understanding of the justice system.

38 www.gov.uk/government/uploads/system/uploads/attachment_data/file/98438/fs-cj-films.pdf Point 7 (accessed 17 February 2017).

39 http://news.sky.com/story/924682/sky-bbc-and-itn-call-for-cameras-in-court (accessed 17 February 2017).

> As representatives of the country's main broadcasters, we welcomed this proposal and the Government's commitment to bring greater transparency to our courts. We hope that timely progress can now be made to ensure that the Bill lifting the prohibition on cameras in court is included in the Queen's Speech in May.
>
> The administration of justice is a key part of a democracy. It shapes and defines a civilised society. The ability to witness justice in action, in the public gallery, is a fundamental freedom. Television will make the public gallery open to all.
>
> If legislation is announced to lift the ban within the next few months, it will still be some time before we see the first case on TV. There will have to be detailed discussions about what can be shown, and in which courts.
>
> A great deal of work needs to be done by the judiciary and court officials, civil servants and the media working together to ensure that the change succeeds in its chief aim of opening up courtrooms to make the judicial process more understandable and accessible.
>
> Each of our organisations fully accepts that there must be limitations on what can be broadcast and we agree that the presiding judge should have complete control of what is shown from the courtroom. We recognise that concerns have been raised about the impact television coverage will have, particularly in controversial cases.
>
> However, we believe that the outcome can only be positive. The experience over the last two years of live streaming from the Supreme Court has shown that the presence of cameras has not affected the course of justice in any way. Instead it enhances public understanding and allows everyone to see justice being done.
>
> Everyone who believes in transparency should support this proposed change in the law. This is a long-overdue reform. For too long the UK has lagged behind much of the rest of the world on open justice. The time has come for us to catch up.
>
> We hope that you share our view of this important issue, and that you will welcome the introduction of a Government Bill to change the law. Colleagues from each of our organisations will be in touch with key members of your party to explain our position in more detail, but in the meantime please do not hesitate to contact any of us personally if you have any questions or would like to arrange a meeting.[40]

It is quite interesting to note that the letter starts with a reference to September 2012, when the Government announced its intention to change the law. One may want to look at the government statement again, point 9 here, and compare what the broadcasters stated in their letter with the guidelines contained in the document, and note the resemblance between the two, and, according to the

40 http://news.sky.com/story/924682/sky-bbc-and-itn-call-for-cameras-in-court (accessed 17 February 2017).

chronology, the strong probability that broadcasters have, in fact, been involved in the design of the legislation. The discourse of the broadcasters involved has been welcoming and it is quite important to further analyse some of the sentences here. We find, for a start, some reference of course to transparency which seems to be the main argument for everyone: 'As representatives of the country's main broadcasters, we welcomed this proposal and the Government's commitment to bring greater transparency to our courts'. Then we have some rather condescending expressions where the broadcasters become teachers and human rights advocates:

> The administration of justice is a key part of a democracy. It shapes and defines a civilised society. The ability to witness justice in action, in the public gallery, is a fundamental freedom. Television will make the public gallery open to all.

The broadcasters are showing some 'responsible' arguments: 'There will have to be detailed discussions about what can be shown, and in which courts'. But also:

> A great deal of work needs to be done by the judiciary and court officials, civil servants and the media working together to ensure that the change succeeds in its chief aim of opening up courtrooms to make the judicial process more understandable and accessible', 'Each of our organisations fully accepts that there must be limitations on what can be broadcast and we agree that the presiding judge should have complete control of what is shown from the courtroom. We recognise that concerns have been raised about the impact television coverage will have, particularly in controversial cases.

And finally, they are showing that they are helping us by being both modernist and pushy: 'This is a long-overdue reform. For too long the UK has lagged behind much of the rest of the world on open justice. The time has come for us to catch up'.

Meanwhile, newspapers reacted quite critically to the move. As cited in a one of the leading British newspapers:

> It is important to preserve the majesty of the law; but this is gradually being diminished. Some courts, though not the criminal circuit, have dispensed with wigs on the grounds that they are old fashioned. Since criminal trials are open to the public it is hard to object in principle to televising judgments and sentencing, with appropriate safeguards. But going any further must promote transparency and justice, not prurience.[41]

What is really meant by transparency in the case of cameras in courts?

41 'TV cameras in court must promote transparency, not prurience', *The Telegraph*, 7 June 2016, www.telegraph.co.uk/opinion/2016/04/07/tv-cameras-in-court-must-promote-transparency-not-prurience/ (accessed 17 February 2017).

Transparency and open justice

Transparency remains the main argument here with cameras and with courts. One term is very important because of its similarity to transparency: open justice. As stated by Stepniak:

> Broadcasting . . . make[s] it possible for a virtually limitless public audience to view proceedings and access court documents. It may be interesting to reflect on whether public access via audio-visual broadcast or Internet posting of civil proceedings and their documents can be justified in terms of the principles of open justice.[42]

What hides behind open justice?

Open justice was recognised as essential to ensure public scrutiny of the operation of the court system as well as provide information to the public as argued in *Scott v Scott* [1913] AC 417.[43] It therefore has two sides: public scrutiny, which means opening the courts to allow the public to check what is going on, and public information, and, in a way, education. Lord Diplock mentioned the point of courts opened to the press and the public in *Attorney General v Leveller Magazine Limited*:[44]

> If the way that courts behave cannot be hidden from the public ear and eye, this provides a safeguard against judicial arbitrariness or idiosyncrasy and maintains the public confidence in the administration of justice. The application of this principle of open justice has two aspects: as respects the court proceedings, it requires that they should be held in open court to which the press and public are admitted and that, in criminal cases, all evidence communicated to the court should be communicated publicly.

In *Guardian v Westminster Magistrates*,[45] Toulson LJ gave his definition of open justice and related it to transparency (although referring to the open justice principle as well later on):

> Open justice. The words express a principle at the heart of our system of justice and vital to the rule of law. The rule of law is a fine concept but fine words butter no parsnips. How is the rule of law itself to be policed? It is an age old question. Quis custodiet ipsos custodes—who will guard the guards themselves? In a democracy, where power depends on the consent of the people governed,

42 Stepniak, 'Technology and Public Access to Audio Visual Coverage and Recordings of Court Proceedings: Implications for Common Law Jurisdictions', esp. p. 819.

43 *Scott v Scott* [1913] AC 417. See also Joseph Jaconelli, *Open Justice: A Critique of the Public Trial?*, Oxford: Oxford University Press, 2002, Chapter 1.

44 *Attorney General v Leveller Magazine Limited* [1979] AC 440 at 450A to C.

45 *In R (Guardian News and Media Ltd) v City of Westminster Magistrates' Court* (Article 19 invervening) [2012] EWCA Civ 420; [2013] QB 618.

> the answer must lie in the transparency of the legal process. Open justice lets in the light and allows the public to scrutinise the workings of the law, for better or for worse. Jeremy Bentham said in a well-known passage quoted by Lord Shaw of Dunfermline in Scott v Scott [1913] AC 417, 477: 'Publicity is the very soul of justice. It is the keenest spur to exertion and the surest of all guards against improbity. It keeps the judge himself while trying under trial.'

In *Kennedy v The Charity Commission*,[46] the link with transparency goes further:

> It has long been recognised that judicial processes should be open to public scrutiny unless and to the extent that there are valid countervailing reasons. This is the open justice principle. The reasons for it have been stated on many occasions. Letting in the light is the best way of keeping those responsible for exercising the judicial power of the state up to the mark and for maintaining public confidence: *Scott v Scott* [(above)]; *R (Guardian News and Media Ltd) v City of Westminster Magistrates' Court (Article 19 intervening)* [(above)].

Open justice is more than merely opening the doors of places of justice and the observation of the process; it has to do with publicity (and therefore more with transparency).[47] Indeed, in *Bank Mellat v Her Majesty's Treasury* Lord Neuberger, described the common law principle of open justice as fundamental to the dispensation of justice in a modern, democratic society (para 2) while Lord Reid recognised that 'the principle of open justice is inextricably linked to the freedom of the media to report on court proceedings'.[48] The connection with the 2013 act is quite striking: transparency is linked to media. Ultimately, here, as in court architecture, what is needed is 'to see justice being done'. To render the court process visible, the courts need to be opened, and the media (press in *Attorney General v Leveller Magazine Limited,* media generally in the latest cases, i.e. press and TV) are the instrument of that new interpretation of transparency. That transparency is erected as a moral principle, but because of what transparency does, i.e. opening up something, spaces such as private and public spheres, it also erases the divide between those private and public spheres, contributing ultimately not to opening up and democratising but rather to a totalitarian trend.[49]

'Their perceptions will be derived from TV dramas that more often than not give a distorted view of reality' and 'increased transparency'[50]

Court of Appeal hearings are now more or less systematically filmed and broadcasted. The first one to be seen on TV was 31 October 2013. One court

46 *Kennedy v The Charity Commission* [2014] UKSC 20; [2015] AC 455

47 Masons, *Criminal Visions*, pp. 260–262.

48 *Bank Mellat v Her Majesty's Treasury* [2013] UKSC 38; [2013] 3 WLR 179

49 Pingeot, *Dictature de la Transparence*, p. 73

50 Masons, *Criminal Visions.*

channel on Sky News has also been set up and appears on the Law Society website www.lawgazette.co.uk/analysis/court-on-camera/. The first 'use' of the 2013 Act was for a programme called The Murder Trial. The British newspapers around the time of the broadcasting of that programme sensed that:

> The prospect of American-style televised courts has moved a step closer after Channel 4 announced that it is to show a British murder trial in its entirety for the first time. Remotely-operated cameras were installed in an Edinburgh court room to film the trial of Nat Fraser, a Scottish man accused of murdering his wife, Arlene, whose body was never found. After three years of negotiation, the Scottish High Court granted permission for the trial to be filmed. The results will be screened as a 90-minute Channel 4 documentary called The Murder Trial.[51]

It was the first example of 'the reality' shown as in fiction. Or perhaps was it the first example of fiction that looked like reality. In fact, the process was not as transparent as it was supposed to be. What really was presented was a reality TV style of programme using real footage of a trial. Instead of the promised transparency, of the promised unmediated footage, there was mediation, but *technological* mediation. The programme had all the flavour of something fictional but with bits and pieces that were taken from reality.

The current results of filming, recording and broadcasting resemble a new legal Janus, with one positive side and one negative side. It appears on the one hand as a continuation of the (real) audience, the public present at a trial, through a 'techno-legal' transparency; while on the other hand it may seem to be drifting towards voyeurism. It also appears as a substitute for fiction, permanently creating and recreating a circular situation: reality, fiction, reality, fiction. This has to be kept in mind as we know that what seemed important from officials was to tackle the distortion created by TV dramas, in order to increase transparency, although they probably never considered the question of voyeurism.

Transparency and voyeurism

The entire operation of filming and broadcasting, rather than fostering transparency, feels rather like the expression of a neoliberal manipulation than anything else. We may draw a parallel between what the giant media corporations have been doing and my comments about the architects in the previous chapter. Here too, they are using and abusing the public when they voice that transparency of a building (literal transparency) or of the process of filming and broadcasting equates to phenomenal transparency (real one).[52] No care has been given to the 'ambivalence' aspect of a notion that crucially oscillates between transparent

51 www.independent.co.uk/news/media/tv-radio/americanstyle-televised-courts-move-a-step-closer-channel-4-to-show-a-british-murder-trial-for-first-time-8541108.html (last accessed 17 February 2017).

52 See previous chapter

visible and transparent *invisible*.[53] However, one may want to consider the matter as reflective and be less critical against neoliberal aspirations, so easily condemned. If the media is pushing this, perhaps it is because we, the public/masses or what is referred to as 'the public', have a need to fulfil. We may therefore turn towards the literature that makes the connection between cinema/TV and psychoanalysis for help. Watching, looking, gazing, is a source of pleasure, while there is also pleasure in being looked at. As reported by Professor Laura Mulvey,

> The cinema offers a number of possible pleasures. One is scopophilia. There are circumstances in which looking itself is a source of pleasure, just as, in the reverse formation, there is pleasure in being looked at. Originally, in his *Three Essays on Sexuality*, Freud isolated scopophilia as one of the component instincts of sexuality which exist as drives quite independently of the erotogenic zones. At this point he associated scopophilia with taking other people as objects, subjecting them to a controlling and curious gaze.[54]

We will extend these comments to the TV. One of the crucial aspects of voyeurism using people as objects through cameras is, in fact, watching them. What more can be right about watching a trial in one's living room? Scopopholia, literally 'the love of looking' is synonymous with voyeurism. Voyeurism is therefore associated with seeing other people as objects, subjecting them to a controlling and curious gaze. Voyeuristic activities of children for instance, their desire to see, revolve around the private and the forbidden.

> In this analysis scopophilia is essentially active. (Later, in *Instincts and their Vicissitudes*, Freud developed his theory of scopophilia further, attaching it initially to pre-genital auto-eroticism, after which the pleasure of the look is transferred to others by analogy. There, is a close working here of the relationship between the active instinct and its further development in a narcissistic form.) Although the instinct is modified by other factors, in particular the constitution of the ego, it continues to exist as the erotic basis for pleasure in looking at another person as object. At the extreme, it can become fixated into a perversion, producing obsessive voyeurs and Peeping Toms, whose only sexual satisfaction can come from watching, in an active controlling sense, an objectified other.[55]

What Mulvey spotted is crucial for an analysis of the introduction of cameras in courts, because she clearly highlights the links between cinema and TV dramas and

53 Pingeot, *Dictature de la Transparence*, esp. p. 152.

54 Laura Mulvey, 'Visual Pleasure and Narrative Cinema', *Screen*, Autumn 1975, vol.16, pp. 6–18. Re-edited as Mulvey, Laura, 'Visual Pleasure and Narrative Cinema', *Film Theory and Criticism: Introductory Readings*, edited by. Leo Braudy and Marshall Cohen, New York: Oxford UP, 1999, pp. 833–844, esp. p. 835.

55 Ibid.

the operation of control through transparency. For Mulvey, cinema, and we may extend her remark to TV here, 'would seem to be remote from the undercover world of the surreptitious observation of a watching unknowing and unwilling victim'.[56] In that sense, what we watch, what we see on TV or on screen, gives us, the audience, the public, pleasure, because we know that the people we are watching cannot know we are watching them. That is how, and again I want emphasise the link with transparency in court buildings, 'control trough transparency' actually unfolds. What is seen of the screen is manifestly shown.

> [T]he mass of mainstream film, and the conventions within which it has consciously evolved, portray a hermetically sealed world which unwinds magically, indifferent to the presence of the audience, producing for them a sense of separation and plan on their voyeuristic phantasy.[57]

That is happening to every one of us, the audience, the public. Consider, for a moment, that we are actually not present, but are the (absent) audience of a (remote) court, an (absent) audience, separated, segregated, by screens. We would, at the same time, be peeping, hiding, behind a screen, and yet be, in fact, so very much present through TV screens. It illustrates how cameras and TV screens operate as a mediation device that produces, as written by Mulvey, a sense of separation, making the mainstream transparency argument irrelevant. This isolation, separation, seems to be created by the 'contrast between the darkness in the auditorium (which also isolates the spectators from one another) and the brilliance of the shifting patterns of light and shade on the screen helps to promote the illusion of voyeuristic separation'.[58] We are facing the binary conflict of 'darkness of the auditorium' (or the darkness of the soft ambiance of a living room) v. 'light of the screen', in fact what is projected. The movie is (really) shown. It is there to be seen: the conditions of screening, the way things are organised, but also the specific narrative conventions (and we may, by analogy, include what has been included in the various documents concerning who operates and how it is operated by video-journalists) give the audience (i.e. the ensemble of spectators or the public/masses) an illusion of 'being', through what is 'seen' of a private world. It is even more exacerbated when we consider the cosy ambience of a home for a TV show, with the TV most of the time nowadays occupying the focal point in a living room, reproducing that effect somehow.[59] Does it make watching a court hearing a pleasant experience? Of course, TV and cinema have something to do with the pleasure of looking too. Watching a court hearing,

56 Ibid.

57 Ibid., pp. 835–836.

58 Ibid., p. 836.

59 I suspect that these considerations must be nuanced according to the cultural identity of the audience and the way the justice process is conducted. What similarities and differences then do we have in the TV fictions? We may offer a safe answer by acknowledging differences in French cinema and TV programmes, where we have either a very slow process, where the French police

watching a trial, goes further than simply 'watching'. It has to do with developing the narcissistic aspect of voyeurism based on what the public is used to see of the courts in cinema or TV fictions.

Narcissus looks at himself in the water, as we look at ourselves in a mirror. As he looks at himself, he gets closer and closer to the water. But the water that constitutes the mirror is also a window. Narcissus does not know it but, by going further, by passing 'through' the 'water-mirror', and considering it as the 'water-window', he will pass a point of no return, a definitive move that opens onto his destiny, his death. What pushes Narcissus to act is more his loneliness than the search for the origin of his image.[60] There are connections between Narcissus story, the mirror, the water, and the birth or feelings of a society. The screen operates surely as a mirror too. As Mulvey remarks and as I have already mentioned, Lacan describes the mirror stage as the moment a child recognises its own image in the mirror and considers it the crucial operation for the constitution of the ego.[61] The mirror phase occurs when the child wants more than what his body can really achieve. It also is a fundamental moment the child sees an image of himself as a complete body for the first time. This mirror image appears here more complete than the reality of his own body, or perhaps of the expectation he may have of himself. Because this image of himself has been conceived as the reflected body of the self and is a recognition of himself, it is a recognition that is also a misrecognition. That is due to the projection of his body outside itself as an ideal ego (the alienated subject), re-introjected as an ego ideal that will start the identification with others. This image of course has to be considered as a topical element here, an element that is crucial for the imaginary, for the binome recognition/mis-recognition and for identification. As the subject is empty, it will look at others, to identify.[62] The mirror stage is in fact the first experience of the 'I', the one of subjectivity, which revolves around the experience of the fascination

is involved and/or an investigating magistrate is very active or pro-active. But here, no one never really see what is inside the courts. The British equivalent is a much more active process with verbal exchange in courts. We go back to the crucial difference between legal culture of verbal and written, of openness and secrecy. That said, the influence of Anglo-American TV and cinema in France has created a craving for Anglo-American style of justice. Popular culture creates a distortion of reality. That is a crucial element to be considered in the reality becoming a fiction. Perhaps a fiction is creating not only a new reality and it certainly helps the public to depart from the dominant culture of one jurisdiction. How can I not remember this apprentice *avocat* wrongly telling a French judge '*objection votre honneur*!' These examples are simply to illustrate the problem of representation and re-representation. What is what we refer to as 'reality' may not be what is going to be expected, truly expected, by the public.

60 David Marrani, 'Althusser in Avatar: comparative law as a science and the haunting of the subject', in Laurent de Sutter (ed.), *Althusser and Law*, London: Routledge 2013, esp. p. 107.

61 Laura Mulvey, 'Visual Pleasure and Narrative Cinema', pp. 833–844, esp. p. 836. See also my comments in Marrani, *Confronting the Symbolic Postition of the Judge in Western Legal Traditions*.

62 Maria Aristodemou, *Law, Psychoanalysis, Society*, London: Routledge 2015, esp. p. 77.

of looking at the mother's face for example, and which collides with the initial consideration of self-awareness. This may be compared to the first step of a journey of 'self-reflecting and self-perpetuating delusions', a 'first wishful misrepresentation of herself [or himself] as a subject'.[63] We, as subjects, will not acknowledge the misrepresentation but will try to find others to ratify and endorse it.[64] We look at others in order to find, to perpetually find something that is not. The complex relationship between image and identification is strongly present in the cinema and TV of course, with the interaction screen-like-mirror/self-like-cinema audience.

Interestingly, for Barthes, 'The spectacle or the tribunal, which are both places where the Other threatens to appear in full view, become mirrors'.[65] We should then rightly consider similarities and differences between screen, that opaque structure that separate spaces, even the most remote ones, and mirror. A screen is at the same time a mirror and not a mirror. Indeed, the cinema does not create a mirror and a self-recognition as such but has the power to fascinate so much that one may lose itself in it for a while, and become inserted in the movie, like Narcissus, falling into the water and drowning. Losing oneself appears then to be the same experience than the one of the mirror stage, the pre-subjective moment of image identification describe above. But the screen is like the mirror. What the public sees as a fiction will be expected in a very similar way as what a child expects in an image of him or herself. The mirror stage here would appear to be the public recognising the image or a certain image of (its) judges and of (its) justice on the screen. We should consider it a crucial operation for the constitution of an image, and further for the perception of the judge and justice. Ultimately, that is something that we could consider as crucial for the creation of a specific space. The image presented becomes fundamental. It becomes what is expected by the public, conceived as the reflection of the law itself, of a legal system, of what a legal culture (we should remember that the mirror stage is the entry of the child in culture) of one place is based on. The major issue here is really what the public expects and not what is really happening. On the basis of identification, and of the recognition, like Barthes mentioned, of man's inability to imagine the Other, we end up with us wanting to reduce otherness to sameness: 'one never tries anybody but analogues *who have gone astray*'.[66]

What is on the screen becomes what is 'real'. It is therefore a recognition of what is there but also a misrecognition. Here, too, the projection of a cultural reality, the narcissistic imagination of what judge and justice should be, becomes a sort of ideal ego (the alienated subject of the mirror stage), that is re-introjected as an ego ideal starting identification with what is there. This crucial image for the legal imaginary, for the binome recognition/mis-recognition and for identification permits to develop perceptions but also and more importantly here expectation of

63 Ibid.
64 Ibid.
65 Barthes, *Mythologies*, esp. p. 151.
66 Ibid., pp. 151–152

what a real trial broadcasted not is but should be, of what the actors, judges, lawyer and parties, should be, should do, of the specific scene, of how it should be. But in addition, we should not forget that to show justice being done, being seen rendered, according to a democratic ideal, imaginary or not, something transparent seems adequate. There should therefore be nothing more transparent than filming and broadcasting in places that are said to be opaque. But to show the interior of the process of justice, to show its intimate mechanism, to reach deep inside the process of justice, one has to be able not to see, even though it seems *prima facie* contradictory. These things have to be hidden, as this is through opacity rather than through transparency, as we have seen for palaces of justice, that the most intimate is reached. To complete that brief argument, I suggest that psychoanalytic theory tells us that transparency does not give us access to the inside. A transparent palace of justice and furthermore cameras do not bring a glimpse of the democratic process, for instance, or shows a fair trial.[67]

Transparency renders the opposite effect to the one we are in fact expecting. It does not really open the interior onto the exterior, but it makes the interior permanently available to the exterior, opened. Transparency equates here to openness. Therefore the use of TV/cinema becomes the seed for revolution. But will it redress the fictional seeds that have been planted in our mind? We may keep in mind that if the domination of US cinema carries on, the expectation of the European audience will be that a trial should be conducted like the public/masses knows, and therefore like a trial in the US (even though we may soften this assumption due to the vast amount of 'real' jurisdictions in the US), because their knowledge is being fuelled by images of what the public/masses have seen on screen. The imaginary, the expectation will simply be one of a US trial and not that of their own jurisdictions.

It can be said, and I have argued in previous chapters, that the rituals of justice taking place in the courtrooms have both an individual and a collective function.[68] They contribute to both the resolution of a private dispute and the re-enactment of the original transgression, the patricide.[69] The real audience, the public/masses, needs to have access to the court rooms, as brothers of the primal hordes needed to witness the re-enactment of the original transgression to interiorise, to repress and then suppress this original transgression that is, as I argued, the moment of the beginning of civilisation.[70] But it has another dimension that has to do with the place, space, identity, and language of a community. It is not surprising that access to courtrooms through the transparency of courthouses and the openness of justice has been topical in the debates following the development of post-modern type of courts. Many architects have used and abused the adage 'justice has to be seen to be done' and made both literal and phenomenal transparency

67 See chapter on architecture.
68 See Chapter 2.
69 See Chapter 1.
70 Ibid.

collapsed.[71] In the case of the use of cameras in courts, we should therefore analyse how the scope of this statement may be multiplied or divided. However, at the same time, one needs to consider it critically, at a different angle. Screens operate as mirrors as we have seen, and we need to keep in mind how that point impacts on many issues. They help spectators, the audience, to identify as ego, through primary identification with the camera itself. Spectators are in actual fact not active but passive agents in front of what is going on; what is seen, the process of justice, a naked justice, undressed in front of their eyes. The action that is taking place on the screen fosters identification with the camera that provides the spectator with an illusion of power over what s/he sees (we have to remember the statement of Foucault on control through transparency).

The space of justice constructed by cameras, the onscreen representation of a reality that is supposed to resolve the mistakes of TV fiction, ignores the walls of the palaces of justice and the specific rituals. It also ignores the visual and cultural training that TV and cinema have given to the public. Cameras circumvent walls and bring new dimensions to the ego, through the perversion of (what is) justice, and for the society, with the help of the Althusserian notion of ideology, a political dimension that results from the abolition of the opaque walls of the courtrooms. A dangerous prospect for contemporary democracy, of course, and, to further analyse the question, we may now turn to Baudrillard and his work on media.

Cameras in courts and the implosion of the meaning in the media

We may want to analyse the question of cameras in courts taking a different but truly relevant angle here. We may reconsider the use of video cameras in courts through the work of Baudrillard, *Simulacra and Simulations*, and specifically Chapter VIII, 'The Implosion of Meaning in the Media'.[72]

For Baudrillard, to 'simulate' is to feign having what one doesn't have.[73] Simulation threatens the difference between the true and the false, the real and the imaginary.[74] Simulation envelops the whole edifice of representation itself as a simulacrum.[75] Baudrillard uses the example of Disneyland[76]: it 'exists in order to hide that it is the "real" country, all of "real" America that *is* Disneyland'; it 'is presented to us as imaginary in order to make us believe that the rest is real', but nothing is real in America, it is simply a simulation. Let us try to apply this concept to the use of cameras in courts. It seems, to a certain extent, adequate to apply *Simulacra and Simulation* in (what I believe to be) the representation or even

71 Chapter on architecture

72 Baudrillard, Jean, *Simulacra and Simulation (The Body in Theory: Histories of Cultural Materialism)*, Ann Arbor: University of Michigan Press, 1994, esp. pp. 79–86

73 Ibid., esp. p. 3.

74 Ibid.

75 Ibid., esp. p. 6.

76 Ibid., esp. pp. 12–13.

double representation taking place in the broadcasting of a trial. In the beginning of Chapter VIII, we find this statement: 'We live in a world where there is more and more information, and less and less meaning'.[77] That is truly why it is relevant to analyse the entire operation of filming and broadcasting in court in the light of this statement. We need to be conscious that as soon as we film and broadcast anything, including a trial, it becomes 'like' any other type of information. Baudrillard considers three hypotheses that we will look at here in turn.

In the first hypotheses, we learn that 'information produces meaning (a negentropic factor), but cannot make up for the brutal loss of signification in every domain'.[78] Therefore, what is transmitted in our case, when the trial is filmed and broadcasted, the 'message and content', is re-sent, 'reinjected' as Baudrillard puts it, but it loses meaning in the process. In the second hypotheses, Baudrillard mentions that 'information has nothing to do with signification'.[79] If it has nothing to do with signification, then it is not linked to meaning and is positioned 'outside meaning and of the circulation of meaning strictly speaking'.[80] What we have is something 'purely functional, a technical medium that does not imply any finality of meaning'.[81] We end up either with a complete disconnection between 'the inflation of information and the deflation of meaning' or 'a rigorous and necessary correlation between the two, to the extent that information is directly destructive of meaning and signification, or that it neutralises them'.[82] When we film and broadcast a trial, the retransmission of a trial inflates information. There is more information sent to the public/masses, the virtual audience, information that used to be only available in (as in inside) court, and is in fact not widely available. But at the same time, it decreases the meaning of what is happening. That is to do with the fact that transparency is indeed deflating the true symbolic meaning here. In the third hypotheses, Baudrillard analyses the measure of socialisation through the exposure to media. There is a point made about correlation between socialisation and media: 'Whoever is underexposed to the media is de-socialised or virtually asocial'.[83] We may just want to consider how for instance, we very quickly forget about the winner of the X-Factor finale every year, even though for weeks and weeks, the judges and all the singers of the show are an integral part of the Saturday or Sunday family routine for millions of viewers. When we are told that we need to see justice being done or being rendered, when we are told that this is good for the administration of justice, we have something similar happening. We need to film and broadcast trials because justice can only exist if it is seen. But as soon as we stop, we may just simply forget about it. This is inverting the meaning of this very statement: if we don't see justice being done, it is not done; it we don't see justice

77 Ibid., p. 79.
78 Ibid.
79 Ibid.
80 Ibid.
81 Ibid.
82 Ibid.
83 Ibid., esp. p. 80.

being done, it does not exist. There is also here a correlation between information and acceleration of the circulation of meaning. From information comes communication, with 'an excess of meaning'.[84] A filmed and broadcasted trial does not simply inform us, it communicates something, via a complex mechanism of meaning. We are all complicit in this myth. It is the alpha and omega of our current modernity, without which the credibility of our social organisation would collapse. And yet, the fact is that it *is* collapsing, and for this very reason: because when we think that information produces meaning, the opposite occurs.[85] To sum up, a filmed and broadcasted trial contributes to the circulation of specific information (we need to see justice being done) in order to avoid our social organisation collapsing. In addition, we believe that the meaning produced by that information is needed to avoid the collapse of our society.

We now have many examples of trials that were filmed and then broadcasted. But, perhaps, we may want to use here, for an illustration, the experience of the highly mediatised trial of Pistorius, the *State v. Oscar Leonard Pistorius (Pistorius)*. The trial in South Africa of the Paralympian was not televised until the ruling, incidentally a televised ruling, in Pretoria's High Court in February 2014.[86] Judge Dustan Mlambo declared at that time that it was vital that impoverished South Africans who feel ill-treated by the justice system be given a first-hand look at the trial. Judge Mlambo had to balance conflicting constitutional rights (expression v. fair trial), but this is not what initiated the filming and broadcasting process but rather the issues of open justice and social elements:[87]

> I have further considered the extensive interest that the pending criminal trial has evoked in the local and international communities as well as in media circles. My view is that it is in the public interest that, within allowable limits, the goings on during the trial be covered as I have come to decide to ensure that a greater number of persons in the community who have an interest in the matter but who are unable to attend these proceedings due to geographical constrains to name just one, are able to follow the proceedings wherever they may be. Moreover, in a country like ours where democracy is still somewhat young and the perceptions that continue to persist in the larger section of South African society, particularly those who are poor and who have found it difficult to access the justice system, that they should have a first-hand

84 Ibid., esp. p. 80.

85 Ibid., esp. p. 80.

86 www.justice.gov.za/docs/other-docs/pistorius-judgment-10193-2014.pdf (accessed 17 February 2017).

87 It is quite interesting here to note that on the contrary Stepniak links right to a fair trial and open justice: 'New technology, in particular the Internet, appears to provide courts with viable means of addressing the long-standing concerns regarding the media's audio-visual coverage of court proceedings, and of securing the balance between the rights to a fair trial and those of the open and public administration of justice.' Stepniak, 'Technology and Public Access to Audio Visual Coverage and Recordings of Court Proceedings: Implications for Common Law Jurisdictions', esp. p. 823

> account of the proceedings involving a local and international icon. I have taken judicial notice of the fact that part of the perception that I allude to is the fact that the justice system is still perceived as treating the rich and famous with kid cloves whilst being harsh on the poor and vulnerable. Enabling a larger South African society to follow first-hand the criminal proceedings which involve a celebrity, so to speak, will go a long way into dispelling these negative and unfounded perceptions about the justice system, and will inform and educate society regarding the conduct of criminal proceedings.

This statement has, we may all agree, more the flavour of a statement from a politician than the statement of a judge on a point of law. We find very few remote connections with 'law' in this. But we sense an echo of Baudrillard's vision: allowing Pistorius's trial to be broadcasted super exposes this vision to the media. It increases the socialisation, and Mlambo's argument is quite clever here, a perception. Meanwhile, it is clear that retransmission of the trial does not create meaning in the way Mlambo really desires it. Because of the inversion that occurs in the creation of meaning, we are left with emptiness rather than clear signification. One of the issues is that, as Mlambo, we believe that information will create a meaning. Therefore, filming and broadcasting the Pistorius trial should not simply be a transmission of information, but a transmission of meaning, the meaning of justice, its administration, etc. Instead, 'Information devours its own content. It devours communication and the social'.[88] In consequence, a televised trial does not convey the expected meaning but simply the misery of the emptiness of signification. There are two reasons for this and I will base these on ideas developed by Baudrillard.

Primarily, information, and I want to note again here that I am focusing on the retransmission of trials via audio-visual technique, does create neither communication nor meaning. Instead, it exhausts itself in the act of staging communication and in the staging of meaning.[89] To sum up and use Baudrillard's terminology, it simply 'simulates'. Assuming the desire of the public/masses, the audience, as I mentioned earlier, becomes an 'antitheater of communication'.[90] That is a heavy machinery of simulation that is put in place to avoid a de-simulation. This simulation masks the 'obvious reality of a radical loss of meaning' and as such participates to the avoidance of that discovery.[91] What becomes quite obvious then is that a televised trial, seen in your living room, is a deception, a simulation of a real trial. It becomes a simulation, but it also becomes hyperreal, an abolition of 'the real': 'More real than the real, that is how the real is abolished'.[92] There is a great and large volume of information but a total loss of communication, and therefore a re-enforcing of the simulacrum. As mentioned earlier about the Pistorius case, not only communication

88 Baudrillard, *Simulacra and Simulation*, p. 80.
89 Ibid., p. 80.
90 Ibid., p. 80.
91 Ibid., p. 80.
92 Ibid., p. 81.

but also social functions are lost. We present the televised trial not as a televised trial but as 'the trial'. In doing so, the 'more real than the real' abolishes 'the real'. It is clear that what is before us is not what is seen or what it seems. It is certainly not the important re-enactment of the original transgression and its punishment.[93] It is something else. However, we are pushed to believe in the information and in its social function (see the declaration of Mlambo or what we have been told during the Crime and Courts bill debates in 2012–2013). As Baudrillard puts it, 'Belief, faith in information attach themselves to this tautological proof that the system gives of itself by doubling the signs of an unlocatable reality'.[94] This tautology is interesting because it triggers a reaction from the public or the audience, one of disaffection, but also one of 'enigmatic belief'.[95] At the same time, there is a crucial assumption that the audience or the public, that Baudrillard calls the masses, will not exercise any critical thinking because of the 'naivete and stupidity of the masses'.[96] We may suspect that to address the question of disaffection and enigmatic belief, one may want to turn to statistics. How many of us watch trials on TV? In a recent survey, it was striking to see that 51 per cent would not watch a criminal trial on TV. We may be quasi-certain that this assumption would be correct for UKSC TV programmes as well.[97] Interestingly enough, in the pure demonstration of Baudrillard's thoughts, what is interesting may not be the statistics, or the content of the article, but rather its title: 'Many would watch criminal trials on TV'. While we are told so, we get quite a different feeling from the statistics and their presentation: in effect, we are informed that 'A significant minority (39 per cent) would watch television coverage of UK criminal trials if they could'. The significant majority of 39 per cent is a very interesting postulate. One would believe that a majority of 51 per cent should be in fact the 'significant majority' or that at least the expression a relative majority of 39 per cent should be used to change the title to 'Only a few would watch criminal trials on TV'. Journalists are here again masking the reality: that in fact a majority is/was against watching a trial on TV. In a similar, and in my opinion related, branch of the argument, there is certainly great analysis to be done on 'real court' television. Real court shows involve actual, unscripted disputes between real people. To sum up, in that sort of programme, a judge hears the testimony; after a commercial break, the judge hands down a decision. The judge handles the trial in an inquisitorial manner. There are no lawyers. The judge fires questions at the litigants (or the occasional non-party witness) in an attempt to get at the truth.[98] What do we in fact have there? Do we have real courts or hyperreal courts?

93 See Chapter 1.

94 Baudrillard, *Simulacra and Simulation*, p. 81.

95 Ibid., p. 81.

96 Ibid., p. 81

97 Many would watch criminal trials on TV. https://yougov.co.uk/news/2014/03/03/many-would-watch-criminal-trials-tv/ (accessed 17 February 2017).

98 Real Court Television, *Michael Asimow, UCLA Law School* (September 1998), http://usf.usfca.edu/pj//articles/realcourt.htm

The second reason for Baudrillard is that 'Behind this exacerbated *mise-en-scène* of communication, the mass media, the pressure of information pursues an irresistible destructuration of the social'.[99] The risk, if we move to televised trial, is to see the flux of 'information dissolve[ing] meaning and dissolve[ing] the social'.[100] Contrary therefore to what we are pushed to believe, either in the UK or in other jurisdictions, as illustrated with the account of Judge Mlambo, the result of the mediatisation of a trial is not socialisation but rather the contrary. For Baudrillard, it means that the implosion of the social (at macro level) is also the implosion of meaning (at micro level).[101] In consequence, 'all contents of meaning are absorbed in the only dominant form of the medium. Only the medium can make an event'.[102] The content of the meaning of the process of justice is then absorbed in the TV itself. In addition, the implosion of that meaning also marks the implosion of the social. The event of a trial on TV transforms the trial: it makes the trial an event. The trial therefore becomes an event. From the latin -e, out, plus -venire, to come, an event involves a movement from outside to inside, which according to Lamizet, as mentioned previously, marks a limit.[103] This limit is a wall, including a glass wall or a camera, which frames the place of the happening of time, linking space and time.[104] This is valid primarily in the matter of a 'general' event. For Nietzsche, 'an event is nothing other than the time when being appears in all its neutrality'.[105] That neutrality is present and reaffirmed by Baudrillard, too, through the operation of making something neutral, the neutralisation of all content of meanings, where the medium replaces the real form. In a TV trial, the cameras in the court rooms replace the real form.[106] In the legal field, one comes to a trial, the legal event, enters a courtroom that delimits, marks boundaries, and defines. As argued previously, the human subject outside is anonymous. S/he enters the courtroom, and becomes defined, named, identified as judge, or advocate, or accused. The idea of the event merges time and space through theatrical ritualisation. As mentioned, and to go back to the example of the legal event, the courtroom is precisely a theatrical place where a play is performed. Actors are all dressed and everyone plays a part, their life (and sometimes death), in a representation of the original transgression. Courthouses are similar to temples where what is sacred, magical, operates with ritual(s), in a fusion between space and time. But what takes place in this re-enactment of the original transgression is a re-birth, a 'new beginning', the end of the (psychoanalytical) cure.[107] Simulation

99 Baudrillard, *Simulacra and Simulation*, p. 81.
100 Ibid., p. 81.
101 Ibid., p. 81.
102 Ibid., pp. 81–82.
103 Lamizet, B., (2006), *Sémiotique de l'Evénement*, Paris: Hermes, Lavoisier.
104 See Chapter 2.
105 Zupancic, A., (2003), *The Shortest Shadow: Nietzsche's Philosophy of the Two*, London: MIT Press, esp. p. 60.
106 Baudrillard, *Simulacra and Simulation*, esp. p. 82
107 Lacan, J., (1999), 'Le temps logique et l'assertion de certitude anticipée. Un nouveau sophisme', *Écrits 1*, Paris: Point, Seuil, esp. pp. 195–211. See Chapter 2.

destroys. It does so because of the dissolution of the meaning through the media. The important part that is played by the parties/audience in the tragedy taking place in the courtroom does not transfer in the simulation. The result is a) the implosion of the message in the medium, b) the implosion of the medium itself in reality, and c) the 'implosion of the medium and of the real in a sort of hyperreal nebula, in which even the definition and distinct action of the medium can no longer be determined'.[108] The hyperreal nebula is also a hyperreal confusion of everything. If we once again carefully consider McLuhan's formula, as interpreted and explained by Baudrillard, we clearly see that the medium is the message, is the key formula of the era of simulation: the medium is the message, the sender is the receiver, there is a circularity of all poles, the end of panoptic and perspectival space.[109]

Using cameras in court does therefore bring some confusion. The hyperreal confusion is that the information (justice) and the TV that shows it are the same. The courts and the audience in the living room become the same. Subjectivity plays a crucial part on what is received, because in a similar way to what is taking place when we are looking at a painting, the viewer gives corpus to what is seen. The true meaning of the trial is then given by the receiver; by whoever will watch the trial. That is the true dilemma that faces that alleged exercise of transparency taking place through the entry of cameras in courts. The open justice argument, a continuation of transparency, but also the great understanding of the process of justice argument, (a very condescending pedagogical rhetoric of the elites concerned with the education of the audience argument) does not take into consideration the real inversion taking place: the audience gives the meaning of the televised trial. Is this a perversion or simply a proper interpretation of what happens in the process of trials retransmitted by TV? Here we have a clear example of the issues of transparency. The walls of the courthouses explode during the implosion of meaning and medium. That is confirmed by Baudrillard's concerns that not only the contents and messages have been volatilised in the medium but also the medium itself is volatilised as such.[110] Information still gives credibility to what is seen, to the medium, to the TV, including its status as medium. For us, the TV is 'the intermediary of communication'.[111] It also confirms what I feared about touching the 'real': transparency, including what is brought by and through TV, destroys mediation. Indeed, 'A single model, whose efficacy is immediate, simultaneously generates the message, the medium, and the "real." '[112] And we arrive at the end of everything, TV is the message, and therefore there is no information anymore. It is the end of both TV and information, 'the end of the message, but also the end of the medium'.[113] Both are needed to appear and exist,

108 Baudrillard, *Simulacra and Simulation*, esp. p. 82.
109 Ibid.
110 Ibid.
111 Ibid.
112 Ibid.
113 Ibid.

and both disappear when this is done. Watching a trial on TV is destroying both the TV as medium (because it does not exist anymore as a medium) and the message, the information, what is seen (justice been done), vanishes in what is communicated. Baudrillard demonstrates that there is no media anymore, 'in the literal sense of the word', no 'mediating power between one reality and another, between one state of the real and another'.[114] The only situation is the one of the hyperreal nebula merging medium and content: the trial televised is a television programme showing a 'real' trial but it simulates it, even though it is appearing or happening somewhere. When we watch it, we do not have any mediation, we are absorbing what we see as if we were present in court . . . but we are not there at all, we are absent, and we cannot 'see' the truth, the judicial truth, we are only left with this nebula; 'the medium and the real are now in a single nebula whose truth is indecipherable'.[115]

Of course, and this is highlighted by Baudrillard, we have idealised meaning and communication and this is according to this sort of standard that we apprehend information and as this is not going according to that standard, then we think about it as a 'catastrophe', where and when 'nothing takes place that has meaning for us'. This understanding we have about meaning, is now a limit, a border, a horizon like in the words of Baudrillard, a 'liminary', or a point of no return of the meaning, which collapses social into masses, because it destroys the 'social': 'Beyond the horizon of the social, there are the masses, which result from the neutralisation and the implosion of the social'.[116] The absorption of what is arriving on TV does trigger many questions, starting with the one of posture. The question of the condescending posture of elites for instance, highlights what must be looked at, the sort of dynamic elites/masses and how this dynamic operates, as mass-communication tools that control the masses. On one side, we have the few, the elites, the subjects supposed to know, and on the other side we have the masses, subjects supposed to believe, or at least supposed to follow the leaders without answering. The mass media and the masses interact in an 'inextricable conjunction of the masses and the media', where one tries to decipher whether 'the media neutralize[s] meaning and produce uninformed [*informe*] or informed [*informée*] masses, or is it the masses who victoriously resist the media by directing or absorbing all the messages that the media produce[s] without responding to them?'[117]

114 Ibid.
115 Ibid., p. 83.
116 Ibid.
117 Ibid. Of course, Baudrillard applies some radical Marxist outcome here: This absence of response is not a strategy of power but a counterstrategy of the masses themselves when they encounter power. That brings you up to the dynamic elites/masses, orchestrated by the media, as confirmed with the many arguments voiced around trials on TV, using the power confer by images to 'carry meaning and countermeaning' and therefore to 'manipulate in all directions at once' (ibid, p. 84). It is the strategy of the masses: it is equivalent to returning to the system its own logic by doubling it, to reflecting meaning, like a mirror, without absorbing it. This strategy (if one can still speak of strategy) prevails today, because it was

At that stage, moving from Baudrillard, it may be relevant and helpful to consider another side of the argument with the introduction of an interpretation based on Barthes's writings. One of the merits of this last interpretation is the introduction of a third level of explanation, a third meaning.

A third level, as additional and last issue to be considered for cameras in courts.

If we have noticed with Baudrillard the place of media and the role mediation plays in communication and information, together with the explosion/implosion of meaning, Roland Barthes brings an additional layer with the notion of a third meaning.[118] Barthes refers to Eisenstein's movie *Ivan le Terrible* to analyse not two but three meanings in movies. Let us just assume that the points he made in his analysis are strongly relevant to filming and broadcasting in court. It is quite simple to consider that everything relating to film may have connection to our question. That said, one objection to the use of Barthes' ideas here could be that specifically, he is referring also to stills. To evacuate that objection, it may be easy to explain that the judicial rituals impose not a permanent dynamic and movement such as the one we have in movies but rather long still scenes. As mentioned above, Barthes considers not two but three meanings of a scene, two that are more, or less, relevant and similar to Baudrillard discussion, communication and signification, and the third meaning.

The first level Barthes calls the 'informational level' (or communication). Here we can learn 'from the setting, the costumes, the characters, their relations, their insertion in an anecdote with which I am (even if vaguely) familiar'.[119] At this level, what is important is communication but not simply as an operation of communication. It has more to do with an operation of education through communication. It is particularly interesting to note that this is rather similar to all the explanations we received from officials concerning the education and pedagogical side of filming and broadcasting in court in regards the Crime and Courts Act. The argument is found not only in the official documents cited at the start of this chapter, but also in literature on the topic.[120] We want to see justice being done,

ushered in by that phase of the system which prevails. To choose the wrong strategy is a serious matter. All the movements that only play on liberation, emancipation, on the resurrection of a subject of history, of the group, of the word based on 'consciousness raising', indeed a 'raising of the unconscious' of subjects and of the masses, do not see that they are going in the direction of the system, whose imperative today is precisely the overproduction and regeneration of meaning and of speech (ibid, p. 86).

118 Roland Barthes, *The Third Meaning, Image, Music, Text*, London: Fontana, 1977, esp. pp. 52–68.

119 Ibid., p. 52.

120 See Stepniak, 'Technology and Public Access to Audio Visual Coverage and Recordings of Court Proceedings: Implications for Common Law Jurisdictions', esp. pp. 806 and 813; but also, more recently, Edward L. Carter, Supreme Court Oral Argument Video: A Review of Media Effects Research and Suggestions for Study, *BYU L. Rev.* (2012), pp. 1719–1758.

being rendered. In all examples seen on the Law Society gazette website of court on cameras,[121] it is obvious that the work of the cameras is around the setting (the court room), the costumes (the gowns/wigs), the characters (judges, lawyers and even parties), their relations, their insertion in an anecdote with which one may be (even if vaguely) familiar (that relates to the point made by Barthes in *Mythologies*: one never tries anybody but analogues *who have gone astray*.[122]) That is the level of the message and, indeed, this is what transpires from the point made by the officials on filming and broadcasting. The informational level is also a level clearly connected to rituals. It is concerned with the decorum, what is presented to us and how clear it makes us 'feel' justice. As such, the operation of communication is truly alike the one found in baroque rococo churches: a rococo building communicates.[123] Then comes the second level.

Barthes calls the second level the 'symbolic level' (or signification or the obvious meaning[124]).[125] In *Ivan the Terrible*, the referential symbolism is the imperial ritual of baptism by gold. We may, by analogy, use our specific judicial rituals in courts. Those rituals are extremely important to the correct administration of justice, because of the meaning that they bring, a meaning that is obvious. Then there is the diegetic symbolism as the theme of gold, of wealth. Here all the elements including law and justice itself contribute to the theme of justice such as an elevated position for the judge, or the presence of a crest or a cross behind the judges. Many themes can be found but the most obvious are law and justice. Then again there is the Eisensteinian symbolism in Ivan. That reflects the personal input of the director and that is an important element, which touches the subjectivity of the person filming. That is a crucial point that we touched upon earlier in this chapter: who uses the cameras, how are the cameras used, etc. The subjective dimension, so well spotted by Barthes, is a dimension removing the argument of absence of mediation. The system 'camera-director' is a system that is not neutral. It does mediate: the camera has technology that is not neutral, particularly when it is used by 'someone'. And there is an historical symbolism, what is brought here 'in a (theatrical) playing, a scenography of exchange, locatable both psycho- analytically and economically, that is to say semiologically'.[126] I have argued in many of my papers the link between the process of justice and psychoanalysis.[127] That is the level of *signification*. The place, or space, of justice has an intimate connection with this. The position of things, the place of the actors, their costumes, are all related to the necessary creation of the good distance, one that psychoanalysts

121 www.lawgazette.co.uk/analysis/court-on-camera/ (accessed 17 February 2017).

122 Barthes, *Mythologies*, esp. p. 151.

123 Karsten Harries, *The Ethical Function of Architecture*, Cambridge: MIT Press, 1998, esp. p. 92. The first meaning of a rococo church is a church, the second is something else that has more to do with education and communication.

124 Barthes, *The Third Meaning*, p. 54.

125 Ibid., pp. 52–53.

126 Ibid., p. 52.

127 See Chapter 2.

consider fundamental for the symbolic. But as in the communication level, the signification is participating in the education of the public, but as a second stage. First, we need to *see*, so the courts are showing. Then we need to ***integrate***. Therefore, the more that is shown (hence strong rituals are crucial), the more that is understood and integrated, again in the same way as what we have in rococo churches. We have finally arrived at Barthes' description of the third meaning.

For Barthes, we have a third meaning (the obtuse meaning[128]). That meaning is unknown but is felt: 'I am not sure if the reading of this third meaning is justified – if it can be generalised – but already it seems to me that its signifier . . . possesses a theoretical individuality'.[129] It goes therefore further than the scene communicating and signifying. It is a meaning that forces interrogation, 'on the signifier not on the signified, on reading not on intellection'.[130] In addition, it is a meaning that leaves us unsatisfied. It is 'significance, a word which has the advantage of referring to the field of the signifier (and not of signification) and of linking up with, via the path opened by Julia Kristeva who proposed the term, a semiotics of the text'.[131] That is a more complex meaning that needs to be considered, particularly because we need to keep in mind that we have an aesthetic dimension in the meaning of justice when we refer to 'justice to be seen to be done'. An image of a courtroom has therefore a signification that is obvious and one that is obtuse. Inside the court, the process of justice takes place with all the decorum and rituals. It is obvious because it has to be seen to be done. What is seen is obvious, it is symbolic and signifies. But with the third meaning, the obtuse meaning, Barthes tells us about 'something to do with disguise'.[132] We are likely to look at the process of justice when we watch a broadcasting of court operations and apply a similar second signification, the significance. 'The characteristic of this third meaning is indeed . . . to blur the limit separating expression from disguise, but also to allow that oscillation succinct demonstration'[133] that is 'an elliptic emphasis . . . a complex and extremely artful disposition (for it involves a temporality of signification)'[134] that is 'just short of the cutting edge'.[135] When one watches a hearing, the cutting edge is indeed present as a phenomenon blurring the reality of the process, the signification, the obvious meaning of the administration of justice, what we are told is the pedagogical aspect of the broadcasting of the 'real' court hearing. The obtuse meaning, the 'spectacular', that is disguised under the uniform of the judges and the specific settings of the rituals. The obtuse meaning opens up an infinity that Barthes says extends further than culture, knowledge and information.[136] This is an emotional

128 Barthes, *The Third Meaning*, p. 54.
129 Ibid., p. 53.
130 Ibid., p. 53.
131 Ibid., p. 54.
132 Ibid., p. 58.
133 Ibid., p. 57.
134 Ibid.
135 Ibid., p. 58.
136 Ibid., p. 55.

meaning.[137] A meaning that is not representing anything. The obtuse meaning is a signifier without a 'signified', hence the difficulty in naming it. My reading remains suspended between the image and its description, between definition and approximation. If the obtuse meaning cannot be described, that is because, in contrast to the obvious meaning, it does not copy anything – how do you describe something that does not represent anything?[138]

We may want to check again what the Law Society website offers and watch some of the videos to grasp the totality of the meanings in fact. The obtuse meaning has to do with something different than the sole symbolic of the wigs and gown or even of a court ritual. It may relate to the ambience of the court room, the atmosphere of the law, its serenity, its solemnity. But law is not all here. Or maybe law is nothing here. The most important 'part' of it is what the voyeur wants to see in the image, still or slowly moving, of the courts. What exactly are we expecting? Do we want to see the law or do we want to see the sanctions? It may well be a sort of implied echo to early positivists such as Austin, and to the command sanction theory. As we know, and as stressed by Cotterel, the threat of sanctions, the punishment, is essential to Austin's theory.[139] That point is not without relation to the idea of Marcusse, that 'the history of man is the history of his repression'.[140] Law and justice 'seen to be done' equates them, because of what has to be seen to be done, for the sanction that is attached to the law. The voyeur does not really care about justice or about the law. The voyeur wants the 'spectacular'. Meanwhile, the officials and the elites want to educate us. The directors and broadcasters may also want to do so, although they are experts in their field and certainly, we reasonably may expect, well-aware of the voyeur aims. The spectacular dimension needs to be embraced as a crucial dimension here. The filming and broadcasting of the court operations take another level, the third meaning. The atmosphere of what is happening rather than what is seen (communication and obvious meaning), but also what is expected rather than the reality of the law being displayed. These are not representing anything. We want sanctions rather than law. In fact, we do not really care about the law at all: we only want (to see) sanction. That sanction is disguised behind the law, a law that is not really present here, even though it is everywhere. It is not present because the third meaning goes way beyond the law, without giving much consideration to it, only regarding the result. That said, by doing so, it completes the law because it reaffirms the compulsory element, echoing Austin, of the necessary punishment. The judges are in front of us, rendering justice, so when we watch them, we see justice being done. But when we film that process, it has another dimension. Again, according to Cotterell on Austin, 'the judge as delegate of the sovereign entails a straightforward recognition that judges legislate no less than do legislatures'.[141] Let us remember that some

137 Ibid., p. 59.
138 Ibid., p. 61.
139 Roger Cotterrell, *The Politics of Jurisprudence*, Oxford: OUP, 2011, 2nd edn, p. 58
140 Marcusse, *Eros and Civilisation*, p. 29.
141 Barthes, *The Third Meaning*, p. 71.

authors are strongly arguing that judges make law and do not simply render justice. That may be considered as an obvious and obtuse meaning of course. In other words, the third meaning structures the film differently without subverting the story and for this reason, perhaps, it is at the level of the third meaning, and at that level alone, that the 'filmic' finally emerges. The filmic is what is in the film that cannot be described, the representation which cannot be represented. The filmic begins only where language and metalanguage end.[142] That is another important point of filming and broadcasting in court. Though the filmic of the courts, what is actually supposed to take place is concerned. Can we really describe it? We can certainly describe the actors, what they wear, where they are and what it all signifies. But what is represented by that film, by a film of an (legal) event where what is expected is to see sanctions? The point made by all the people involved in bringing cameras in court was to educate and offer a better understanding of the process of justice. It was also to give a twentieth or twenty-first century translation of the 'to be seen to be done' quote and to open justice up to the public. However, what we got is the emergence of the filmic, something that could have been foreseen, but that, in fact, could not have been described. What we should say, with Barthes, is that it is not a representation, it is an obtuse meaning. For Barthes, 'The third meaning – theoretically locatable but not describable – can now be seen as the passage from language to significance and the founding act of the filmic itself'.[143] We know where to locate the meaning of what is filmed in court. We film justice that is seen to be done. We film actors of a legal play, actors of a real play. But we cannot describe what we see altogether, when we move from language that describes what is seen, i.e. justice being done, to the significance, i.e. what is happening in the scene we are watching. We film law as well as justice and retransmit 'things' that have meanings that overspill 'traditional' meanings.

The third or obtuse meaning is 'discontinuous, indifferent to the story and to the obvious meaning (as signification of the story)'.[144] The court hearing is like a story. We should consider the question of chain novel, where 'a judge is like a writer trying to continue a story started by earlier writers'.[145] It is easy to understand that there is a signification of that story for an individual and for a group of individuals (a community or a society). Notably because that story, the additions a new judge makes on top of a previous one, is 'the best interpretation of the meaning of what went before'.[146] The judge must make the best story with the best legal meaning.[147] But when we see what we see, we do not need to link either the (best) story or its signification (the best legal meaning). Let us go back to the notion of the voyeur. Does he or she really need to know the story? Is he or is she interested in signification? Or is there something else, more emotional, something even perverted? Is there an emptiness that is filled with what we

142 Ibid., p. 64.
143 Ibid., p. 65.
144 Ibid., p. 61.
145 Roger Cotterrell, *The Politics of Jurisprudence*, p. 167.
146 Ibid.
147 ibid.

interpret as voyeurism? The third meaning keeps something empty and yet not empty.[148] Because what we see is not simply a court hearing, it goes further, we see more than we have but we do so because we do not see anything that signifies. We expect emotionally to see something that does not happen. We emotionally see justice being done but we actually see nothing. If we see the application of the law, or more precisely the law becoming the law through the (expected) punishment, we see literally everything: 'the obtuse meaning can be seen as an accent, the very form of an emergence, of a fold (a crease even) marking the heavy layer of information and signification'.[149] Here we have the demonstration that this is something that subverts the meaning. We receive the information of what is going on in the court room. We see the actors of the play of justice. We understand that there is something going on that had to do with justice and perhaps the law. But the entire film of the play is highlighted to become super- or hyper-real here too. The film of the court, we know, is not the court. It is a representation of something that is happening somewhere. We cannot even really say we are watching a trial, although this may well be said. We cannot say so because what we see is only a part of what is really happening somewhere else. We are only watching a small portion, subjectivised (by the person filming), of a trial, a tiny part of the process of justice. We may want to name what we see 'justice', and we may, through the film, give full effect to the law, because of the argument that the punishment is seen. Then, not only is our expectation as voyeur fulfilled, but, we also have the law 'in full', complete. It marks, in essence, what we see, but also crucially highlights that what we have is not what it is.

148 Barthes, *The Third Meaning*, p. 62.
149 Ibid., p. 62.

5 Conclusion

In the various chapters of this book, I have tried to explore an inter-disciplinary approach towards the question of justice. I have looked at intersections between philosophy, psychoanalysis and law, and sometimes art and architecture theory, film theory, structuralism and esoteric writings to present thoughts and reflections on spaces of justice.

But one may consider after reading these chapters that my ideas have only been looking gently at law and justice as objects of study and have never really dissected either. But perhaps that was the point of this book, because if justice is to be seen to be done, what we can only consider is what can be seen, and as a side but critical issue, how it is perceived, how we perceived those very complex and abstract concepts. This, then, unfolds another connected issue: how systems of values use archaic connections through rituals, conveying the idea of power and authority through time.

In Chapter 1, I considered the (original) transgression and the fundamental law 'you shall not kill'. Using psychoanalysis and specifically the killing of fathers and brothers and its repression, I analysed how it is re-enacted during the legal event, highlighting how fundamental that moment is for the law. In turn, the spaces of justice where this re-enactment is taking place become also fundamental, because it is a place of the re-creation of the original transgression, the first step of social organisation. I then looked, in Chapter 2, at the relationship between time and space in the legal event and tried to decipher how we may connect the judge, 'totem' and the Oedipus complex, particularly necessary in defining the symbolic position of the judge. That chapter offers a connection between time and space through ritual(s). In Chapter 3, I focussed on the architecture of the spaces of justice and the link between those spaces and the law (at individual and community/society levels). I specifically introduced an in-depth examination of the use (and abuse) of transparency, the new opacity, even though one may believe that transparent walls are 'OK', before moving to the complete absence of walls in Chapter 4. Here, the question was how the psycho-social perspective on the legal event may be challenged by the use of technology, such as cameras in courts. I considered, then, how filming, recording and broadcasting trials, through a 'techno-legal' transparency, affects the spaces of justice.

To sum up briefly what has been written in these chapters, we could use the words of Linda Mulcahy, 'the fundamental principle [is] that justice should be seen to be done',[1] or of Supreme Court Justice Felix Frankfurter, 'Justice must satisfy the appearance of justice', but also the essay of Michael Stolleis's *The Eye of the Law*. As Douzinas puts it, we need to keep in mind the *ars juris*, the old aesthetic side of the law.[2] Maybe we should remember that, as I mentioned a few times, applying the law is exercising a power, the power to decide the meaning of words. We seem to have forgotten that in order for words to be spoken, a specific space, something like a scene should be carefully crafted. The words then take their full, solemn meaning, because of the *where* and *when* they are spoken. Therefore, one must critically be aware of the importance of buildings, time, ritual or rituals and ceremony. The question, deeply connected to the aesthetic of justice, ultimately relates also to art. In the essay the 'Age of Technological Reproducibility', Benjamin defined art in terms of its cult value:

> originally, the embeddedness of an artwork in the context of tradition found expression in a cult. This fits well here with the idea of the space of justice being a temple illuminated by the light of the truth. As we know, the earliest artworks originated in the service of rituals – first magical, then religious.[3]

Art was created for the purpose of ritual but then a shift happened in artwork's value. It moved from cult to exhibition that allowed for 'the emancipation of specific artistic practices from the service of ritual'.[4] The increase in investment in exhibition value has also affected how art is conceived by the artist himself and in his mode of representation.[5] The aesthetic side of justice relates to this art value and exhibition value defined by Benjamin. There are some connections between a vision of justice rendered that may come from the 'magical-cult' and emerge in the 'exhibition-rational'. The point has been made by and about architects – the exhibition-rational value of images of a trial for a broadcaster. In addition, we have seen, with Latour, that the divide of religious/secular seems to vanish or to have vanished, while spaces where the ritual or rituals of justice used to develop are evidence of the vanishing of this divide: 'post-modern' courthouses have become transparent and the ritual(s) absent; the meaning of the process has imploded and exploded with the use of cameras in courts.

One may want to consider the symbolism of Justice through, for example, the number 8 in Tarot cards that

1 Mulcahy, L., 'Architects of Justice: the Politics of Courtroom Design', *Social Legal Studies*, 16, 3, (2007), pp. 383–403, esp. p. 383.
2 Stolleis, M., *The Eye of the Law: Two Essays on Legal History*, CRC Press, 2008.
3 Benjamin, W., 'The work of Art in the Age of its Technological Reproducibility', in *Selected Writings* Vol. 3, 1935–1938, USA: Harvard University Press 1996–2003, pp. 101–133, esp. p. 105.
4 Ibid., p.106.
5 It may also give rise to a wish for a return of investment through profit.

Figure 5.1 A representation of Justice by Sadb Marrani.

> [s]tresses a harmonious union of opposite forces. Sitting on a throne, this large female figure symbolizes superhuman feminine power. Yet she holds a sword and wears a warrior's helmet, indicating that masculine discrimination and courage are also involved in her work.[6]

The balance, the very important equilibrium between forces, is the only security for the proper, orderly functioning of a complex society. But it is a balance that may be forced upon us, as the symbol shows that justice brings not peace but the sword.[7] Maybe what we really should remember about spaces of justice is that

> [c]ourts of law are useful tools for achieving certain kind of compensation and social equilibrium. But sometimes it seems that what is sought in the courts is actually not on trial there. At times, perhaps, we mistakenly turn to a human court in search of answers which can only be found in a heavenly one.[8]

6 Nicolls, S., *Jung and Tarot: An Archetypal Journey*, Red Wheel/Weiser; New edition, 1985, p.154.
7 Ibid., p.153.
8 Ibid., p162.

Bibliography

Abraham, G., 'The Sense and the Concept of Time in Psychoanalysis', *The International Review of Psycho-Analysis* 3, (1976).

Adams, G.B., 'The Descendants of the Curia Regis', *American Historical Review*, 13 (1) (1907), pp. 11–15.

Addo, M.K., 'Are Judges beyond Criticism under Article 10 of the European Convention on Human Rights?' *ICLQ*, 47 (2) (1998), pp. 425–438.

Agamben, G., *State of Exception*, Chicago, University of Chicago Press, 2005.

Aristodemou, M., *Law, Psychoanalysis, Society*, London: Routledge, 2015.

Ascher Barntones, D., *The Transparent State: Architecture and Politics in Postwar Germany*, London: Routledge, 2005.

Asimow, M., *Real Court Television*, UCLA Law School, 1998, http://usf.usfca.edu/pj//articles/realcourt.htm

Assier-Andrieu, L., *L'Autorité du Passé, Essai anthropologique sur la common law*, Paris: Dalloz, Les sens du droit Essai, 2011.

Austin, J. and Campbell, R., *Lectures on Jurisprudence, Or, The Philosophy of Positive Law*, Volume 1, Clarck: The Lawbook Exchange Ltd, 2005, p.444.

Badiou, A., 'The Problem of Evil', in Badiou, A., *Ethics: An Essay on the Understanding of Evil*, London and New York, Verso, 2001.

Balibar, E., *The Invention of The Super-Ego: Freud and Kelsen 1922*, Univérsité de Paris X Nanterre and The University of California, Irvine.

Barthes, R., *Mythologies*, Paris: Seuil, Point Essais, 1957.

Barthes, R., *The Third Meaning, Image, Music, Text*, London: Fontana, 1977.

Baudrillard, J., *Simulacra and Simulation (The Body in Theory: Histories of Cultural Materialism)*, Ann Arbor: University of Michigan Press, 1994.

Baum, F., *Dorothy and the Wizard of Oz*, Boston: MobileReference, 1908 (2008).

Benjamin, W., 'The Work of Art in the Age of its Technological Reproducibility' in *Selected Writings*, Vol. 3, 1935–1938, Cambridge: Harvard University Press 1996–2003, pp. 101–133.

Bessire, D., 'Transparency: A Two-Way Mirror?' in D. Pettman (ed.), *Thirty Years of IJSE: Festschrift in Honour of Professor John O'Brien*, Bradford: Emerald Group Publishing, 2005, pp. 424–438.

Bettelheim, B., *Psychanalyse des Contes de Fées*, Paris: Pocket Lafont, 1976.

Bourdieu, P., 'The Cult of Unity and Cultivated Differences' in Bourdieu, P., *Photography: A Middle-brow Art*, Cambridge: Polity Press, 1990.

Bouvresse, J., *Wittgenstein Reads Freud: The Myth of the Unconscious*, Princeton: New French Thought, 1995.

Bowie, F., *The Anthropology of Religion*, London: Blackwell Publishing, 2000.
Breger, C., 'The Leader's Two Bodies, Slavoj Zizek's Postmodern Political Theology', *Diacritics,* 31 (1) (2001), pp. 73–90.
Bronx County Hall of Justice, 2011, http://architypesource.com/projects/61-bronx-county-hall-of-justice/description
Bruner, J.S., *Law, Culture and Ritual: Disputing Systems in Cross-Cultural Context*, New York: NYU Press, 2005.
Brunet, P., 'Humpty Dumpty a Babel? Les juges et le vocabulaire juridique', *Chronique de Droit Européen et Comparé (Les Petites Affiches),* 17 (2008), pp. 1–9.
Brunet, P., 'Approche Critique du Vocabulaire Juridique Européen: Le Pouvoir des Juges', *Chronique de droit européen et comparé,* 17, Centre d'études juridiques européennes et comparées (CEJEC – Université Paris Ouest – Nanterre La Défense), Les Petites Affiches, 2008, pp. 7–12.
Bud, R., 'On the Social Production of Visual Difference, the Myth and the Machine: Seeing Science through Museum Eyes', in G. Fyfe and J. Law (eds) *Picturing Power: Visual Depiction and Social Relations*, London: Routledge, 1988.
Bullen, P.A., 'Assessing Sustainable Adaptation of Existing Buildings to Climate Change', *Cobra,* 2004, Leeds: Royal Institution of Chartered Surveyors.
Cardozo, B.N., *The Nature of the Judicial Process*, New Haven: Yale UP, 1921.
Carnwath, R. (Lord), 'ECHR Remedies from a Common Law Perspective', *ICLQ*, 49 (3) (2000), pp. 517–528.
Chase, O. and Bruner, J., *Law, Culture and Ritual: Disputing Systems in Cross-Cultural Context*, New York: NYU Press, 2005.
Chasseguet-Smirgel, J., *The Ego Ideal*, London: Free Association Books, 1985.
Chaumon, F., *Lacan, le Sujet et la Jouissance*, Paris: Michalon, Le Bien Commun, 2004.
Commaille, J., *L'Esprit Sociologique des Lois*, Paris: PUF, 1994.
Cotterrell, R., *The Politics of Jurisprudence*, London: OUP, 2011.
Davidson, J., 'Bronx Clear, How a Courthouse Polices Us Through the Glass', 4 February 2008, http://nymag.com/news/intelligencer/43599/
Derrida, J., *De la Grammatologie*, Paris: Les Éditions de Minuits, 1967.
Derrida, J., *Force de Loi, Le fondement mystique de l'autorité*, Paris: Galilée, 1994.
Derrida, J., *La Voix et le Phénomène*, Paris: PUF, Champs, 3rd edn, 2005.
Derrida, J. and Laboussiere, P.J., *Alterités*, Paris: Osiris, 1986.
Dews, P., *Logics of Disintegration, Post-Structuralist Thought and the Claims of Critical Theory*, London: Verso, 2007.
Dicey, A.V., *Introduction to the Study of the Law of the Constitution*, London: Macmillan and Co., 1927.
Discours de Lord Phillips of Worth Matravers, Chief Justice of England and Wales, 'Alternative Dispute Resolution: An English Viewpoint', India, 29 March 2008. www.judiciary.gov.uk/media/speeches/2008/speech-lord-phillips-lcj-29032008 www.judiciary.gov.uk/docs/speeches/lcj_adr_india_290308.pdf
Duncan, C., 'Art Museums and the Ritual of Citizenship' in I. Karp and S.D. Lavine (eds), *Exhibiting Cultures: The Poetics and Politics of Museum Display*, Washington and London: The Smithsonian Institute, 1991, pp. 279–286.
Duncan, C., 'The Art Museum as Ritual', in C. Duncan, *Civilising Rituals, Inside Public Art Museums*, London: Routledge, 1995, pp. 7–20.
Dworkin, R., *Law's Empire*, Cambridge: Harvard University Press, 1986.

Eastlake, C.L., *A History of the Gothic Revival*, London: Longmans, Green and Co, 1872.

Eliade, M., *Aspects du Mythe*, Paris: Gallimard, Idées, 1963.

Eliade, M., *Rites and Symbols of Initiation: The Mysteries of Birth and Rebirth*, Putnam, Spring Publication, 2009.

Eliot, C. and Quinn, F., *English Legal System*, London: Pearson, 7th edn, 2006.

Feigenson, N. and Spiesel, C., *Law on Display*, New York: NYU Press, 2009.

Fish, M., 'An Eye for an Eye: Proportionality as a moral principle of punishment', *Oxford Journal of Legal Studies* 28 (1) (2008), pp. 57–72.

Foucault, M., 'The Eye of Power', in C. Gordon (ed.), *Power/Knowledge: Selected Interviews and Other Writings, 1972–1977*, New York: Pantheon Books, 1980, pp.146–165.

Foucault, M., *Surveiller et Punir*, Paris: Gallimard, Tel, 1975.

Freud, S., 'Screen memories', *SE* 3 (1899), pp. 299–322.

Freud, S., 'The Unconscious', *SE* 14 (1905), pp. 160–215.

Freud, S., 'Identification' in 'Group Psychology and the Analysis of the Ego', *SE* 28 (1921), pp. 105–110.

Freud, S., *Civilisation and Its Discontents*, London: Penguin, 2002 (1930).

Freud, S., 'Moses and Monotheism: Three essays', *SE* 23 (1939), pp. 1–138.

Freud, S., *Totem and Taboo*, London: Ark, 1950.

Freud, S., 'The Group and the Primal Horde', in 'Group Psychology and the Analysis of the Ego', *SE* 18, London: Vintage Hogarth Press, 2001.

Friedel, W., 'Sigmund Freud: the loss of transparency', in *Copernicus, Darwin and Freud: Revolutions in the History and Philosophy of Science*, Oxford: Wiley-Blackwell, 2008, pp. 185–270.

Furneaux Jordan, R., *Western Architecture: A Concise History*, London: Thames & Hudson, 1993.

Fuss, D. and Sanders, J., 'Bergasse 19: Inside Freud's Office', in J. Sanders (ed.) *Stud: Architectures of Masculinity*, Princeton: Princeton Architectural Press, 1998, pp. 112–139.

Garapon, A., 'Le Droit mis à l'Epreuve', *Esprit,* August-September 2007.

Garapon, A., 'What Should one Think of Judicial Ritual in Law?' in Ralph Lindgren, J. and Knaak, J., *Ritual and Semiotics*, New York: Lang, Critic of Institutions 14, 1997.

Garapon, A., *Bien Juger*, Paris: Odile Jacob, 2001 (1997).

Garapon, A. and Allard, J., *Les Juges dans la Mondialisation, la nouvelle révolution du droit*, Paris: Seuil, La République des Idées, 2005.

Glenn, P., *Legal Traditions of the World*, Oxford, OUP, 2007.

Goodrich, P., 'Europe in America: Grammatology, legal Studies, and the politics of transmission', *Columbia Law Review* 101 (8) (2001), pp. 2033–2084.

Guarnieri, C. and Pederzoli, P., *The Powers of Judges: A Comparative Study of Courts and Democracy*, Oxford: OUP, 2003.

Guinchard, S., Brandac, M., Lagarde, X. and Douchy, M., *Droit Processuel, Droit Commun du Procès*, Paris: Dalloz Précis, 1st edn, 2001.

Halmos, C., *L'autorité Expliquée aux Parents*, Paris: Nil, 2008.

Harries, K., *The Ethical Function of Architecture*, Cambridge: MIT Press, 1998.

Hart, H.L.A., 'Positivism and the Separation of Law and Morals', in R.M. Dworkin (ed.), *The Philosophy of Law*, Oxford: OUP, 1977.

Heidegger, M., *Being and Time*, Oxford: Blackwell, 2007 (1927).

Heidegger, M., *Introduction à la Métaphysique*, Paris: Gallimard, 1967 (1935).
Heidegger, M., *Qu'appele t'On Penser*? 3rd edn, Paris: PUF, 1959.
Heidegger, M., *The Basic Problems of Phenomenology*, Bloomington: Indiana University Press, 1988 (1927).
Heidegger, M., *The Metaphysical Foundations of Logic*, Bloomington: Indiana University Press, 1984 (1928).
Hilferty, R., *Jury Beauty*, 26 February 2008, www.nysun.com/arts/jury-beauty/71877/
Hoebel, E.A., *The Law of the Primitive Man*, New York: Atheneum, 1976.
Holm, L., 'What Lacan Said re: Architecture', *Critical Quarterly* 42 (2000), pp. 29–64.
Holm, L., 'The New Yorkers', *Architectural Theory Review* 12 (2) (2007), pp. 104–120.
Jabloner, C., 'Kelsen and his Circle: The Viennese Years', *European Journal of International Law*, 9 (1998).
Jauffret Spinosi, C., 'Comment Juge le Juge Anglais?' in *Droits, la fonction de juger*, Paris: PUF, 1989.
Jencks, C., *The New Paradigm in Architecture: The Language of Postmodernism*, Cambridge: Yale University Press, 2008.
Kant, E., *Idées d'une Histoire Universelle au Point de Vue Cosmopolitique*, Paris: Bordas, 2006 (1784).
Kantorowicz, E.H., *The King's Two Bodies, a Study in Mediaeval Political Theology*, Princeton: PUP, 1997.
Kelsen, H., *General Theory of Law And State*, Clarck: The Lawbook Exchange Ltd, 2009.
Kelsen, H., 'The Conception of the State and Social Psychology – With Special Reference to Freud's Group Theory', *International Journal of Psycho-Analysis* 5 (1924).
Klein, M., *L'Amour et la Haine*, Paris: Payot, 2001 (1937).
Klein, M., *Le Complexe d'Oedipe*, Paris: Payot, 2001 (1945).
Krier, L., *Architecture: Choice or Fate*, Winterbourne: Papadakis Publisher, 2007.
Krips, H., 'The Politics of the Gaze: Foucault, Lacan and Zizek', *Culture Unbound* 2 (2010), pp. 91–102.
La Fontaine, J., 'Le Juge arbitre, l'Hospitalier et le Solitaire', Livre XII fable 25, in *Fables*, Paris: Hachette, 1929.
Lacan, J., 'Les Fondements de la Psychanalyse', in Lacan, J., *Les Quatre Concepts Fondamentaux de la Psychanalyse*, Livre XI, Paris: Seuil, 1973 (1964).
Lacan, J., *Le Séminaire I: Les écrits techniques de Freud*, Paris: Seuil, 1975, p. 178.
Lacan, J., *Le Séminaire II: Le moi dans la théorie de Freud et dans la technique de la psychanalyse*, Paris: Seuil, 1978.
Lacan, J., *Le Séminaire XVII: L'Envers de la psychanalyse*, Paris: Seuil, Champs Freudien, 1991.
Lacan, J., 'The Insistence of the Letter', *Yale French Studies, Structuralism*, 36/37 (1996), pp. 112–147.
Lacan, J. and Miller, J.A. (ed.), *The Four Fundamental Concepts of Psycho-analysis*, London: Vintage, 1998.
Lacan, J., *Écrits 1*, Paris: Point Seuil, 1999.
Lacan, J., *Écrits 2*, Paris: Seuil, Points Essais, 1999 (1966).
Lacan, J., *Écrits: A Selection*, translated by A. Sheridan, London: Norton, 2004.

Lacan, J., *Écrits: A Selection*, translated by A. Sheridan, London: Routledge, 2005.

Lacan, J., *My Teaching*, London: Verso, 2008.

Laclau, E. and C. Mouffe, *Hegemony and Socialist Strategy: Towards a Radical Democratic Politics*. London: Verso, 2001.

Lamizet, B., 'Sémiotique de l'Evénement dans l'Espace Euro-méditerranéen', *Actes du Colloque International 'l'Evénement dans l'Espace Euro-méditerranéen, Mémoire, Identité et Communication'*, Toulon, USTV, 2006, pp. 17–26.

Lamizet, B., *Sémiotique de l'Evénement*, Paris: Hermes, Lavoisier, 2006.

Latour, B., 'Visualisation and Social Reproduction: opening one eye while closing the other . . . a note on some religious paintings', in G. Fyfe and J. Law (eds), *Picturing Power: Visual Depiction and Social Relations*, London: Routledge, Sociological Review Monograph 35, 1988, pp. 15–38.

Lecourtois, C., ' "Espace de la conception" d'architectures judiciaires: les nouveaux palais de justice (Caen, Melun, Nantes, Grenoble et Pontoise)', *Diagonale Phi. n°4, Université Lyon 3*, 2010, pp. 31–52.

Lecourtois, C., 'Perception Architecturale et Image', *Colloque International 'Images et citadinité'*, Alger, 2005, pp. 1–10.

Legendre, P., *Le Crime du Caporal Lortie, Traité sur le Père*, Paris: Champs Flammarion, 1989.

Legrand, P., 'How to Compare Now', *Legal Studies* 16 (1996), pp. 232–242.

Legrand, P., *Droit Comparé*, Paris: PUF, Que Sais Je, 2nd edn, 1999.

Lévi-Strauss, C., *Totemism*, London: Merlin, 1964.

Levinas, E., 'Reflections on the Philosophy of Hitlerism', *Critical Enquiry* 17 (1990).

Levinas, E., *Le Temps et l'Autre*, Paris: PUF, 1983.

Lucien, A., *Médiation et modernité, Approche communicationnelle de l'institution judiciaire*, Toulon: USTV, Thèse, 2007.

Lyotard, J.F., *Le Différend*, Paris: Éditions de Minuit, Critiques, 1983.

Macdonald, C.F. 2003, 'The Palaces of Minos at Knossos', *Athena Review*, 3 (3) (2003), www.athenapub.com/11knoss.htm

Mack, K., '*Legal Architecture: Justice, Due Process and the Place of Law* by Linda Mulcahy: *Representing Justice: Invention, Controversy, and Rights in City-States and Democratic Courtrooms* by Judith Resnik and Dennis Curtis', *Journal of Law and Society* 39 (2) (2012), pp. 317–325.

Major, R., *Lacan avec Derrida*, Paris: Flammarion, Champs, 2001.

Marcuse, H., *Eros & Civilisation*, London: Abacus, 1972.

Markus, T., *Buildings and Power, Freedom and Control in the Origin of Modern Building Types*, London: Routledge, 1993.

Marrani, D., 'Althusser in Avatar: comparative law as a science and the haunting of the subject', in L. de Sutter (ed.), *Althusser and Law*, London: Routledge, 2013.

Marrani, D., 'Confronting the symbolic position of the judge in western European legal traditions: A comparative essay', *European Journal of Legal Studies* 3 (1) (2010), pp. 1–31.

Marrani, D. and Farah, Y., 'ADR in the Administrative Law: A Perspective from the United Kingdom', in *Alternative Dispute Resolution in European Administrative Law*, Heidelberg: Springer, 2014, pp. 259–279.

Mason, S., 'Cameras in the courts: why the prohibition occurred in the UK?' *Amicus Curiae* 91 (2012), pp. 22–27.

McQuire, S., 'From Glass architecture to Big Brother: Scenes from a cultural history of transparency', *Cultural Studies Review* 9 (2) (2003), pp. 103–123.

Meltzer, D., 'Tyranny', in D. Meltzer, *Sexual States of Mind*, London: Karnac, 1973.

Meltzer, D., 'The Apprehension of Beauty', in D. Meltzer, *The Apprehension of Beauty*, Strath Tay: Clunie Press, 1988.

Merleau-Ponty, M., *Le Visible et l'Invisible*, Paris: Gallimard, 1964.

Miller, J.A., *Theorie de Turin*, www.causefreudienne.net/index.php/ecole/textes-fondateurs/theorie-de-turin

Miller, J.A., 'Extrémité', in M. Bracher, F. Massardier-Kennedy, M.W. Alcorn and R.J. Corthell (eds), *Lacanian Theory of Discourse: Subject, Structure, and Society*, New York: NYU Press, 1997, pp. 74–87.

Moran, L., 'Every Picture Speaks a Thousand Words: Visualizing Judicial Authority in the Press' in P. Gisler, S.S. Borella and C. Wiedmer (eds), *Intersections of Law and Culture*, London: Palgrave, 2012, pp. 31–49.

Mulcahy, L., 'Architects of Justice: the Politics of Courtroom Design', *Social Legal Studies*, 16 (3) (2007), pp. 383–403.

Mulcahy, L., *Legal Architecture: Justice, Due Process and the Place of Law*, London: Routledge, 2011.

Mulvey, L., 'Visual Pleasure and Narrative Cinema', *Screen* 16 (Autumn 1975), pp. 6–18. Reedited as Mulvey, L., 'Visual Pleasure and Narrative Cinema', in L. Braudy and M. Cohen (eds), *Film Theory and Criticism: Introductory Readings*, New York: Oxford UP, 1999, pp. 833–844.

Nader L. and Sursock, A., 'Anthropology and Justice', in R. Cohen (ed), *Justice: Views from the Social Sciences*, Springer, 2006.

Nicolls, S., *Jung and Tarot: an archetypal journey*, Maine: Red Wheel/Weiser, 1985.

Open curtain wall gives transparency to the judicial process. 2011. http://archrecord.construction.com/projects/bts/archives/civic/07_bronxhall/default.asp

Ost, F., 'L'invention du tiers, Eschyle et Kafka', *Esprit* (2007).

Overgaard, S., *Husserl and Heidegger on Being in the World*, Dordrecht: Kluwer Academic Publishers, 2004.

Pareto, V., *The Rise and Fall of Elites: An Application of Theoretical Sociology*, New Jersey: Transaction Books, 1991.

Pingeot, M., *La Dictature de la Transparence*, Nouvelles Mythologies, Laffont Paris, 2016.

Poulantzas, N., *Fascisme et Dictature*, Paris: Seuil, Point Essais, 1974

Pritchard, H., 'Appearances and Reality', *Mind* 15 (58) (1982), pp. 223–229.

Public Perceptions of Working Court Dress in England and Wales, October 2002, 1/3 p. 4 http://www.dca.gov.uk/consult/courtdress/orcreport.pdf (accessed 15 November 2010).

Ravaz, B., 'Le Juge Judiciaire Gardien de la Vérité Historique?' *Champs libres* n° 2, Paris: L'Harmattan, 2002, pp. 225–245

Ravaz, B., 'Vérité Judiciaire et Vérité Religieuse', *Champs libres* n° 3, Paris: L'Harmattan 2002.

Reik, T., *Ritual, Four Psychoanalytic Studies*, New York: Evergreen, 1962 (1946).

Renucci, F., 'Les Voix pour le Dire', *Actes du Colloque International 'l'Evénement dans l'Espace Euro-méditerranéen, Mémoire, Identité et Communication'*, pp. 27–39.

Resnik, J. and Curtis, D., *Representing Justice: Invention, Controversy, and Rights in City-States and Democratic Courtrooms*, Yale: Yale Law Library Series in Legal History and Reference, 2011

Richard, P., *Introduction au Droit Italien: Institutions juridictionnelles et droit procédural*, Paris: L'Harmattan, 2004.

Richard, P., 'Les Apports de Wittgenstein à la Réflexion Comparatiste', *RIDC* 4 (2005), pp. 899–920.

Richard, P., *Le Jeu de la Différence: Réflexions sur l'épistémologie du droit comparé*, Laval: PUL Dikè, 2007.

Ricoeur, P., *Amour et Justice*, Paris: Seuil, Point Essais, 2008

Rowe, C. and Slutzky, R., 'Transparency: Literal and phenomenal', *Perspecta* 8 (1963), pp. 45–54.

Sacco, R., *Anthropologie Juridique, Apport à une micro histoire du droit*, Paris: Dalloz, 2008.

Samuel, G., 'Epistemology and Comparative Law', in M. van Hoecke (ed.), *Epistemology and Methodology of Comparative Law*, Oxford: Hart, 2004.

Schoenfeld, C.G., *Psychoanalysis and the Law*, Springfield: Charles Thomas, 1973.

Sherover, C. (ed.), *The Human Experience of Time, The Development of its Philosophic Meaning*, Evanston: Northwestern University Press, 2001

Stepniak, D., 'Technology and Public Access to Audio Visual Coverage and Recordings of Court Proceedings: Implications for Common Law Jurisdictions', *William & Mary Bill of Rights Journal* 12 (2004), pp. 791–823.

Stepniak, D., 'British Justice: Not Suitable for Public Viewing?' in P. Masons (ed.), *Criminal Visions*, London: Routledge, 2012.

Strydom, P., *Risk, Environment and Society*, Buckingham: Open University Press, 1st edn, 2002.

Sueur, J.-J. and Richard, P. (eds), *La Transgression*, Brussels: Bruylant, 2013.

Sutcliffe, A., *Architectural History of London*, New Haven: Yale University Press, 2006.

Tambiah, S.J., 'The Magical Power of Words', *Man* 3 (2) (1968), pp. 175–208.

Teubner, G., 'Global Bukowina: Legal Pluralism in the World Society', in G. Teubner (ed.), *Global Law Without a State*, Dartmouth: Aldershot, 1997.

Tusseau, G., *Jeremy Bentham, la Guerre des Mots*, Paris: Dalloz Les sens du droit, 2011.

Van Koppen, P.J. and Penrod, S., *Adversarial Versus Inquisitorial Justice: Psychological Perspectives on Criminal Justice Systems*, Berlin: Springer, 2003.

Villey, M., 'Dialogue, Dialectique en Philosophie et en Droit', *Archive de Philosophie du Droit*, tome 29, Paris: Sirey, 1984.

Waldron, J., 'Lex Talionis', *Ariz. L. Rev.* 34 (25) (1992).

Weiner, F. 'Sigmund Freud: the loss of transparency', in *Copernicus, Darwin and Freud: Revolutions in the History and Philosophy of Science*, Oxford: Wiley-Blackwell, 2008.

Wigley, M., *The Architecture of Deconstruction: Derrida's Haunt*, Cambridge: MIT Press, 1995.

Willis, D., *The Emerald City and Other Essays on the Architectural Imagination*, Princeton: Princeton Architectural Press, 1999.

Wirth, O., *La Franc-Maconnerie Rendue Intelligible à Ses Adeptes, Volume II Le Compagnon*, Paris: Dervy, 1994.

Wirth, O., *La Franc-Maconnerie Rendue Intelligible à Ses Adeptes, Volume III Le Maitre*, Paris: Dervy, 2005.

Wittgenstein, L., *Tractatus Logico-philosophicus*, Paris: Gallimard, 1961.

Womack-Weidner, A., 'New York Opens Second Mega-Courthouse', *Benchmark, Journal of the New York State Unified Court System* 2 (3) (2006), pp. 1–2.

Woodhouse, D., 'The Law and Politics: More power to the judge – and to the people?' *Parliamentary Affairs* 54 (2001), pp. 223–237.

Yankelevitch, H., 'Qu'est ce qu'un Concept en Psychanalyse', *Futur Antérieur* 10, (1992), http://multitudes.samizdat.net/Qu-est-ce-qu-un-concept-en.html (accessed 17 February 2017).

Zizek, S., 'The Big Other Doesn't Exist', *Journal of European Psychoanalysis*, Spring/ Fall 1997.

Zizek, S., *The Fragile Absolute: Or, Why is the Christian Legacy Worth Fighting For?* London: Verso, 2000.

Zizek, S., *How to Read Lacan*, London: Granta Books, 2006.

Zizek, S., 'Knight of the Living Dead', *The New York Times*, 24 March 2007.

Zupancic, A., *The Shortest Shadow: Nietzsche's Philosophy of the Two*, London: MIT Press, 2003.

Index

Page numbers in italics refer to figures.

For Product Safety Concerns and Information please contact our EU representative GPSR@taylorandfrancis.com
Taylor & Francis Verlag GmbH, Kaufingerstraße 24, 80331 München, Germany

www.ingramcontent.com/pod-product-compliance
Ingram Content Group UK Ltd.
Pitfield, Milton Keynes, MK11 3LW, UK
UKHW011018180926
475701UK00004B/818
9780367594008